SOUTH HOLLAND PUBLIC LIBRARY

3 1350 00251 9785

W9-AVC-720

DISCARD

South Holland Public
South Holland, Illinois

Rise Up Singing

DOUBLEDAY

NEW YORK

LONDON

TORONTO

SYDNEY

AUCKLAND

Rise Up Singing

BLACK WOMEN WRITERS ON MOTHERHOOD

EDITED BY

CECELIE S. BERRY

SOUTH HOLLAND PUBLIC LIBRARY

PUBLISHED BY DOUBLEDAY
a division of Random House, Inc.

DOUBLEDAY and the portrayal of an anchor with a dolphin are registered
trademarks of Random House, Inc.

Book design by Gretchen Achilles

Library of Congress Cataloging-in-Publication Data

Rise up singing: Black women writers on motherhood / [compiled by]
Cecelie S. Berry.— 1st ed.
      p.   cm.
   1. Mothers—Literary collections. 2. Motherhood—Literary collections.
      3. Mother and child—Literary collections. 4. African American
women—Literary collections. 5. American literature—African American
authors. 6. African American women authors—Biography. 7. American
   literature—Women authors. 8. Mother and child—United States.
                          I. Berry, Cecelie S.
                          PS509.M6R57 2003
                          810.8'035252—dc22
                          2003068823

                    ISBN 0-385-50903-0

Copyright © 2004 by Cecelie S. Berry

Permissions to reprint previously published work appear on p. 279.

All Rights Reserved

PRINTED IN THE UNITED STATES OF AMERICA

May 2004
FIRST EDITION

1   3   5   7   9   10   8   6   4   2

*"One of these mornings
you're gonna rise up singing . . ."*

—"Summertime," from *Porgy and Bess*

I am grateful to my editors, Janet Hill and Clarence Haynes, and my agent, Victoria Sanders, for their enthusiasm and effort in the creation of this work. The talents and professionalism of the contributors will be a light and an inspiration to me always. Marian Wright Edelman, Faith Ringgold, and Jewelle Taylor Gibbs provided words of wisdom and encouragement at critical points. In their energy and generosity they are an example for all women everywhere.

My husband, Scott Flood, has been tireless in coaching, advising, editing, and just plain sacrificing time and energy to this project. Darling, I couldn't have done it without you. And to my mother-in-law, Pastor Mary Lou Flood, I appreciate and admire your commitment to faith and family. You have taught me a great deal.

For my sisters, Christiane and Stephanie, and my "baby" brother, Charles: You all never let me give up on me. I owe you big-time.

For Daddy, who always believed in me and for Mother, who keeps hope alive: There are no words except "I love you."

For Sam and Spenser, my joyful sons: You are my dream come true.

And for all the Black mothers whose heroics went unsung, you are not forgotten; we sing your praises in random acts of kindness, warm glances, and loving rebukes, every day and every hour, forever.

Contents

SECTION III

TORCH SONG FOR MOTHER AND CHILD

SECTION IV

THE ROUND:

ROWING GENTLY DOWN THE STREAM

Rise Up Singing

Foreword

I begin my thoughts for a book on Black mothers by thinking about my own mother, Maggie Leola Bowen Wright. Mama was a pillar of Shiloh Baptist Church in Bennettsville, South Carolina, where Daddy was pastor. She was director of the youth and senior choirs, church organist, fundraiser-in-chief, and founder and head of the Mothers' Club, which she organized to emphasize the importance of mothers' leadership roles at home and in the community. Mama was a natural-born organizer of people. Mama was also the creative entrepreneur in the family. Daddy could not have managed without her. She always had a dime and an idea and a streak of independence that my strong father would try in vain to rein in but could always rely on. He called her "Pal."

As I grow older, I look more and more like her. My mother's strength sustains me whenever I waver in the face of tough challenges. I remember once, after I became a civil rights lawyer in Mississippi, I went home to visit Mama and brought along Jeannie, a small girl who had lost her eye when marauding Mississippi Whites sprayed buckshot through the windows of her family's house. I'd been instructed by Jeannie's mother how to remove, clean, and replace her glass eye, which I felt able to do in theory. When confronted by the reality, though, I quavered. Seeing my hesitation, my mother gently pushed me aside and quickly removed, cleaned, and reinserted Jeannie's eye without missing a beat.

My concern for children without homes or parents to care for them comes from the foster children my mother took into our house after Daddy died. Mama reared nearly a dozen foster sisters and brothers. Years later, when my sister admonished our aging mother to relinquish some of her many church and community responsibilities, including cooking for the aged in a home where most of the occupants were younger than she, Mama replied: "I did not promise the Lord that I was going part of the way. I promised him I was going all the way until he tells me otherwise."

I have always wanted to be half as good, half as brave, and half as faithful as my mother and the other great women who were like her in my community. They represented countless unsung lives of grace, women who carried on day in, day out, trying to keep their families, churches, and communities together and to instill by example the enduring values of love, hard work, discipline, and courage. From the beginning, I was surrounded by strong Black female role models. Black women were steady anchors who helped me navigate every step of my way through childhood, college, law school, and as I tested professional adult wings. They encouraged me by word and example to think and act outside the box and to ignore the low expectations many have for Black girls and women.

I did not come into or get through this life alone. Neither did you. Our mothers had to push to get us here. Those of us who are mothers ourselves now can understand their work in a whole new light. And not every mother's work turns out the same. The mothers writing in this anthology speak in a range of voices. They are joyful, stressed, grateful, ambivalent, determined, disappointed, and, in bad ways and good, overwhelmed. But over and over again in their stories we see mothers struggling with the push: striving to give their children their best and to make sure the world gives their children its best, hard as that fight may be.

I am inspired by these mothers just as I am inspired by the hundreds of thousands of other Black mothers who work every day to give their children, too, the best they can. They carry on the legacy of women like my mother and the other women of my hometown, just as those women were emulating the mothers in their own communities who had come before them. When I returned to Bennettsville in 1984 for my mother's funeral, an elderly White man asked me what I did for a living. I realized in a flash that in my work at the Children's Defense Fund I do exactly what she did, just on a different scale. I am convinced that women—mothers and grandmothers—will lead the way, and Black mothers and grandmothers can set a special example. Black mothers have always been ready and willing to do whatever it takes to transform the world for our children. Our children and all children need us now more than ever.

MARIAN WRIGHT EDELMAN, 2004

Introduction

$\mathcal{R}$*ise Up Singing: Black Women Writers on Motherhood* was just a bubble in my mind when I departed for the Million Mom March on Mother's Day 2000. Approaching my point of departure I could see, in the parking lot of a local university, a fleet of buses shining silver in the dawn. I glanced around the dark interior of our station wagon, my husband at the wheel, in back, my two sleepy sons, Sam and Spenser. They were, respectively, 7 and 5 at that time and distrusted my motives for leaving; they always seemed to suspect that I might sneak off like a thief in the night. I had explained that a demonstration against gun violence might help make the country safer, but they didn't see the connection. "A march?" they exclaimed. "What good's a march gonna do?"

I was reminded then that one of my missions as a mother was to connect the dots from the past to the present, to weld the link between our heritage and our future. My boys had been introduced to the civil rights movement in school, but that would not suffice. I wanted to show them that our comfortable lives had not been won without effort, nor had they secured us a perch above the world. The price of change will always be sacrifice.

By attending the march, I also wanted to demonstrate to myself that I had not, as I'd feared, become obsolete in my years as a stay-at-home mother. Now I know that fear was an illusion. Motherhood certifies one's importance in the world. Every tear wiped, every skinned knee bandaged makes you at least as relevant as the voluble defenders of civilization, and a whole lot more powerful. The march was a celebration of the fact that mothers and motherhood, with its menial tasks and countless sacrifices, count. I could not pass up a chance to honor that truth. By doing so, I sensed that the march, like motherhood itself, would lead me someplace new. Not knowing where that might be, I got on the bus.

Another force, well known to African American mothers, propelled me onward: fear. I was perpetually worried that the world would destroy my sons before I could see them become men. All Americans must now cope with the possibility of international terrorism, but African Americans add to that threat an awareness that racial terrorism and police brutality can happen virtually anywhere. The statistics haunt African American mothers like a spectre, and gun violence is but a single blight. Gang warfare, babies having babies, poor schools for the underclass and persistent underachievement of Black middle-class kids, prisons overcrowded with men of color, and the media, the media, the media, all seem to threaten our children's future. When Slam poet Patricia Smith visits her son in prison she writes in *Dancer of the World* of "carrying the card," her induction into the sorority of despair. So many lives, so many sons, lost.

One might see these dangers as macroscopic, headlines unlikely to be actualized in the comfortable lives of most of the writers here. But as mothers, we see the larger forces in miniature daily in our neighborhoods and schools. In *Elementary Lessons* Rita Coburn Whack investigates the mark on her son's face when she picks him up from his progressive, predominantly White nursery school and finds the machinery of stereotyping already at work. I have met with immensely popular White and Asian teachers who've informed me through clenched teeth that my children are bright and well behaved. It hurts them to say as much because they'd feel so much more at ease, and less threatened, if my boys were problem children as stereotypes suggest. This reaction is part of the fulminating resentment, the "you're-not-better-than-me" animus of racial hostility. Nobody talks about it, though, and it contributes mightily to the alienation of the Black middle class. Black mothers must be able to spot the wolf in sheep's clothing, the smiling face that seeks to crush their children's spirit and undermine their progress—or, just as damaging, to with-hold the recognition fairly won. And we must do so without allow-ing our children to cry wolf, to view themselves as victims of discrimination whenever they are challenged to do better. It is a high-wire act and our unique burden.

As if confronting racial hostility were not enough, there is the myopia of Blacks who label African Americans of different beliefs or values as traitors. In 2002, when civil rights activist Harry Belafonte publicly accused National Security Advisor Condoleezza Rice and Secretary of State Colin Powell of being no more than house servants of the Bush administration, he practiced litmus-test politics that seeks to force African Americans to conform to a liberal political tradition or risk ostracism. Whether or not we agree with the ideas expressed, African Americans must accept and, indeed, celebrate the diversity of voices in our community, or we will stifle creativity and undermine progress. It is still common for Black children to be pressured to con-form to a narrow and demeaning definition of Blackness propagated chiefly by us. Black mothers must inculcate their children with the idea that to be anything less than uncompromising in their individual values is to dishonor their hard-won freedom. On this point, it is not enough to talk the talk, we must walk the walk.

"Making it," as many African Americans have in recent years, does not always heal the very wounds that drive us to achieve. Some of us self-destruct, as though there were a ticking time bomb in our heads. My husband and I were shocked to learn of a Harvard Law School classmate, a Black man of great promise, who, one morning while his children were in private school and his wife was out shop-ping, walked into his luxury car–filled garage, doused himself with gasoline, and set himself on fire. You never would have thought it possible; the guy was a rock. Of course, we didn't know that his fa-ther had done the same thing at his exact age, 40. The demons that hounded him were not exorcised by success. We can buy the best, and still find ourselves bereft. We can earn doctorates in African

American history, but until we take a personal journey back through the shame, neglect, abuse, and trauma that is often the bitter sap of our family trees, we—and our children—will wither. The mothers of this collection honor their past by sharing its burdens as well as its victories.

Materialism can be a form of addiction in which upwardly mobile African Americans seek to repair our experience of being devalued, but there are many addictions. Black mothers must be particularly attendant to the multiplicity of ways we may telegraph the message to our children that, whatever our status, we may nurse these dependencies because we still feel inferior. After a sustained effort on behalf of political correctness, we cannot forfeit our obligation to speak well of—and to—one another. "Nigger" is not and never will be a term of endearment. When one mother picked up her daughter after a swimming party in our backyard pool, I overheard her say, "Oh, now you've gone and gotten all *dark.*" I have explained to my sons that inferiority is a disease of the mind and they are not to let anyone infect them with it. African Americans may not be able to rid ourselves of racism, but we would deal it a crippling blow if we cured ourselves of our self-hatred and its assorted addictions.

The hydra of mainstream racism and Black self-hatred work together in the same way that external forces converge with private sentiments, the way society's values reinforce family values or their absence. Black mothers must connect these dots, to hone a consciousness about the dyad of dangers, physical and psychological, societal and personal, that beset Black children. If mothers are said to need eyes in the back of their heads, Black mothers must have veritable searchlights.

Even now at the dawn of the 21st century, many challenges remain for African American families, but mothers, of all people, cannot be seduced by negative conditions into negative thinking. Too many of our ancestors have overcome great obstacles for us to despair in these comparatively halcyon times. As Gwendolyn Brooks writes in her poem "The Children of the Poor," our history proclaims that "reaching is the rule." Brooks reminds us that motherhood—and childhood—are precious enclaves where we may share with our children the "joy of undeep and unabiding things." The simple joys of shared lives—the purchase of a new bike for Florence Ladd by her son in "A New Balance"—inform the relationship between mother and child as, through their lives, each subtly changes and challenges the other. These small but incandescent moments are testified to throughout *Rise Up Singing*, but they are the focus of Section IV, "The Round: Rowing Gently down the Stream." The writers of this section find that our best hope for the future lies not in the tides of political change, but in the personal moments that bind generations together and form the backbone of our moral character.

Still, historically, politics has impacted our lives, more perhaps than any other group of Americans, so Black motherhood compels us to strive for a radical spirituality that resists, defies, and transcends oppression. Accordingly, *Rise Up Singing* opens with "Aria of the Matriarch" and Maya Angelou's epic poem, "Our Grandmothers," which pays tribute to the matriarch's sojourn against injustice. In "Margaret: A Mother for All Seasons" by Jewelle Taylor Gibbs, and "My Daughters and Me" by Faith Ringgold, both writers celebrate and emulate the indomitable spirit of the black matriarch.

Motherhood also awakens in us the creative spirit to find in the ordinary, extraordinary gifts. On the bus to the march I sat back and in daydreaming, entered the "little room for thinking" evoked in Rita Dove's poem "Daystar." Those precious moments of surrender that weary mothers wrest from chore-filled days are the crucible in which we distill our unique mission and sometimes find our heart's desire. In "Daystar," it is at baby's naptime that her mother, Beulah, enters a state of "nothingness," when she is brilliantly attuned to the quiet epiphanies of her world.

In the little room for thinking, Black mothers find internal refuge and emerge more self-knowing, proud, and emboldened. Section II,

"Dream Song: A Mother's Interior World," explores its resonant, contemplative moments and elemental comforts. Andrea Lee in "Mother" and Martha Southgate in "An Unnatural Woman" find rich metaphor for living, suffering, and joy in the mundane, a bowl of pasta, a spiced, raw roast. Alice Walker's classic short story "Everyday Use," proffers the quilt, a trope of female community and interdependence, in celebration of the ordinary. The peace restored to mother and daughter at the story's end reflects a newfound respect for their humble traditions, and themselves.

"The personal is political" is a phrase I often heard in college, and it was uttered more than once by speakers at the Million Mom March. It was popularized in the 1970s by feminists who equated woman's presumed fate as homemaker with exploitation. Feminism was distrusted then by some Black leaders, who believed it to be divisive at a time when unity was our greatest and, arguably, our only weapon against a patriarchal, racist culture. Feminism seemed to place Black daughters at loggerheads with their long-suffering mothers, and Black men, who have been doubly victimized by gender and color, with Black women. When affirmative action expanded job and educational opportunities, and Black women moved in force to scale the economic ladder, they were accused of "cutting the line," displacing Black men in pursuit of gender equality. The feminist movement also seemed to focus principally on the needs of middle-class White women who wanted the right to work. Black women had always worked, usually raising other people's children as well as their own. If White women tired of the pedestal, Black women longed for respite for the double yoke of being breadwinner and nurturer. If White women felt men were expendable, most Black women—regardless of their socioeconomic or educational level—continued to feel that a man, particularly a "do right" man, was a luxury worth almost any price.

In fact, feminism has served Black women—and all women—by elevating the discourse on womens' lives and by challenging us to forge bonds based on cooperation and mutual respect. Ten years ago, the editors of *SAGE: A Scholarly Journal on Black Women* took up this gauntlet and edited the volume *Double Stitch: Black Women Write about Mothers and Daughters. Double Stitch,* a fusion of literary criticism and feminist scholarship, dissected Black women's relationships at their nucleus, the mother/daughter bond. It initiated an intracommunity dialogue that was both constructive and informative.

Feminism also brought to the fore what was otherwise quietly kept. It challenged the fairy-tale illusions that made the absence of choice in work, love, and childbearing palatable. Feminism propagated the heresy that tradition did not always work out as promised: A man does not make you secure, motherhood may not make you happy. Not a pretty message, certainly not what women, all steeped in the "happily ever after," wanted to hear. But where would we be now without those who dared reveal ugly truths? This subject makes hallowed ground of Section III, "Torch Song for Mother and Child." In this section, the late June Jordan writes in her essay "Many Rivers to Cross" of what it meant in 1966 to be a single, divorced mother, a trained but unemployed Black, female professional, the daughter of a mother whose life as a "good woman" ended in suicide. The fortitude of writers like her won for women the right to defy the "fate" of motherhood, a choice Erin Aubry Kaplan weighs in her essay "Mother, Unconceived."

The writers of *Rise Up Singing* speak in a range of personal voices, but we are far more than "political." We are women—from all over the country, diverse in every aspect and agenda, who can speak to the truth of our experiences and let the ideological chips fall where they may. When Lorraine Hansberry was interviewed in the early 1960s, she was asked whether she was Black first or a writer first, a question commonly leveled at Black artists of the time. The writers here aren't always Black first, or women first, mothers first, or careerists first. Gone are the days when we had to lock ourselves into a hierarchy of self-definition. Our *conception* of ourselves has changed. We evolve over the course of a lifetime, wearing different hats, veils, or head-dresses. Some writers here have raised children, and some have declined the privilege; some are novelists, journalists, and social critics; many, like Maxine Clair and AJ Verdelle, have had not one successful career but two. They have circumnavigated the ocean of choice and found that, while our lives are rich with opportunity, what we choose is still not always what we really want. Carolyn Ferrell conveys in "Linda Devine's Daughters" that choice has not made us omnipotent; we still must yield to the vicissitudes of love and memory, to the grip of history and desire, and the yet-formidable enigmas of Mother Nature.

It was a beautiful day on the mall that Mother's Day, rich with early summer's primary colors. Eventually, I elbowed my way back through the languid, contented crowds and rested in the marble shadows of the National Gallery of Art. There I ran into a White mother from Spenser's kindergarten class. She was a politically active mom-about-town, attending the march with one of the local clubs. "Who're you with?" she asked me.

I told her that I came by myself. She looked shocked. "You mean you're alone?" In the milliseconds that followed, I saw a constellation of feelings orbit in her eyes, the same feelings a man might have felt when confronting an independent woman a century ago. There was pity, grudging admiration, and suspicion: What was I up to?

There wasn't time just then to explain to her that while I was unaffiliated, I was far from alone. I got back on the bus, took out my pad, and sketched the outline for the proposal that led to this anthology. I had, that day, found a new mission; I'd heard the voices of the brave writers here. I invite you to listen to them. They make a rousing chorus, a call that will draw from faithful readers a soulful response. All comers are welcome, but particularly those African American mothers who feel alone. It was Hansberry who wrote in *To Be Young, Gifted and Black* that "the thing that makes you exceptional, if you are at all, is inevitably that which must also make you lonely." The isolation that motherhood sometimes imposes is meant to make you be still, so that you can hear the melodies and cadences of your life. It is meant to help you refine your purpose and resuscitate your spirit so that you might better know yourself and guide your children. It is immensely useful to be alone; to turn your back on the world for a while; to build with love the home and the family of your dreams is the ultimate revolution. As you do, you march forward, shoulder to shoulder with other mothers, as we connect the dots, bear witness, share the wisdom, give thanks, express the love, remember, forgive, endure, and rise up singing.

CECELIE S. BERRY, 2004

Aria of the Matriarch

The Black grandmother is an icon of spirituality and endurance. She is both a quiet sufferer and an inexhaustible warrior. In this first section, her transcendent spirit is reflected in the experiences and reminiscences of these writers. It is most appropriate that any examination of motherhood begins with a tribute to our grandmothers, the shepherdesses of generations. Their hands have urged us on to deeper understanding and their leadership has provided a moral compass for family, community, and country.

Our Grandmothers

BY MAYA ANGELOU

She lay, skin down on the moist dirt,
The canebrake rustling
with the whispers of leaves, and
loud longing of hounds and
the ransack of hunters crackling the near branches.

She muttered, lifting her head a nod toward freedom,
I shall not, I shall not be moved.

She gathered her babies,
their tears slick as oil on black faces,
their young eyes canvassing mornings of madness.
Momma, is Master going to sell you
from us tomorrow?

Yes.
Unless you keep walking more
and talking less.
Yes.
Unless the keeper of our lives
Releases me from all commandments.
Yes.
And your lives,
Never mine to live,
will be executed upon the killing floor of innocents.
Unless you match my heart and words,

saying with me,
I shall not be moved.

In Virginia tobacco fields,
leaning into the curve
on Steinway
Pianos, along Arkansas roads,
in the red hills of Georgia,
into the palms of her chained hands, she
cried against calamity,
You have tried to destroy me
And though I perish daily,

I shall not be moved.

Her universe, often
summarized into one black body
falling finally from the tree to her feet,
made her cry each time in a new voice.
All my past hastens to defeat,
and strangers claim the glory of my love,
Iniquity has bound me to his bed,

yet, I must not be moved.

She heard the names,
Swirling ribbons in the wind of history:
nigger, nigger bitch, heifer,
mammy, property, creature, ape, baboon,
whore, hot tail, thing, it.
She said, But my description cannot
fit your tongue, for

I have a certain way of being in this world
And I shall not, I shall not be moved.

No angel stretched protecting wings
above the heads of her children,
fluttering and urging the winds of reason
into the confusion of their lives.
They sprouted like young weeds,
but she could not shield their growth
from the grinding blades of ignorance, nor
Shape them into symbolic topiaries.
She sent them away,
underground, overland, in coaches and
shoeless.
When you learn, teach.
When you get, give.
As for me,

I shall not be moved.

She stood in midocean, seeking dry land.
She searched God's face.
Assured,
She placed her fire of service
on the altar, and though
clothed in the finery of faith,
when she appeared at the temple door,
no sign welcomed
Black Grandmother. Enter here.

Into the crashing sound,
into wickedness, she cried,

No one, no, nor no one million
Ones dare deny me God. I go forth
alone, and stand as ten thousand.
The Divine upon my right
Impels me to pull forever
at the latch on Freedom's gate.

The Holy Spirit upon my left leads my
feet without ceasing into the camp of the
righteous and into the tents of the free.

These momma faces, lemon-yellow, plum-purple,
honey-brown, have grimaced and twisted
down a pyramid of years.
She is Sheba and Sojourner,
Harriet and Zora,
Mary Bethune and Angela,
Annie to Zenobia.

She stands
before the abortion clinic,
confounded by the lack of choices.
In the Welfare line,
reduced to the pity of handouts.
Ordained in the pulpit, shielded
by the mysteries.
In the operating room,
husbanding life,
In the choir loft,
holding God in her throat.
On lonely street corners,
hawking her body,
In the classroom, loving the

children to understanding.
Centered on the world's stage,
she sings to her loves and beloveds,
to her foes and detractors:
However I am perceived and deceived,
however my ignorance and conceits,
lay aside your fears that I will be undone,

for I shall not be moved.

Ernestine: A Granddaughter's Memories

BY JEWELL PARKER RHODES

Grandmother Ernestine was born in Georgia, raised in a rural backwater ("way down the road from Athens," she would say) with clear, blue skies, in a huge house with a screened-in porch, and a half-acre of pecan trees in the backyard.

"We didn't live in these nasty, brick houses with cement for backyards. Many black folks held land in the South. Come North, we rent, struggle, trying to make a fair dollar. We go to stores to buy our greens."

Grandmother always told me stories about this southern heritage I had. Telling me, passing down tales was her way of making it real for me. Telling was her way of keeping it real for herself. It wasn't until Grandmother died, that I realized how out-of-place she must've felt in Pittsburgh. What lure was there in steep hills covered with brick and trolley steel rails? What ease in a land of more rain and snow than was good for her arthritis-stricken hands and knees? What pleasure in soot cascading from the steel mills' furnaces? Even for Easter services, Grandmother never wore white.

"What sense?" she'd ask. "When it'll only turn gray. Now, in Georgia—"

I'd groan, "Not another Georgia story."

"—white stayed white. White shoes. White gloves. White pearls."

It didn't matter where you were—in the basement shoveling coal; in the kitchen, making designs with your breakfast grits. Or, outside on the front steps, trying to suck salt sprinkled on ice cubes. Grandma told stories. Didn't matter if she told you before. Didn't matter if you didn't want to hear it. Telling tales seemed Grandmother's mission in life. Her grandchildren, especially, had to hear her tales. Sometimes I wondered whether Grandmother's tales were all true, whether she'd made them up, imagined more than she knew or whether memory and time had created a South more glimmering and glinting than any reality.

This is true. Grandmother raised me, my sister, and my cousin. When she wasn't telling tales, she fed, clothed, and cleaned us, three little girls in a three-storied, battered and broken-down house. My Dad and aunt were single parents and Grandmother did the cooking, cleaning, laundry, and instructed us kids with her stories. She'd boil Argo starch then trudge down to the dank basement to add it to the rinse water. She didn't trust the washing machine or dryer my Dad had given her. She still did laundry on the wooden and metal washboard and used a manual wringer. Then, she'd hang the clothes to dry in the basement.

"Georgia has clean air, clean water. Nothing like sheets flapping on the line, flapping in the wind." She persisted washing by hand, hanging our clothes indoors, though surely it must have made her tired and sore.

"Down South," she'd sometimes say, leading into one of her stories. "Down South, we'd make pecan pies like you wouldn't believe. I'd split nuts all day and my mother would make the pies with butter, syrup. Better than any Christmas toy. Pie made with love and a 350 degree oven." This story invariably came after a Christmas of unwrapping presents from under our tinsel tree. Disappointed as kids, mourning what we did and didn't get (nothing worked like it did on TV) we'd settle into ill humor until Grandmother got her burlap sack, sent "up" from down South by her remaining relatives. She'd spill the pecans on the table, letting some of them roll, drop to the floor and she'd send us kids scurrying after them. Then, she'd hand us silver nutcrackers, saying, "The first piece of pie to whoever shells the most." Christmas was always saved by Grandmother's spirit and pies.

It would take me years to understand that as surely as us grand-

kids could jump double-dutch and play a mean turn of jacks, we kept
Grandmother from her beloved "down South." She wouldn't leave us
until we were filled with her stories, sayings, and wisdom.

"Down South—" she'd whisper especially on summer nights
when we could watch fireflies gleam-blink and wave to neighbors sitting on their front stoops.

"Down South . . . in Georgia—"

"I know Georgia's down South. You've done told me."

Grandmother would stare at my sassy young self, then start again,
"Down South . . . IN GEORGIA—"

I'd roll my eyes.

"—everybody in the family was a nice, chocolate brown with lots
of fine black hair. Chocolate and silky-haired 'cause a handsome
Seminole left his seed in my great-grandmother, Ruthie. Sure did. As
I witness. Ruthie's parents were newly freed slaves. They went to
church nearly every day to testify about how their 'brighter day' had
done come.

"One Sunday in August, when flies, thick and drowsy, hovered
in humid air; cousin Ruthie pleaded sick to stay home from church.
Nine months later, great grandfather was born. Birthing, Ruthie told
her story about her Indian. Said they didn't need words. Some
folks said she was crazy, out-of-her mind. Knocked up by a local boy.
Her baby was beautiful. Ruthie raised her son. When he was grown,
folks say, Ruthie took to her room like a ghost. She never married.
No one knows why. I suspect the men who came courting talked
too much. The Indian just got busy with his hands and mouth." (I
was thirteen when I finally understood her comment enough to
blush.) "Her son became my grandfather, Wade. Your great great-
grandfather."

I remember, as a child, loving the feel of her smooth chocolate skin,
her high cheekbones and silky black hair. I remember climbing on

the toilet seat to comb her hair and to see myself in the mirror, rising out of my grandmother's head:

"Grandma, can I do it? Please? Pretty please?"

"No," said Grandma, taking the tufts of hair from my cupped hand.

I stood beside the sturdy, grease-splattered range. "Tell me why you do it."

"I've done said it before."

"Tell me again. And say it like you said the first time."

Grandma turned the flame on high.

"Why do you burn it, Grandma? What for?" I asked, staring at the hungry, blue fire.

Grandma inhaled, spun around, opened her eyes wide and said, "Jewell, child, what if I didn't? Why if I didn't burn my hair some tweety bird might catch hold of it and use it for some nest and as soon as the motherbird's speckled eggs started hatching and the little birds squeaking for meat, my hair would fall right out."

I giggled as the singed hair stank up the air.

I would also cry at night because my hair was quite kinky next to Grandmother's silk. Even when her hair grew white, it stayed smooth, looking like strands of crystal. My hair always had a million, nappy braids. I always felt I was less beautiful than my sister who took after Grandmother Ernestine, Wade, Ruthie and that Seminole Indian. I seemed to take after no one.

Nights when Grandmother tucked me in, she'd sometimes say, "Down South, the peach is rock hard, then fine weather . . . summer heat makes it bloom. You'll bloom. See if you don't."

Grandmother Ernestine was gorgeous as a girl, more legs than trunk. Her bosom just the right size for a baby or a man to rest his head upon. I know. I've seen pictures of Grandmother—young, with her lips pulled in a wide smile, and her eyes, black and sparkling. Grandmother was gorgeous—maybe too gorgeous, in a small town where colored folks prospered and valued respectability and manners.

Grandmother also talked about education. "Read," she'd say. "Read," though I'd figured out long ago, she couldn't read well.

"Down South, my folks felt eight grades of schooling was enough. After all, I was already pledged to be a clerk's wife. I knew how to cook and clean. I served in the church, passing out fans with portraits of Jesus, to folks who cried and shivered with the Holy Spirit."

Ernestine—her parents' blessing. Obedient. Dutiful. Clean. Ernest.

"I was supposed to be just the right gal to help uplift the race. But one summer I met a sailor—so light he could pass for white. Like great-grandmother Ruthie's beau, he didn't talk much. But I was charmed by him and his visions of moving North for better opportunities, for more freedom.

"South had its race problems, but so does the North. Too, too true. I should've known better. I shouldn't have listened to a man who passed for white so the Navy could make him a Lieutenant. What's the sense of pretending who you're not?"

In Pittsburgh, she had two babies in quick succession which she struggled to keep dressed and fed while Grandfather James sailed out (or so he said) and forgot to mail his pay. Later, it was discovered Grandfather James was a bigamist; he'd married a white woman just across Pittsburgh's three rivers and raised five kids.

Grandmother Ernestine never talked much about Grandfather James. One time she did, she'd brung a care package of food to my college dorm.

"Don't let a man lead you astray from your roots."

I wondered what roots I had.

" 'A bee gets busy even when the flower's still young.' 'One mistake today mean sorrow tomorrow.' 'Don't do as I did, just do as I say'."

Then before she left, she reminded me to take my cod-liver oil.

Like telling her stories, Grandmother had a habit of flooding folks with "sayings." "Her 'tiny wisdoms'," she called them.

After she left my dorm, I realized she'd been advising me not to get pregnant. I suspected then she had another tale about Grandfather James she would never tell.

Just as she'd never tell me further details about race. Except to say, "Be careful"; "Be self-respecting"; "Wear clean underpants and socks." I never understood the latter until the day I flew over the top of my bike, breaking a rib and collarbone. White policemen, three feet away, saw me slam hard onto concrete, the bike crashing on top of me. A middle-aged black man pleaded with me to allow him to take me to a hospital. I was wary of strangers, but, finally, consented because the pain was too much. He took me to Allegheny General, not Mercy, known for the nuns care of the poor and brown, the only hospital where colored doctors could work on staff. "Allegheny was closer," he said.

Grandmother came to see me all dressed up like she was going to church. When she was satisfied I'd live, she whispered low, "Clean underwear?" I nodded. "Good. Don't let them think you ignorant. Poor or dirty." She sat with me until visiting hours ended and nurses came to shoo her. Regal, Grandmother declared, "Give my grandchild the best care." Then, winked at me, saying, "If they don't treat you right, let me know. I'll learn them. Down South, we know a thing or two."

Astafedia bags for sore hearts and bones, mint tea for headaches, bark root for infections, and dandelion leaves for nausea.

For the most part, Grandmother's "down South" was just as segregated as "our North." Except for the occasional teacher or the grim-riding policemen, we lived in a black working-class world with peeling linoleum, plastic-covered sofas, and church fans painted with images of Jesus.

If violence shattered our neighborhood, I never knew it. Like a sentry, Grandmother kept ill tidings at bay—*"Hurt and harm stay outside our door."*

But issues of *Ebony* or *Jet* were always scattered about our house, never hidden. Their photographers never flinched at racism's bitter harvest. And Grandmother who wouldn't let me see a fistfight on a street, let me see pictures of violence down in her beloved South. I'd sit on the porch steps, studying grainy, black-and-white photos of men hanging from trees, of men tarred and feathered splayed on the road, hands tied, knotted to a car. I still remember one naked soul, dead, his chin resting on his chest, and his body marked with holes from a screwdriver.

When I asked, "Why?" Grandmother would sing, "Were You There When They Crucified My Lord?" The song was heartbreaking but Grandmother would sing it, at first, low and deep in her throat, then it would soar to upper registers and she would start to clap her hands and before I knew it, me, my sister, and cousin would holler and clap and sing and what had been sorrow turned to a strengthening joy. Words by themselves were of little use, but music soothed, and with Grandmother, now long dead, I still hum and sing when hurt seems too much to bear.

"Spirits never die. Every goodbye ain't gone. Like light shimmering through clouds, leaves swept up by wind, water rushing over rock, there is a touch so light it brings tears, reminding us, there is life—always, forevermore, life. Preacher tells me so. Mother told me so."

"How'd your mother die?" I once asked, a brave eight.

"She died while I was here. Up North. 1962. I had just gotten you kids off to school. I was hanging laundry outside when a ladybug crawled along the wire line to my arm. As kids, we sang, "Ladybug, ladybug, fly away home. Your house is on fire, your children are gone." And I felt something, someone clutch my heart and I knew my mama was gone."

"Did you cry?"

"I bawled into the sheet. Then sang. For women would've circled 'round her bed, singing too. My aunts, second and third cousins. Nieces too. Women would've washed her body down and shrouded the clock when she died."

"How'd she die?"

"Heart gave out."

I didn't ask whether it was brokenhearted.

Grandmother looked up quick, then turned the tide by whispering, "Did I ever tell you folks can call the dead?"

I shrieked. "Really? Truly? Can you call your mother?"

"I could. She wouldn't appreciate it. 'Sides, she's with me every day. That's how I know she forgave me. But that ain't the tale."

Inhaling, I leaned closer.

"My aunt (on my father's side) played the numbers and relied on dreams to tell her what to bet. Five dollars on 462. Ten on 765. Eleven on 891. One whole summer, when I was eight like you, no dreams came to her. Down South, everybody cherishes dreams. In dreams, this world and the next mix, like sugar and grits. So Aunt Hattie called the dead. Put a glass of water under her bed, right beneath her pillow, quoted from the Bible and chanted some slave prayer. She wrote 'Give me a number,' and slipped it on top the water glass and slept."

"Did you see?"

"My mother told me. Told me, too, the spirit was so angry, she slapped Aunt Hattie's face, leaving a black, hand-shaped mark and gave her the number 337. The number hit and aunt Hattie gave our town a party with marshmallow yams, watermelon, barbecue, and smoked corn. She never played the numbers again and her mark never faded."

'Scratch a wall, somebody die.' 'Do good and it'll fly right back to you.'
'Walk the right side of the street, memories stay sweet.' 'Never go backward,

only forward.' 'Curse an enemy, curse yourself too.' 'When I die, I'll be with you. Standing two steps behind.'

I always wanted to know who says such things? Who taught Grandmother to believe such things?

"Down South, in Georgia, everybody knows what I say is true. Miracles abound." Then, Grandmother would hush me, hush all us kids, and say, "Ray Charles. On TV." And there Ray Charles would be, shielded behind dark glasses, rocking, singing, "Georgia." It never mattered to Grandmother that he was singing about a woman. For her, he was singing *Georgia*—peaches, pecans, tall grasses, clear streams, stately willows, and damp nights.

Grandmother toiled raising us kids and some nights, she'd fall asleep in the chair watching late night movies—*Carmen Jones, Imitation of Life, All God's Children Got Wings*. Us kids, liberated from bedtime, would laugh and play and when we got too rowdy, she'd wake, scoot us off to bed. Climbing the stairs, favoring her sore left side, I'd hear her mutter softly, "Down South, women don't leave kids." I knew the complaint was directed at my mother and though I didn't know where my mother was, I only knew she wasn't "down South."

The only time Grandmother sounded like she came from a mysterious state called Georgia was when she and us grandkids sat knee to knee on our pitiful front steps while Grandmother told stories. "My grandmother told my mother, my mother told me, I told my children. Now I'm telling you."

We knew better than to ask why *our* parents weren't passing along their mother's stories. This was another difference in "up North."

Telling tales, Grandmother's voice would slow like molasses; her vowels growing wide; her tone, caressing, humming, conjuring pictures.

We were in childhood heaven listening to tales about B'rer Rabbit falling down a deep well, about lazy spiders who spun stories for slavery's children, and about a pig-tailed girl smarter than little Red Riding Hood, smart enough to outwit egg-stealing foxes. As the night turned velvet and the moon smiled on high, she'd whisper about haints lost in swamps, about High John the conqueror who slayed enemies, and the Devil who couldn't outsmart guitar-strumming blues men.

We hated to go to bed, but Grandmother would soothe us with one more story, then one more, hustle us to brush our teeth, then, in the darkened bedroom, hum a wordless song which clung to our very souls.

"Good night," she'd whisper. "Say your prayers. Remember: the world is alive. Everything has a living spirit." *Animate. Inanimate.* It didn't matter. Grandmother believed a sensibility, a soul existed in everything. Many a night, I suspected the rocking horse near the bedroom window was alive and watching me, daring me to ride it past dark.

In all the years Grandmother lived up North, she only returned home, "down South to Georgia," once.

I hated every minute of the trip. We drove fourteen hours straight and went to the bathroom on the side of the road. I didn't understand then there were few places for "coloreds" to stay. We drove and drove (three adults up front; three kids in the backseat) and each mile, Grandmother seemed more fidgety, nervous; her skin, flush.

Today, long grown, I barely remember the humid July, the rope-swing in the yard, running barefoot through grass, chasing chickens, and catching lightening bugs in washed-out jars. I barely remember relatives who pinched my cheek, patted my hair, and offered me plat-ters of bright, pepper-spiced food. But I do remember Grandmother growing more languid, moving with a grace I'd never seen. It was as though the wet heat had soothed aches in her bones, soothed lines which creased her brow.

Grandmother was the prodigal child come home and relatives

waited on her, fed her, and kissed her a thousand times. An old suitor, now a carpenter with blunt and scarred hands, came to call. The Preacher praised Grandmother's return in church. The sewing circle made her a quilt. All the while, the Georgia sun shone bright, making the dampened air shiver with rainbows.

While I know Grandmother loved sitting on the wide, bright-white porch, rocking in a wicker chair, staring at the point where the grass gave way to groves of trees, she spent many hours in a back room, tending her elderly dad. Shriveled, seeming older than Moses, his eyes near blind with cataracts, Grandmother stayed beside him each moment he was awake. She straightened his pillows, washed his body, changed his soiled sheets, and fed him mashed peaches. Us kids never went farther into great-granddaddy's room than the threshold. The room was too dark; it smelled of camphor and sweat. But, at night, when us kids were camped out on the porch, we could hear Grandmother murmuring stories to her Dad. Never about Pittsburgh, but always about childhood "down South."

"Do you remember Daddy teaching me to fish? I caught my finger in the line and nearly lost my thumb."

"Do you remember Baptismal Day—me crying, afraid to put my head under water? You promised me pie if I wiped my tears."

"Do you remember Christmas, our money low, you hunted squirrel for Mama? Whenever Mama looked sad, you tickled her, making her laugh."

"Do you remember carrying me on your shoulders when I turned five? You bounced, twirled me 'til I was dizzy."

"You remember teaching me to harvest? Working before dawn well into night?"

Sometimes we'd hear chuckles amid coughs and even, sometimes, a cry of pain. The keening would sound so lonesome, so beyond this world, that us kids would shiver, and begin to bet whether it was some spirit. I suspected it was great-grandfather. But, once, seeing Grandmother close her father's bedroom door, then lean back against the wood, her hands covering her eyes, her mouth trembling, I thought maybe the wails came from her.

One morning, it was "Time to go. I got to go." Grandmother made us pack our clothes; box our new-found toys of pecan shells, dried snake skin and marbles. We left with a wicker basket of chicken, biscuits, peach cobbler, and plastic cups and spoons. Kool-Aid was in a jug. Grandmother made everyone kiss her father and after her last kiss, she said, quietly, "I got to go."

The drive home was killing; us kids, bored, squabbling, and the adults in the front seat speaking nary a word.

I was thrilled to be home. The North side of Pittsburgh with its hardened poverty and sun-starved weeds, nonetheless, seemed magical to me. I raced up our front stairs barely conscious of the grown-ups unpacking, of Grandmother gingerly stepping down the basement stairs to start the first of many loads of laundry.

But, in truth, if Pittsburgh ever had any magic, it was because of my grandmother. All the children in the neighborhood were her children. She scolded and doled out sugar cookies and meringue, peach, pumpkin or apple pie. No person was ever turned away from her door. If you needed, Grandmother, who really had so little, found a way to provide. She was funny, generous and the very glue which kept our ragged family rich in love rather than bitterness.

We, in turn, teased her about her "southern ways," laughed when she simmered black-eyed peas and greens on January 1 to bring our family luck and money. On chitlin' days, everyone complained about the skunky smell. "Slave food isn't always bad food," she said. After Grandmother fried them chitlins, smothered them in hot sauce, she'd eat her fill, then carry pounds of leftovers to the neighbors.

"Down South, in Georgia," Grandmother's father died. Parentless, she kept parenting us, her second set of children, her grandchildren. And like all children, I hurried to grow up. Each of us grew older, though, usually not wiser. And like a blink in time, Grandmother was caring for my cousin's children. Three generations of kids she helped raise.

I called Grandmother on a Sunday from my college dorm's phone. I said, "I'll visit next week." Grandmother sounded tired but happy. Another Christmas had passed, but winter was still holding on and Good Friday was weeks off.

"In Georgia, I'd be planning my garden. Pole beans, sweet peas, and early tomatoes. I'm too old to be raising kids. One day, down South, I'm going to put my feet up and watch my garden grow."

"Next week, when I see you . . . will you tell me about cauls?"

"Why you want to know about that?"

"Research. I'm writing a novel."

"Cauls are special. In Georgia, Mama's midwife would talk about cauls. Meant the baby had the gift, the sight. None of Mama's babies were born with it, but the midwife kept hoping. Midwife said her Mam had told her just what to do with it."

"What's that?"

"I'm not sure I remember. Bury it. Light some candles. Save a piece and boil it with tea. I don't know what all else. Down South, folks can be funny."

"Are you funny?"

Grandmother laughed and her voice sounded years younger. In my mind's eye, I could see her in the hallway, just beyond the vestibule, sitting in the telephone chair, her arms draped on the small table. Flowery house dress. Pink, terry-cloth slippers. Her hair squeezed tight in curlers.

"I was always funny. So were you. Do you remember the time when you thought the Big and Little Dippers were a sign from God? You were too cute. You asked me for the Bible."

I laughed.

"But it's true, you know. Everything in life is a sign." She sighed. "Love you. Got to put the kids to bed."

"Love you. See you Friday."

Tuesday, walking from the store with her new children (my second cousins: two boys, 7 and 10), Grandmother collapsed onto the sidewalk, clutching at her heart. I imagine the boys jumping up and down, waving, hollering for help.

This is the tale I was told:

"A kind man stopped his car and offered a ride to the hospital. Ernestine was still conscious. She asked for Mercy. Mercy Hospital.

"When they got to Mercy, the nurses made her wait. Ernestine was having trouble breathing. The eldest boy answered questions: 'Yes, she has pressure problems. Diabetes. Pains in her chest.'

"Ernestine was taken upstairs for heart monitoring. They rolled her wheelchair into the elevator. By the time they got to the right floor, Ernestine was dead."

I was dazed, shaken, guilty that I hadn't seen Grandmother. Hadn't said a proper good-bye. Later, our family doctor said, "They should've taken Ernestine to Allegheny. Poor Mercy only had one heart monitor and cardiac machine. That's why they took the elevator—they were taking her to it. Allegheny, a rich county hospital, would have had a machine in Emergency. Would've been able to save her right then and there."

I don't know if that's true. I don't know if Grandmother's heart could have been saved. At the funeral, all her many children cried.

———

I have been to Georgia. I stayed in the Peachtree Atlanta Hyatt and stared out the windows on the 21st floor looking at a skyline of concrete, steel, glass, and a light blue sky. Clouds drifted west to further horizons I could only dream about.

I did not rent a car. I did not visit the ancestral home. I was afraid Grandmother's home would be a will 'o wisp, a mirage cloaked by humid heat. I was afraid the soil which had nurtured Grandmother's love, would appear only barren and dry like a desert to me.

Older, I understand better the complex weave of how generations of children chained Grandmother like steel. I understand, too, Grandmother would not, could not have behaved any other way. She would mother us all as long as she believed we needed her. I know I needed her. I need her still.

The dead are with us.

I speak with Grandmother nearly every night. And I hear echoing through time, through memory, her stories, sayings, and "little wisdoms." I conjure her loving hands, her big-hearted smile, and generosity. I try to "live right" because that is how a southern gal raised "in Georgia," raised me.

"We make our own sweet dreams. One life in this world; another, in the hereafter."

Telling this tale, telling the tale Grandmother lived to tell me, I am South. *Warm, enveloping steadfast love. Abiding faith in human goodness. Charity to all.*

Grandmother is standing behind me, slightly to the right. "Read, read," she murmurs. (I swear I feel her breath glance off my ear.)

I smile because I *am* reading, reading these words I have typed, just as you're reading about Grandmother's precious "down South."

"Words and good deeds learn us all. 'Tis true."

"Tell it to me again, Grandmother."

"I've done said it before."

"Tell it like you told it the first time."

"*Tales and memories are never-ending. Why, down South, in Georgia . . .*"

. . . and so on and so on, passing from one generation to the next.

You tell them, Jewell, girl.

I do. I will.

Amen.

My Daughters and Me

BY FAITH RINGGOLD

In 1961, the girls, Mother and I went to Europe for the first time. They were on a sight-seeing vacation and I was on an expedition to seek out the great masterpieces of European art, of which I had seen only reproductions. At the time, I was questioning my future as an artist. Somehow I felt that being in Europe—where Picasso, Matisse, Monet and the other great painters had lived—would lead me to the answer.

We sailed for France aboard the S.S. *Liberté* one cool morning in mid-July. *The Liberté* was on its last voyage, and we reaped the benefits of its final gust of glory; sumptuous French feasts, wine three times a day. Mother liked her food plain and felt that wine was for winos. Our first meal began with *soupe a l'oignon gratinée*. Although she spoke no French, Mother animated her way through the language, waving her hand over the waiter's tray as if the gesture could make the whole thing vanish.

Our waiter had a beautiful smile but spoke only a few words of English. He returned with escargot. "Madame is pleased?" he asked, and then trailed off in a profusion of French. But Mother's eyes were closed now, her face passionate with resignation. "Please, please listen to me," she said slowly and clearly in her most articulate English. "I want just a little plain broiled chicken." Our next course was beef fillet with Madeira sauce. The waiter appeared smiling again, but Mother did not. The girls were enjoying it all.

Using her hands and face in a dramatic presentation of "perfect" slowly articulated English, Mother fluttered her hands like a bird and then took on the posture of a broiled chicken in a pan. Thus, Mother "spoke French" to the waiter. Finally, he understood and was delighted. She got what passed for "a little plain broiled chicken" twice a day for the duration of our trip.

My daughters, Barbara and Michele, refused Mother's "Franco-American diet," preferring to pick and choose among the courses, ending every meal except breakfast with a dish of ice cream. They were eight and nine years old on this first trip to Europe, and the ship was made for them. There is something very carefree about the ambience of a ship at sea, and the children picked it up immediately. Before we were an hour out, they had met up with a marauding band of children whose parents allowed them total freedom from morning until night. The children had a great time swimming and plotting a scheme to find Bob Hope, who was also on the boat. Each morning the kids got together with a new plan to catch at least a glimpse of the famous comedian—and perhaps get a signature, too. Bob Hope stayed out of sight in his suite of rooms, hidden on the other side of the boat where the public was forbidden to go. I wonder if he knew there was a group of children (two little black girls among them) who were looking for him. They never saw him, but the hunt filled their days and nights with anticipation, and mine with peace.

At mealtimes, I would watch all the gaiety at the surrounding tables, which were littered with empty wine bottles. Finally, I requested that our waiter open the bottle on our table just to see what it was all about. After all, in Harlem wine was for winos, but could all these nice-looking white people be winos? "No," I thought, raising my wineglass for my first taste.

"Is Madame pleased?" the waiter inquired.

"Oh yes, it's fine," I said, evading my mother's disapproving glance and trying not to seem like a wino. The discovery of "wine with meals" and the peace and quiet of lemonade on a shaded sun deck supplied me with an afterglow that floated me to Europe.

I wanted my daughters to know about art, music and literature; to know about other people's cultures and history as well as their own and to be well traveled. I wanted them to be little "continental colored girls" with a future—if they chose—outside Harlem or, indeed, America. Most of all, I wanted my daughters to have choices.

Obviously, high on the "to do" list in Paris was the Louvre. *Mona Lisa*, here we come—Mother, Barbara, Michele, and I, three generations of blackness from Harlem, U.S.A. The day we went to see the *Mona Lisa* was the same day the girls discovered a *glacé* (French for ice cream) wagon in the courtyard outside. The French ate very little ice cream at this time, so it was a rare thing to see someone selling it. "We have come to the Louvre to see the *Mona Lisa, The Death of Marat*, and certain other masterpieces, not to eat *glacé*," I told Barbara and Michele, trying to sound warm but firm. After all, we had already begun to attract attention just by being there and I didn't want to cause a scene over anything as "American" as ice cream. A crowd was beginning to form around us, and the man selling *glacé* held out two containers in a vain attempt to connect with Barbara and Michele's outstretched hands. "When we come out," I promised, and took their hands in mine, hurrying them into the Louvre against their will.

I had to almost drag Barbara and Michele through the museum; they knew all too well that my art museum tours could take hours, since they had already been on many museum trips to the Metropolitan and the Museum of Modern Art in New York. We were now followed by a crowd of curious French museum goers. Mother pretended that she was not with us, as the magnificent halls of the Louvre echoed with the girls' desperate pleas for *glacé*. Finally we found the *Mona Lisa*, whereupon I began to lecture the girls on "The Smile" and the history of this great painting. Our French audience was politely attentive but the girls were unimpressed. Barbara and Michele found the smile as well as the painting too small, and its pursuit far too time consuming a distraction. The next time I saw Mother, she was outside the Louvre eating *glacé* and shaking her head in disbelief.

———

The rift between my daughters and me began a few years later, in the middle of the 1960s, when I was in my mid-thirties. As I look back, the Sixties provided a fantastic revelation, an inspiration, and a milestone in my development as both a woman and an artist. In the summers, when I wasn't teaching art, I painted. Throughout the decade, I had begun to explore the idea of a new palette, a way of expressing on canvas the new "black is beautiful" sense of ourselves. Although trained to paint in the Western tradition, I was now committed to "black light" and subtle color nuances and compositions based on my new interest in African rhythm, pattern and repetition.

For my teenaged daughters, however, the 1960s involved a youthful power blast. The world was looking and listening to youth. "What the young people are saying" prefaced everything that certain adults had to say. I, on the other hand, was outraged when I first heard my daughter announce, "but, Mother, everybody is . . ."—as if this youthful viewpoint was the criterion upon which we should all judge our actions.

In the summer of 1969, I was preparing for a one-person show and desperately in need of time to paint. Michele and Barbara were sixteen and seventeen, respectively, and in open rebellion. Michele was the friend of a white girl whose mother had a black boyfriend, a jazz musician, and they all got high together. My kids thought that was great family unity. "You're too emotional on the subject. Everybody who uses drugs is not a drug addict," the girls informed me. I was outraged. I was haunted by the deaths of my first husband, Earl, the girls' father, and Andrew, my brother. Both died from heroin overdose.

One day I heard the girls discussing some so-called revolutionary remarks Stokely Carmichael had made in a lecture, "The only position for women . . . is prone," he had said.

"Please don't allow yourselves to be used by anyone, male or female," I begged them. But Michele had a super crush on Stokely Carmichael and Barbara was excited just to hear that she had met him. It was obvious neither girl had heard a word I said. They had already been told by movement leaders that mother was the undisputed enemy of all revolutionary ideas. My daughters didn't seem to sense the contradictions. "Have a baby for the revolution!" was a supposed battle cry for women of the movement. Would they then be revolutionary mothers—or merely women, with the added burden of a child to bring up, possibly alone?

My husband Birdie was very expressive on the baby issue. "We don't want a baby. If we did, we could have one ourselves. Your mother and I [then aged thirty-five and thirty-six] are not as old as we seem. Hold those boys off. The revolution, my ass! All they want to do is fuck and run."

"But, Daddy," Barbara argued, "you don't know the boys of today. They are honest. We're not into the lies of your generation."

Our family could no longer take a vacation together, but I got an idea I thought they would like: summer study abroad at the University of Mexico in Mexico City. They could both study their favorite subjects—Barbara, Spanish and Portuguese, and Michele, art and literature. Though Mother disapproved of my allowing the girls to go to Mexico, she admitted that they really had enjoyed studying French on their last trip to Paris with her. Although Birdie and I were separated at the time, I knew that if I were to call him he would caution me: "Don't let those girls go away alone. Keep them with you and give up your art. Postpone the show. They'll be back in school in a few months anyhow."

But then, so would I.

In Mexico, I believed they could live in a student house where they would be supervised, but still be somewhat on their own with other young people. A sense of freedom was apparently what they yearned for. I told myself that maybe what they needed was an opportunity to show how mature they were. I thought the trip would be a good test, at any rate.

Before the girls left for Mexico I gave them a thorough briefing: "Remember to lock your door ... be careful when you meet strangers ... stay together, and most of all look out for each other."

Michele was older by eleven months; therefore, she was to be responsible for Barbara.

I began to assemble my canvases and paints to start work. For the first day or two I did nothing else and before long I was totally absorbed in my art. The girls had called to tell me that they had safely arrived in Mexico and were starting school the next day. Everything seemed perfect. A pattern for my summer was set up.

The girls had been gone less than three weeks when, at 2 A.M. on a hot July night, Barbara was on the phone. She was in New York at Kennedy Airport on her way uptown in a taxi. "I'm all out of money. Be downstairs to pay the taxi driver," she demanded, and hung up. I waited in front of the building for Barbara. I was out of my mind with worry. Barbara home . . . barely two weeks . . . Where's Michele? Out of money . . . Oh, God, what has happened . . . ? When her cab arrived, I embraced Barbara. My baby looked adorable, acting so grown up in a new white Mexican dress with embroidery on it. I wanted to hold her and kiss her again and again, but she wasn't for it. She was cool and in a hurry to get the greeting over with. She had on her "cut-the-kid-stuff-I'm-a-woman-now" face.

Finally Barbara got down to the story. She and Michele had met some Mexican "revolutionary" students the first day of classes and decided to go and live with them at their commune in the suburbs of Mexico City. There were three men and two women, all in their middle to late twenties, and Ramos, the leader of the commune, was thirty-two years old. I was told that Michele would not be coming home. She had fallen in love with Ramos and had joined the movement. They intended to live at the commune and be happy forever after. Michele had turned over all of her money to Ramos, who would take care of everything. Barbara came home because she didn't fit in. As for the nature of these revolutionary activities, the story was vague. They were doing some takes in the nude for a movie. Otherwise they smoked a lot of pot. The "girls" did housework, and the men "worked" one day a week in town.

I called Michele immediately, ordering her to come home. I could feel her coolness through the phone.

"As far as I am concerned, I am home," she informed me. If I'd feel any better about it, I could send permission so that she could get married. That was all she had to say. Ramos was there to explain matters further if I didn't understand.

Ramos then got on the phone and proceeded to inform me that I was "a reactionary individualist artist, a domineering self-serving woman, a pawn of the capitalist system who had to be destroyed." I was a menace. My children should leave me because I was a dangerous negative influence. People like me were beyond hope.

A lifetime of careful speech and whitey-fied intonations went right through the window. I reached back to my native Harlem street language.

"Me? You motherfucking . . . bastard, son of a honkey bitch. You have taken advantage of my child. Whoever said a white racist full-of-shit creep like you could—"

"Mrs. Ringgold," he said, his Mexican accent seeming heavier now and his voice out of control, almost cracking, "your daughter has left you—"

"Let me warn you," I screamed, "you're not fucking with a fool. Your honky ass will be hotter than hell if—"

Ramos interrupted again, "There is nothing you can do. Michele is—"

"Listen, you murky-white cracker junky half-ass revolutionary pimp motherfucker, what have you given her? Some of your dope? Barbara tells me you have a fucking drug store there. Well, you dopey freaked-out sack of shit, you'd better not take me lightly. This black capitalist bitch will cause you more trouble than it's worth. What kind of revolutionary are you, you freak? You haven't seen no revolution! The best you can do, you motherfucking drug addict bastard, is send my daughter home or—"

"Good day, Mrs. Ringgold," Ramos said, and hung up the phone.

I called the American embassy in Mexico. The ambassador was conveniently out of town, but his assistant spoke with me. I told him the story, that I was rescinding my permission for Michele to be in Mexico, waving in my hand a copy of my letter of consent (which he, of course, could not see). The assistant attempted to explain to me that it would not be possible to make Michele leave Mexico unless she was doing something unlawful.

"Unlawful?" I screamed. "What do you think they are doing over there? Watching the sun set?"

"I don't know, Mrs. Ringgold," came the disinterested voice of the assistant.

"And you don't care either, do you? Well, if you know what's good for you, you'll get your ass over there and see what they—"

Suddenly I realized I was raving to a dial tone. The assistant had hung up on me. I had to get a grip on myself. I called the State Department in Washington, D.C., and then I called the White House and tried to get through to President Nixon. Then I sent the following telegram to all the appropriate officials:

MY DAUGHTER IS A MINOR BEING HELD IN A MEXICAN COMMUNE AGAINST MY WILL. I AM HER MOTHER AND A BLACK WOMAN, AN AMERICAN CITIZEN, A REGISTERED VOTER AND A TAXPAYER, AND I DEMAND IMMEDIATE ACTION OR ANY HARM THAT COMES TO HER IS THE RESPONSIBILITY OF ALL OF YOU WHO DO NOT ASSIST ME IN BRINGING HER HOME IMMEDIATELY. SHE HAS A RETURN FLIGHT TICKET. I EXPECT HER IN AMERICA BY SUNDOWN TOMORROW.

Now the assistant to the ambassador was calling me. He was at the commune. And he wanted to know what Michele looked like. "She's black," I bellowed. "Can't you see? Now what are you going to do?"

He hesitated. His voice softened. "Well, what do you want me to do?"

"Take her out of there right now. Put her in a hotel where she will be safe for the night, and tomorrow put her on the first flight home. That is all. Don't leave her there. She doesn't even speak their language. Can't you see they are adults taking advantage of a young black girl?"

The next day Michele flew back to America, with no ticket, no identification or papers of any kind, and no money. When she arrived home, Michele looked pretty much as Barbara had: dressed in a beautiful, white, hand-embroidered Mexican dress that seemed made for her. She was a little thinner but she looked pretty and healthy. She was very hostile, however, admitting nothing about the drugs. As far as she was concerned, I had destroyed her chance at happiness; and like Barbara, she had nothing but contempt for me. As soon as her friends from Mexico came for her, she announced defiantly, she would be off again to the commune.

Back in Mexico at that very time, hundreds of young, white Americans were being arrested on marijuana charges. Many were later forced into heroin addiction in Mexico's prisons, their parents compelled to send thousands of American dollars each year to maintain drug habits forced upon them by unscrupulous prison personnel. A large group was released in 1979 in exchange for Mexican prisoners serving time in American jails. So I was lucky I got my girls out of there, although I didn't realize how lucky then.

I wanted both Michele and Barbara examined for drugs and mental and physical health. I searched the Yellow Pages for family services, someone to talk to who knew more than I did about all this. I found the name of an agency I recognized and called. "I'm having trouble with my daughters and I'd like to talk to someone about it. They have just come from Mexico where they joined a commune and I don't know what . . ." There was an accommodating silence on the other end. Embarrassed, I rambled on. "I don't know why my daughters did this. . . . I thought we all knew what our struggle was, and what we should be. . . . I didn't think young black people had time for. . . . We have so many other more important—"

"Mrs. Ringgold, please come down to see us. We will talk." From the way she responded, I knew she must be a black woman and I could feel that she understood what I was going through. The wait through the night began. A quiet desperation crept over me. What would become of us?

At the social service agency we never saw the black woman I had spoken to on the phone. Instead, we were greeted by a cold, pale, white young woman from the old school of social workers. She established my ability to pay and then fell into a dead silence. She had us all figured out. When she finally spoke, she advised us to go home and wait for all hell to break out. Only then, I surmised, would she feel comfortable talking to the police and hospital caseworkers and perhaps placing Barbara or Michele with another member of the family.

I needed immediate help. Michele had to be placed somewhere, because she clearly couldn't stay with me and there was no one else who could keep her. She was going to Howard University in September. If she wanted to leave from there and go back to the commune, so be it—I wouldn't even have known when she left. But for now I wanted her to be somewhere else. More than pain, I felt anger for the waste of energy, time and resources. It is the "feminine ghetto" that drives so many young women, no matter how richly endowed and carefully brought up, they seek out the enemy and give themselves over to him. Why can't we ever disappoint the bastard and leave him standing there as we sashay on by?

At my request, Michele was put in a Catholic girl's home where she had to remain until it was time for her to go to college in five weeks' time. If she promised not to run away with the Mexicans, she could come home and we would try again. She refused.

At Howard University, Michele took to spending money recklessly and not attending classes. Birdie went down to see her and then came to see me. He was concerned about Michele's education. He felt she was jeopardizing it by her casual "party" attitude, which he was able to detect easily in one short visit. I was very glad he came to see me. We had not been together for almost two years. The girls demanded too much of my time to share myself with anyone; only Birdie could understand what I was going through. At that point all I could do was teach and try to get a little painting done in between bouts with Barbara and late-night calls from Michele demanding money.

In September, with Michele at Howard University, it was Barbara's turn to act out at school. I guess we were lucky she chose her senior year in which to do it. Her SAT scores placed her in the upper 99th percentile of graduating high school seniors. Several Ivy League colleges requested her application, but she was—in keeping with the mood of the 1960s—ready to "turn off and drop out." Although we were proud of her achievements, her rebellious spirit hardly gave us a chance to enjoy them. Later I discovered she had taken LSD and was giving her teachers a bad time. Because of my well-known aversion to drugs, I was not told, but I knew something was very wrong with Barbara.

By 1970, Birdie and I were officially back together again. He was very supportive, and acted as a buffer between the girls and me, shielding me from their constant tyranny. He listened to their recklessly youthful ideas and became a sounding board for their madness. Birdie told me to ignore them: "Cut the cord or they will destroy you," he advised. Yet he was ambiguous about how to do it. I was still "Mommy Faye" (my girls' name for me), and the ultimate burden was still mine. He could only make the pain more bearable. Even my mother couldn't help me now. The Sixties youth said "no, no" to extended families.

In the Sixties, well-meaning parents were as confused about drugs as they were about the white power establishment, the black man, the poor, the war in Vietnam, and everything else. They were reluctant to guide, restrict, or set standards for their children. They practically pushed the kids to rebel, as if through their children's actions they could achieve some form of redemption for being rich. My children were no better off despite my standards of appropriate dress, behavior and ghetto smarts. What I had to say, as far as my children were concerned, just didn't count.

If I had found 1969 difficult, 1979 was worse. Michele's book on black feminism was published, *Black Macho and the Myth of the Superwoman*, and I received a great deal of negative public attention. I remember tuning in to a national radio program just in time to hear the interviewer announce that she was talking to Michele Wallace, "the woman whose mother had put her in a home." In her book, Michele "whitewashed" the Mexican commune incident and made me look like a controlling, stereotypical black matriarch whose daughter became a feminist in spite of her. She gave me no credit as a role model for learning how to be both a woman and a political activist. There is no greater defeat to a woman who is a mother than to have her value as a mother denied. I had produced two very talented children; why not give me credit?

Instead, Michele made no mention of the fact that I was an artist, an activist, or a feminist. A caption to a photograph of Michele, her two grandmothers, and me appeared in *Ms.* Magazine. it was a quote from Michele's book: "By the time I was fifteen there was nothing I dreaded more than being like the women in my family."

As a young mother I thought that if I gave my girls lots of love and attention, a good home and education, and a wealth of cultural experiences, they would be trouble free. But there is no guarantee of what kids will pattern their lives after. There is only one certainty in the mother-daughter relationship: No matter how hard you try, mother will make mistakes and daughter will, too, but the mistakes daughter makes will probably be "all mother's fault."

A wonderfully gifted writer, Michelle continues to thrive as a teacher, lecturer, and a much-sought-after conference participant. She has become a major presence nationally in the articulation of cultural criticism and is an associate professor of English and Woman's Studies at the City College of New York, and the City University Graduate Center CUNY. Michele authored her second book in 1991, a collection of essays, titled *Invisibility Blues: From Pop to Theory.*

In the late Seventies, Barbara also became an accomplished scholar. After receiving her undergraduate certificate from the University of London, Barbara became interested in sound and syntax in East African languages. Later she won a summer fellowship to attend a linguistics conference where she met other East African linguists at the University of Illinois in Champagne-Urbana. In 1980, Barbara won another fellowship from City University to do research on East African languages at the Yale Library, where she read in Italian and German all they had on structure, sound and syntax of East African languages. With three master's degrees in linguistics, Barbara now teaches—she is a brilliant and inventive fourth-grade teacher in an elementary school in Harlem—and has three beautiful daughters, Faith, Theodora and Martha.

I've been told I am demanding and I don't deny it, but I am also generous and giving of my time, love, energy and resources. My mother made many demands on me and I complied. She would have been devastated if I had ever shown disloyalty toward her. Lack of trust was unthinkable in our relationship as mother and daughter. By contrast, my demands on my daughters, even of loyalty, have often been a burden to them.

Of Michele and Barbara, Mother used to say: "Today they are around your feet; tomorrow they'll be around your heart." However, it never occurred to me that in a few short years, between that trip to Paris in 1961 and the debacle of Mexico City in 1969, they would change so much. Don't get me wrong: they are still beautiful, personable and smart. Although we don't have the same bonds my mother and I had, we continue to try.

To make up for some of the closeness I missed in my relationship with my daughters, I made a number of works of art. Through art, I tried to create the peace we could not achieve in real life. (There is a kind of eternal insidious competition between me and my daughters—a women's war that never seems to end.) In my Couples Series, I created wedding installations for each of my daughters, in an attempt to resolve a charged issue that confronts so many mothers and daughters: Daughters' love relationships. In another series, the first Slave Rape Series, I created portraits of Barbara, Michele, and me: Barbara in *Fear: Will Make you Weak*, Michele in *Run: You Might Get Away*, and me in *Fight: To Save Your Life*. Michele mentioned recently that I had once said that all of the women in my paintings were based on the likeness of one of the three of us. I don't remember stating this, but I do know that all of my story quilts about families have been in some way based on my own experience of family.

The text of my performance/five-part story quilt *The Bitter Nest* (which I created in 1985 and 1987, respectively) is a fictitious response to our mother-and-daughter feuds. In the story, everything is resolved in the end with the death of the family patriarch, Dr. Prince. Although there is no reigning patriarch in our own family, the men in my daughters' lives have been a continuing issue over which we have struggled. Michele's marriage in 1989 to Eugene Nesmith, a talented actor, director, and theater professor, has relieved some of that old tension between us and helped us to be closer than we have been in years. Barbara's three children, my glorious grandchildren, have welded Barbara and me. Despite the fact that we sometimes pull apart, we have Faith, Theodora, and Martha, the next generation, to give us hope and keep us together.

Margaret: A Mother for All Seasons

BY JEWELLE TAYLOR GIBBS

"To everything there is a season, and a time for every purpose under heaven."

ECCLESIASTES, 3, VERSE 1, OLD TESTAMENT

*O*n Christmas Eve, 2002, my Mother died peacefully at the age of ninety, surrounded by two generations of her children and grandchildren. In the aftermath of her death, there were the usual preparations, the familiar rituals, and the intermittent spasms of grief. But it was not until I had returned to California a few days after her funeral, that I was finally overwhelmed by feelings of loss, and flooded by memories of our relationship over the seasons of our intertwined lives.

My Mother's obituary in the *New York Times,* describing her as "the product of a multiracial, multiethnic family" afforded only a surface glimpse into her fascinating life that began in 1912, the year the *Titanic* sank, and ended in 2003, the year the space shuttle *Columbia* exploded. Born only a few blocks from the Capitol in Washington, D.C., my Mother was the fifth child of fair-skinned mulattoes of modest means. At the age of four, her own Mother died prematurely of cancer and she was shortly abandoned by her Father, who disappeared to "pass for white" along with her four older siblings and their Irish grandmother. Reared by a series of eccentric foster parents, my Mother never completely recovered from the early trauma of loss and rejection, a theme that resonated throughout her life and motivated her lifelong search for family and community.

My Mother's death was neither unexpected nor unpredictable, but her life was a triumph over adversity and a testament to her resilience and courage. As I have reflected on her long life, I have come to understand and to appreciate the remarkable legacy that she bequeathed to all of her extended family. My Mother was thoughtful and compassionate, optimistic and hopeful, energetic and enthusiastic, witty and wise, charming and coquettish, frank and feisty, a true Gemini.

OUR SEASONS OF LIVING

In the weeks and months after my Mother's death, my thoughts of her flickered as images in a videotape rewinding, her story unfolding in reverse with snatches of muffled conversation and dimly remembered scenes. The scenes began to come into sharper focus and then sorted themselves into chronological order, a series of vignettes that vividly captured my relationship with her over the seasons of our lives.

My Mother and Father were married in New York City Hall in January, 1933, in the depths of the Depression, and I was born ten months later in the bucolic town of Stratford, Connecticut, where my Father had been called to serve as the minister of the small and struggling First Baptist Church. It was not easy for my twenty-year-old Mother, a lively and beautiful young woman from cosmopolitan Washington, D.C., to adapt to a small New England town with few Blacks (called Negroes then) and few cultural amenities. But she was fiercely determined to make a home for her new family, even though it meant repressing some of her own desires, and channeling her energies into ensuring my Father's success in his new position.

One of my earliest memories of my Mother was at the age of three, when I was sitting in her lap while she combed my short wiry hair. She was patiently trying to make me Shirley Temple curls and telling me to keep still while I played with her long black wavy hair and ran my fingers along her lovely high cheekbones. After all these years, I still have a strong sensory memory of how soft her ivory-colored skin felt and how wonderfully she smelled. I knew even then that I wanted to grow up to look and smell like my pretty Mother, who put on her makeup and a touch of perfume, and earrings every morning after her bath.

By the time I was four, there were two more babies, my brother, Julian, Jr., and my sister, Shirley Anne, but my Mother still found special time to spend with me, teaching me to read and enlisting me as "Mother's little helper." Though the Depression shadowed our early years in Stratford, my Mother always managed to find joy in small blessings. She spent her days entertaining the three of us with daily adventures, picking green apples off the trees in our yard in the spring, catching crayfish in the creek that ran by our cottage in the summer, and walking down the block to watch the ferries on Long Island Sound in the autumn. It was an idyllic childhood, a time when I first picked up my Mother's sense of adventure and her zest for life.

Our family expanded every summer when my father's two older daughters, Mauryne and Doris, came up from Washington to spend their school vacations with us. Along with my foster sister, Margaret, who had joined our family when I was two years old as a real Mother's helper, they added excitement and adolescent mischief to our active household. Most of all, I remember the sense of being surrounded by people who loved and cherished me, and the sense of the safe haven that my parents provided, most especially my Mother, lasted through all the seasons of my life.

In 1938 my family moved about twenty miles away to Ansonia, Connecticut, where my Father became the pastor of the Macedonia Baptist Church, and my Mother assumed a new role as his helpmate in a church which was rapidly expanding as the town's mills recruited Black workers from the South. Unable to find permanent housing after three years due to racial discrimination, our family moved to a duplex in nearby Waterbury just before my parents' fourth child, Patricia Rose, was born. Coping with four young children and a commuting husband with two jobs, my Mother was sometimes harried and eager for adult company. She befriended the Italian landlady, who taught her how to make authentic Italian spaghetti and meatballs, a favorite family recipe for many years.

Shortly after my baby sister arrived, I was run over by a moving truck as it careened down a hill near our house. I can still envision my Mother, running down the street with Patty in her arms and tears streaming down her face, cradling my head in her lap and reassuring me until the ambulance arrived. My brush with mortality brought our family even closer together and my Mother became even more protective of her brood and more alert to every nuance of threat or danger. It must have been a very stressful time for my Mother, caring for an infant and a temporarily disabled child, but she never seemed to complain or miss a beat. She seemed unflappable, the original "energizer bunny," another trait she clearly passed on to me.

We moved back to Ansonia into the church's new parsonage when I was in the fifth grade and my Mother was delighted to have a larger house for her family, even though it meant sharing her time and her home with the church members. While I was making new friends and competing for grammar school honors, my Mother was entering her thirties and finding her own voice as a youth leader in church and a volunteer in the community. She helped my Father establish a chapter of the NAACP after a young Black man in our church was falsely accused of raping a white girl, and remained an active member of the chapter for the rest of her life.

Because of her early life experiences, my Mother was always keenly aware of injustice and had deep springs of empathy for the underdog. My Mother became involved in the foster care system in Connecticut and soon opened her home and her heart to a teenager named Ethel, who joined our family when I was in sixth grade. Four more foster daughters came to live with us over the next fifteen years—Althea, Jackie, Margery, and Minna—even after we had all left home. My parents welcomed them into our family, educated them, celebrated their marriages, and launched them into adulthood.

My Mother became the matriarch of a growing clan, rarely making any distinctions between family kin and fictive kin.

My Mother also loved animals, so our lively household always included a large dog, stray cats, and later a cranky parrot, who all competed for her attention and affection. Our house sometimes seemed like a petting zoo with noisy animals underfoot and kids in perpetual motion.

Whenever my Mother thought any of her children were treated unfairly, her usually sweet and refined demeanor could suddenly turn into an angry tirade, earning her the family nickname "Toughy Taylor." When I was in the eighth grade, I came home sobbing one day because I had auditioned but failed to make the cut for the annual junior high school operetta. My Mother, suspecting racism in the selection process, went into high dudgeon, called the principal to advise him that I was the lead soprano of our junior choir, and questioned why I hadn't been selected. The next day, I found my name had been added to the cast list for the operetta, called "Huldah of Holland." Needless to say, I was the only brown face on the stage with a blond wig. That incident taught me to stand up for myself and never accept rejection if you feel you are qualified for the job, no matter what it is; it was a lesson that would change the course of my life.

When I entered my teenage years, my Mother was in her mid-thirties and blossoming into a mature, more confident woman, a supportive partner for my ambitious Father, and a charming hostess for the numerous political leaders and candidates who courted the Black vote in Connecticut. As an adolescent, it was exciting for me to meet the First Lady, Eleanor Roosevelt, the flamboyant Harlem Congressman, Adam Clayton Powell, the brilliant lawyer, Thurgood Marshall, and the courtly Judge William Hastie, when my Father introduced them at various political rallies and civil rights meetings in the New Haven area.

With her infectious laugh and coquettish smile, my Mother was also very popular with my beaux; she often served hot chocolate and brownies to them when we returned home from dates. But she made it very clear that she had high expectations for me and didn't want me to "fool around" with boys. In fact, the only sex education she ever gave me was elliptical but effective: "When you go out with boys, keep your skirt down, your panties up, and don't let them touch you below the neck."

Throughout high school my parents encouraged me to put my studies first, and were very supportive of all of my extracurricular activities, subtly encouraging my competitive spirit and rewarding me for being an honors student. I sensed that my Mother wanted me to have the opportunities that she never enjoyed and she frequently extolled my Washington cousins and aunts, who were all teachers and school administrators, as role models for me to emulate. They were so proud when I graduated from Ansonia High School with honors and was admitted to Radcliffe College, the women's counterpart of Harvard University.

While my parents were sending me off to an elite women's college, my Mother was tightening the family budget at home and going without some luxuries herself in order to support me in style. It was years later that I fully realized what sacrifices my parents made to give all of their daughters a first-class education and to prepare us for the opportunities that racial progress would create in the 1960s. My Mother also welcomed my college friends on holidays and for Harvard-Yale games in New Haven. During my freshman year, I brought one of my wealthy white friends home for Thanksgiving, always a festive occasion with a traditional dinner accompanied by spirited conversation and insider family humor. The next day, my Mother insisted that I take my friend Genna to meet an ailing neighbor who lived in a tiny apartment near the church. On the way back to Cambridge, Genna told me that she wished she had a family that was as warm and loving as mine and a Mother who was so compassionate. Again, my Mother had taught me a valuable object lesson on never forgetting about your less fortunate neighbors, no matter how much you may achieve or what friends you may acquire.

After graduation, I worked for a year in Washington, D.C., wanting to bond with my extended family, and also wanting a year of independence before I married. The following year, on August 25, 1956, I married James Lowell Gibbs, Jr., an anthropology graduate student at Harvard. My Mother delighted in helping me plan an elegant formal wedding with twenty-two attendants, reflecting her skill in organizing a large social event while maintaining peace among the various family factions, who all wanted to participate. The wedding was such a happy event for both of our families, yet they were not eager to hear that we would soon be going to Liberia for eighteen months while Jim conducted research on the Kpelle tribe for his doctoral dissertation. Six months later on a damp cold February afternoon, twelve members of our family stood on a Brooklyn pier, waving and crying as we sailed away to Europe on the first leg of our trip to West Africa. Later, we often joked that we could have sailed all the way to Liberia on the ocean of tears they shed that day.

Our time in the Liberian village of Fokwele was fascinating, arduous, and sometimes frustrating, particularly living in the bush in a mud hut without plumbing, electricity, or gas, not to mention television or any of the other amenities young couples expect. Without my Mother's frequent encouraging letters and "care packages," I'm not sure I could have maintained my sanity for the long haul, but she had urged me to stay with my husband and work together to establish a firm foundation for our marriage. Whenever I would feel that the foundation was getting shaky, I would visualize my Mother and think of all the hardships she had endured early in her marriage and I would resolve to stick it out, thatch rats and bush snakes notwithstanding.

When we returned to Cambridge in 1958, Jim completed his dissertation and was offered a job at the University of Minnesota, which seemed like the North Pole to me. Again, my Mother reassured me that, just as she had moved away from her family and friends to begin her married life in Connecticut, so would I adjust to Minneapolis. While I was beginning a new job in market research at the Pillsbury Company and plunging into local Democratic politics in the early 1960s, my parents were deeply involved with John F. Kennedy's campaign for President in 1960. My Father, who had worked his way up to the vice-chair of the Connecticut Democratic Party, was recruited by Sargent Shriver to rally the Black churches for Kennedy in the West Virginia primary, while my Mother worked behind the scenes in Connecticut. One of the most exciting moments in her life was attending Kennedy's inauguration and the inaugural ball in her own hometown. Later she gave the beautiful black and gold gown she wore to me, which I wore only once, then wrapped it in tissue paper and stored it for posterity in one of my closets.

Within four years after we settled in Minneapolis, our two sons were born, Geoffrey Taylor in 1961 and Lowell Dabney in 1963. My Mother came out to help me with both babies, giving me helpful tips about schedules and self-survival, but mainly showing me how to handle the babies calmly and carefully so that they would always feel safe and secure, as we did with her. While my Mother was in her fifties, she welcomed several more grandchildren, as my two younger sisters and my brother produced more progeny. She easily made the transition from mothering to grandmothering, relishing the role of beloved "Nana" to all her thirteen grandchildren and her many adopted grands. But my children didn't have the benefit of Nana's attention and spoiling as much as my nieces and nephews who all lived within driving distance of New Haven, so she would make it up to them on her infrequent visits with special treats and adventures.

On one of those memorable adventures, when we were en route to Liberia for our second field work in the summer of 1965, Nana accompanied us to Europe to help babysit for our active preschoolers.

She proved to be a real trouper, undaunted by language difficulties and reveling in the spectacular scenery and the exotic cultural experiences of Spain and Portugal.

When my husband accepted a position at Stanford University and we moved to the Bay Area in 1965, my parents were sad that we were moving even further away from the East Coast, but my Mother fell in love with California on her first visit and subsequently found every opportunity to visit us. She flew out to celebrate my first graduate degree in social work, our son Geoffrey's high school graduation in 1979, and my doctoral degree in psychology in 1980. Each time, she would provide an elaborate excuse for my Father's absence, but I knew he was gradually getting weaker from emphyesma, and she was basically keeping him functioning with her loving care.

On May 2, 1981, my Father died suddenly twelve days before his seventy-ninth birthday, two months after my Father-in-law died of cancer. It was a double blow to our small family, as we had encouraged both of our sons to choose Ivy League colleges, so that they could spend their college years in the East, where they would get to know their grandparents, aunts, and cousins better. Geoffrey had enjoyed spending weekends with my family in New Haven during his first two years at Harvard, but by the time Lowell entered Cornell, both grandfathers had passed away. My Mother found widowhood very traumatic, as she had grown up with my Father, never worked outside the home, and never lived alone, so it was now our turn to comfort and care for her.

Within the next three years, my foster sister, Margaret, and my brother, Julian, also died prematurely. My Mother's courage and dignity in the face of these multiple losses exemplified true grace under pressure, inspiring the rest of us with strength and faith to move forward.

On the cusp between adolescence and adulthood, Nana's grandchildren quickly stepped in to help fill the enormous void in her life.

Her pride knew no bounds in 1983 when Geoffrey graduated *magna cum laude* from Harvard and was selected as a Rhodes Scholar. Nor was she shy about bragging rights when Lowell graduated from Cornell two years later and joined the Salomon Brothers investment bank as one of the early African American analysts on Wall Street.

Four years after my Father died, my Mother sold her large home and moved in with my younger sister Patty and her family in the suburbs of North Haven. When she came out to see me the following summer, she seemed sad and withdrawn, so I suggested that she needed to get involved with some volunteer work, and she tartly replied: "I know what I need. I need a man, and I don't want an old man who smells like liniment, I want a younger man who smells like Brut." It would be an understatement to admit that I was a little shocked, but it made me realize that my Mother still had a lot of life left in her and she wanted to share it with someone.

It didn't take my Mother long to find a suitable mate and, in the summer of 1986 at the age of seventy-four, she married Graham Hancock, a gentle widower she had met at her new church. My sisters and I gave her a beautiful garden wedding, serving as her attendants, along with our husbands, Jim, Harold Haizlip, and Jim Brown; three of her granddaughters, Deirdre, Melissa, and Julie, as bridesmaids; and six of her grandsons, including my two sons, Dale, Taylor, Jeffrey, and Max, as ushers. It was another happy occasion for a family gathering, but I was painfully aware of how many members were missing and how frail my two elderly aunts seemed.

On my Mother's eightieth birthday, my sister Shirley Haizlip gave her the most precious gift of all—the news that her older sister, Grace, was still alive and living alone in Anaheim, California. Shirley had discovered Grace's whereabouts while researching her book, *The Sweeter the Juice: A Family Memoir in Black and White,* and soon reunited the two sisters by phone. Soon after the book was published in 1994, my Mother was startled by a surprise reunion on the *Oprah* show with two nieces and a grandnephew, who were also living in the white world. She was so thrilled to have *five* years of visits with Grace, her long-lost sister for seventy-six years, and grateful to learn about what had happened to her other siblings, providing some closure to her lifelong quest. She also became a bit of a diva, reveling in the attention she received at Shirley's book signings, finally enjoying the spotlight after a lifetime of being in my Father's shadow.

In the summer of 1992, only two months after they jointly celebrated their eightieth birthdays, Graham Hancock died after a long battle with cancer. My Mother, widowed for the second time, was devastated. Once again, she packed her bags and returned to the suburbs to live with her youngest daughter's family. She didn't have as much energy and her memory was not as sharp, but she still enjoyed going to see her grandsons play football, getting dressed up for a Links dance, and making her annual trek to visit her California family. Even in her eighties, Margaret was always eager for a new adventure, whether it was trying a new restaurant with grandson Lowell, cruising with friends on San Francisco Bay, or seeing granddaughter Melissa in the Los Angeles production of *The Lion King*.

We celebrated my Mother's eighty-fifth birthday with a lovely afternoon tea under a tent on my sister Patty's sweeping lawn. My Mother looked beautiful in a lilac-flowered chiffon dress and matching coat, basking in the attention and affection of her family and friends, even dancing with her new beau. She looked on with pride as all of her grandchildren, now adults, gave tributes to her, reflecting the values she had passed on in their own lives and accomplishments. The memory of that day is now bittersweet, as it marked the beginning of her gradual mental and physical decline. When she came to visit us the following spring, she exhibited the early signs of dementia: the memory loss, the mental confusion, and the sudden mood swings. Her energy and her enthusiasm to try new things were waning, so I realized that old age had finally caught up with her.

Before she left to return home, my Mother gave us a gift of four rose bushes for our forty-first wedding anniversary. Now there are sixteen rose bushes in coral and yellow varieties planted in our sunny garden, blooming profusely from early spring to late autumn. There is a special bush with large canary yellow blossoms named "Margaret," the queen of the garden and the object of my constant admiration and attention.

For the last five years of her life, my Mother spent longer periods in California during the winter months. She complained more about her arthritis, respiratory problems, and other physical ailments, and her joy in life seemed diminished. But she rallied to attend my retirement dinner in February, 2000, entrancing my friends and colleagues with her charm and grace. When she later was diagnosed with chronic obstructive pulmonary disorder (COPD), at the age of eighty-eight, the doctor told me that the disease was destroying her lungs and the prognosis was not good. A year later, too weak to care for herself and needing constant care, she was finally admitted to a nursing home. It was the most difficult decision we ever had to make as a family, and it caused enormous turmoil and tension among us, although none of us was able to care for my Mother at home. But it seemed fitting that my Mother's favorite stuffed animals were her constant bedside companions, providing her with comfort and easing the transition from home to nursing home.

My Mother had long expressed the hope that she would reach the age of ninety, as had her grandmother and her oldest sister Grace. So we planned a small party in the nursing home for her ninetieth birthday in late May. She enjoyed a month-long birthday celebration with her grandchildren from East and West arriving in shifts, even sharing a coveted glass of beer with our son Lowell. Before we rolled my Mother to the lounge in her wheelchair, she turned to our older son and said, "Do I need any lipstick, Geoffrey?" He smiled and said, "No, Nana, you look very pretty." I couldn't help smiling myself at my ninety-year-old, bedridden Mother, who still put on lipstick, perfume, and earrings every day after her bath.

Just six months later, my sister Patty called to tell me that Mother had been transferred to hospice care. My husband and I dropped all of our holiday preparations and flew home immediately to spend the last days with my Mother as her life ebbed away. Her life had come full circle from the cottage by Long Island Sound where she had come as a bride to this peaceful hospice setting overlooking the Sound. We all took turns sitting by her bedside, massaging her thin arms with lotion, and singing her favorite hymns. About six days before she died, Geoffrey called her from Korea to tell her that he had finally found his muse in Brazil and planned to be engaged at Christmas, news that she had been waiting for years to hear. She raised herself slightly from her pillow and muttered, "Oh, my God," with a smile on her face. Those were the last clear words that I ever heard her say, delighted that her second-oldest grandson was finally going to marry.

My Mother died just a few days later on Christmas Eve and we had a poignant celebration of her life in the historic Dixwell Avenue Congregational Church, which she had joined after my Father died. As our extended family gathered from the four corners of the country, I looked around at the lively and talented group and saw my Mother reflected in the beauty of her granddaughters, the self-assurance of her grandsons, the quiet dignity of her cousins, the sophistication of her nieces and nephews, and the loyalty of her close friends, but, above all, in the vitality and joie de vivre that characterizes our family.

Just four months after my Mother's death, our family celebrated a happier occasion of Geoffrey's marriage to Cristina Simone da Silva Angelo, his lovely Brazilian bride. Their marriage took place at a large Presbyterian church in Sao Paulo, Brazil, the bride's hometown, on the groom's forty-second birthday. I wore the elegant lilac chiffon beaded gown that my Mother had worn only once for her second wedding in 1986. As I walked down the aisle with Geoffrey, I felt that my Mother was walking beside us and I could feel her spirit surrounding us. There was a mystical serendipity that Geoffrey became engaged on Christmas Eve in Brazil, about the same time as his Grandmother lay dying a continent away. I envisioned her smiling down on us as we walked toward the altar, happy to know that he would soon begin a family of his own, and hopefully, pass on to a third generation many of the values and traditions that she and my Father had taught us. The pain of losing my Mother was somewhat diminished by our joyful anticipation of gaining a new daughter-in-law. Now it gives me great comfort to remember one of my Mother's favorite biblical passages: "There is a time to be born and a time to die—One generation passes away, and another generation follows." And, as the seasons inexorably pass, we are all connected in an endless cycle of birth, death, regeneration, and renewal.

Everyday Use

BY ALICE WALKER

I will wait for her in the yard that Maggie and I made so clean and wavy yesterday afternoon. A yard like this is more comfortable than most people know. It is not just a yard. It is like an extended living room. When the hard clay is swept clean as a floor and the fine sand around the edges lined with tiny, irregular grooves, anyone can come and sit and look up into the elm tree and wait for the breezes that never come inside the house.

Maggie will be nervous until after her sister goes: she will stand hopelessly in corners, homely and ashamed of the burn scars down her arms and legs, eyeing her sister with a mixture of envy and awe. She thinks her sister has held life always in the palm of her hand, that "no" is a word the world never learned to say to her.

You've no doubt seen those TV shows where the child who has "made it" is confronted, as a surprise, by her own mother and father, tottering in weakly from backstage. (A pleasant surprise, of course: What would they do if parent and child came on the show only to curse out and insult each other?) On TV mother and child embrace and smile into each other's faces. Sometimes the mother and father weep, the child wraps them in her arms and leans across the table to tell how she would not have made it without their help. I have seen these programs.

Sometimes I dream a dream in which Dee and I are suddenly brought together on a TV program of this sort. Out of a dark and soft-seated limousine I am ushered into a bright room filled with many people. There I meet a smiling, gray, sporty man like Johnny

Carson who shakes my hand and tells me what a fine girl I have. Then we are on the stage and Dee is embracing me with tears in her eyes. She pins on my dress a large orchid, even though she has told me once that she thinks orchids are tacky flowers.

In real life I am a large, big-boned woman with rough, man-working hands. In the winter I wear flannel nightgowns to bed and overalls during the day. I can kill and clean a hog as mercilessly as a man. My fat keeps me hot in zero weather. I can work outside all day, breaking ice to get water for washing; I can eat pork liver cooked over the open fire minutes after it comes steaming from the hog. One winter I knocked a bull calf straight in the brain between the eyes with a sledge hammer and had the meat hung up to chill before nightfall. But of course all this does not show on television. I am the way my daughter would want me to be: a hundred pounds lighter, my skin like an uncooked barley pancake. My hair glistens in the hot bright lights. Johnny Carson has much to do to keep up with my quick and witty tongue.

But that is a mistake. I know even before I wake up. Who ever knew a Johnson with a quick tongue? Who can even imagine me looking a strange white man in the eye? It seems to me I have talked to them always with one foot raised in flight, with my head turned in whichever way is farthest from them. Dee, though. She would always look anyone in the eye. Hesitation was no part of her nature.

"How do I look, Mama?" Maggie says, showing just enough of her thin body enveloped in pink skirt and red blouse for me to know she's there, almost hidden by the door.

"Come out into the yard," I say.

Have you ever seen a lame animal, perhaps a dog run over by some careless person rich enough to own a car, sidle up to someone who is ignorant enough to be kind to him? That is the way my Maggie walks. She has been like this, chin on chest, eyes on ground, feet in shuffle, ever since the fire that burned the other house to the ground.

Dee is lighter than Maggie, with nicer hair and a fuller figure. She's a woman now, though sometimes I forget. How long ago was it that the other house burned? Ten, twelve years? Sometimes I can still hear the flames and feel Maggie's arms sticking to me, her hair smoking and her dress falling off her in little black papery flakes. Her eyes seemed stretched open, blazed open by the flames reflected in them. And Dee. I see her standing off under the sweet gum tree she used to dig gum out of; a look of concentration on her face as she watched the last dingy gray board of the house fall in toward the red-hot brick chimney. Why don't you do a dance around the ashes? I'd wanted to ask her. She had hated the house that much.

I used to think she hated Maggie, too. But that was before we raised the money, the church and me, to send her to Augusta to school. She used to read to us without pity; forcing words, lies, other folks' habits, whole lives upon us two, sitting trapped and ignorant underneath her voice. She washed us in a river of make-believe, burned us with a lot of knowledge we didn't necessarily need to know. Pressed us to her with the serious way she read, to shove us away at just the moment, like dimwits, we seemed about to understand.

Dee wanted nice things. A yellow organdy dress to wear to her graduation from high school; black pumps to match a green suit she'd made from an old suit somebody gave me. She was determined to stare down any disaster in her efforts. Her eyelids would not flicker for minutes at a time. Often I fought off the temptation to shake her. At sixteen she had a style of her own: and knew what style was.

I never had an education myself. After second grade the school was closed down. Don't ask me why: in 1927 colored asked fewer questions than they do now. Sometimes Maggie reads to me. She stumbles along good-naturedly but can't see well. She knows she is not bright. Like good looks and money, quickness passed her by. She will marry John Thomas (who has mossy teeth in an earnest face) and then I'll be free to sit here and I guess just sing church songs to myself. Although I never was a good singer. Never could carry a tune. I was always better at a man's job. I used to love milk till I was hooked in the side in '49. Cows are soothing and slow and don't bother you, unless you try to milk them the wrong way.

I have deliberately turned my back on the house. It is three rooms, just like the one that burned, except the roof is tin; they don't make shingle roofs any more. There are no real windows, just some holes cut in the sides, like the portholes in a ship, but not round and not square, with rawhide holding the shutters up on the outside. This house is in a pasture, too, like the other one. No doubt when Dee sees it she will want to tear it down. She wrote me once that no matter where we "choose" to live, she will manage to come see us. But she will never bring her friends. Maggie and I thought about this and Maggie asked me, "Mama, when did Dee ever *have* any friends?"

She had a few. Furtive boys in pink shirts hanging about on washday after school. Nervous girls who never laughed. Impressed with her they worshiped the well-turned phrase, the cute shape, the scalding humor that erupted like bubbles in lye. She read to them.

When she was courting Jimmy T she didn't have much time to pay to us, but turned all her faultfinding power on him. He *flew* to marry a cheap city girl from a family of ignorant flashy people. She hardly had time to recompose herself.

When she comes I will meet—but there they are!

Maggie attempts to make a dash for the house, in her shuffling way, but I stay her with my hand. "Come back here," I say. And she stops and tries to dig a well in the sand with her toe.

It is hard to see them clearly through the strong sun. But even the first glimpse of leg out of the car tells me it is Dee. Her feet were always neat-looking, as if God himself had shaped them with a certain style. From the other side of the car comes a short, stocky man. Hair is all over his head a foot long and hanging from his chin like a kinky mule tail. I hear Maggie suck in her breath. "Uhnnnh" is what it sounds like. Like when you see the wriggling end of a snake just in front of your foot on the road. "Uhnnnh."

Dee next. A dress down to the ground, in this hot weather. A dress so loud it hurts my eyes. There are yellows and oranges enough to throw back the light of the sun. I feel my whole face warming from the heat waves it throws out. Earrings gold, too, and hanging down to her shoulders. Bracelets dangling and making noises when she moves her arm up to shake the folds of the dress out of her armpits. The dress is loose and flows, and as she walks closer, I like it. I hear Maggie go "Uhnnnh" again. It is her sister's hair. It stands straight up like the wool on a sheep. It is black as night and around the edges are two long pigtails that rope about like small lizards disappearing behind her ears.

"Wa-su-zo-Tean-o!" she says, coming on in that gliding way the dress makes her move. The short stocky fellow with the hair to his navel is all grinning and he follows up with "Asalamalakim, my mother and sister!" He moves to hug Maggie but she falls back, right up against the back of my chair. I feel her trembling there and when I look up I see the perspiration falling off her chin.

"Don't get up," says Dee. Since I am stout it takes something of a push. You can see me trying to move a second or two before I make it. She turns, showing white heels through her sandals, and goes back to the car. Out she peeks next with a Polaroid. She stoops down quickly and lines up picture after picture of me sitting there in front of the house with Maggie cowering behind me. She never takes a shot without making sure the house is included. When a cow comes nibbling around the edge of the yard she snaps it and me and Maggie *and* the house. Then she puts the Polaroid in the back seat of the car, and comes up and kisses me on the forehead.

Meanwhile Asalamalakim is going through motions with Maggie's hand. Maggie's hand is as limp as a fish, and probably as cold, despite the sweat, and she keeps trying to pull it back. It looks like Asalamalakim wants to shake hands but wants to do it fancy. Or maybe he don't know how people shake hands. Anyhow, he soon gives up on Maggie.

"Well," I say. "Dee."

"No, Mama," she says. "Not 'Dee,' Wangero Leewanika Kemanjo!"

"What happened to 'Dee'?" I wanted to know.

"She's dead," Wangero said. "I couldn't bear it any longer, being named after the people who oppress me."

"You know as well as me you was named after your aunt Dicie," I said. Dicie is my sister. She named Dee. We called her "Big Dee" after Dee was born.

"But who was *she* named after?" asked Wangero.

"I guess after Grandma Dee," I said.

"And who was she named after?" asked Wangero.

"Her mother," I said, and saw Wangero was getting tired. "That's about as far back as I can trace it," I said. Though, in fact, I probably could have carried it back beyond the Civil War through the branches.

"Well," said Asalamalakim, "there you are."

"Uhnnnh," I heard Maggie say.

"There I was not," I said, "before 'Dicie' cropped up in our family, so why should I try to trace it that far back?"

He just stood there grinning, looking down on me like somebody inspecting a Model A car. Every once in a while he and Wangero sent eye signals over my head.

"How do you pronounce this name?" I asked.

"You don't have to call me by it if you don't want to," said Wangero.

"Why shouldn't I?" I asked. "If that's what you want us to call you, we'll call you."

"I know it might sound awkward at first," said Wangero.

"I'll get used to it," I said. "Ream it out again."

Well, soon we got the name out of the way. Asalamalakim had a name twice as long and three times as hard. After I tripped over it two or three times he told me to just call him Hakim-a-barber. I wanted to ask him was he a barber, but I didn't really think he was, so I didn't ask.

"You must belong to those beef-cattle peoples down the road," I said. They said "Asalamalakim" when they met you, too, but they didn't shake hands. Always too busy: feeding the cattle, fixing the fences, putting up salt-lick shelters, throwing down hay. When the white folks poisoned some of the herd the men stayed up all night with rifles in their hands. I walked a mile and a half just to see the sight.

Hakim-a-barber said, "I accept some of their doctrines, but farming and raising cattle is not my style." (They didn't tell me, and I didn't ask, whether Wangero (Dee) had really gone and married him.)

We sat down to eat and right away he said he didn't eat collards and pork was unclean. Wangero, though, went on through the chitlins and corn bread, the greens and everything else. She talked a blue streak over the sweet potatoes. Everything delighted her. Even the fact that we still used the benches her daddy made for the table when we couldn't afford to buy chairs.

"Oh, Mama!" she cried. Then turned to Hakim-a-barber. "I never knew how lovely these benches are. You can feel the rump prints," she said, running her hands underneath her and along the bench. Then she gave a sigh and her hand closed over Grandma Dee's butter dish. "That's it!" she said. "I knew there was something I wanted to ask you if I could have." She jumped up from the table and went over in the corner where the churn stood, the milk in it clabber by now. She looked at the churn and looked at it.

"This churn top is what I need," she said. "Didn't Uncle Buddy whittle it out of a tree you all used to have?"

"Yes," I said.

"Uh huh," she said happily, "and I want the dasher, too."

"Uncle Buddy whittle that, too?" asked the barber.

Dee (Wangero) looked up at me.

"Aunt Dee's first husband whittled the dash," said Maggie so low, you almost couldn't hear her. "His name was Henry, but they called him Stash."

"Maggie's brain is like an elephant's," Wangero said, laughing. "I can use the churn top as a centerpiece for the alcove table," she said, sliding a plate over the churn, "and I'll think of something artistic to do with the dasher."

When she finished wrapping the dasher the handle stuck out. I took it for a moment in my hands. You didn't even have to look close to see where hands pushing the dash up and down to make butter had left a kind of sink in the wood. In fact, there were a lot of small sinks; you could see where thumbs and fingers had sunk into the wood. It was beautiful light yellow wood, from a tree that grew in the yard where Big Dee and Stash had lived.

After dinner Dee (Wangero) went to the trunk at the foot of my bed and started rifling through it. Maggie hung back in the kitchen over the dishpan. Out came Wangero with two quilts. They had been pieced by Grandma Dee and then Big Dee and me had hung them on the quilt frames on the front porch and quilted them. One was in the Lone Star pattern. The other was Walk Around the Mountain. In both of them were scraps of dresses Grandma Dee had worn fifty and more years ago. Bits and pieces of Grandpa Jarrell's Paisley shirts. And one teeny faded blue piece about the size of a penny matchbox, that was from Great Grandpa Ezra's uniform that he wore in the Civil War.

"Mama," Wangero said sweet as a bird. "Can I have these old quilts?"

I heard something fall in the kitchen, and a minute later the kitchen door slammed.

"Why don't you take one or two of the others?" I asked. "These old things was just done by me and Big Dee from some tops your grandma pieced before she died."

"No," said Wangero. "I don't want those. They are stitched around the borders by machine."

"That'll make them last better," I said.

"That's not the point," said Wangero. "These are all pieces of dresses Grandma used to wear. She did all this stitching by hand. Imagine!" She held the quilts securely in her arms, stroking them.

"Some of the pieces, like those lavender ones, come from old clothes her mother handed down to her," I said, moving up to touch the quilts. Dee (Wangero) moved back just enough so that I couldn't reach the quilts. They already belonged to her.

"Imagine!" she breathed again, clutching them closely to her bosom.

"The truth is," I said, "I promised to give them quilts to Maggie, for when she marries John Thomas."

She gasped like a bee had stung her.

"Maggie can't appreciate these quilts!" she said. "She'd probably be backward enough to put them to everyday use."

"I reckon she would," I said. "God knows I been saving 'em for long enough with nobody using 'em. I hope she will!" I didn't want to bring up how I had offered Dee (Wangero) a quilt when she went away to college. Then she had told me they were old-fashioned, out of style.

"But they're *priceless!*" she was saying now, furiously; for she has a temper. "Maggie would put them on the bed and in five years they'd be in rags. Less than that!"

"She can always make some more," I said. "Maggie knows how to quilt."

Dee (Wangero) looked at me with hatred. "You just will not understand. The point is these quilts, *these* quilts!"

"Well," I said, stumped. "What would *you* do with them?"

"Hang them," she said. As if that was the only thing you *could* do with quilts.

Maggie by now was standing in the door. I could almost hear the sound her feet made as they scraped over each other.

"She can have them, Mama," she said, like somebody used to never winning anything, or having anything reserved for her. "I can 'member Grandma Dee without the quilts."

I looked at her hard. She had filled her bottom lip with checkerberry snuff and it gave her face a kind of dopey, hangdog look. It was Grandma Dee and Big Dee who taught her how to quilt herself. She stood there with her scarred hands hidden in the folds of her skirt. She looked at her sister with something like fear but she wasn't mad at her. This was Maggie's portion. This was the way she knew God to work.

When I looked at her like that something hit me in the top of my head and ran down to the soles of my feet. Just like when I'm in church and the spirit of God touches me and I get happy and shout. I did something I never had done before: hugged Maggie to me, then dragged her on into the room, snatched the quilts out of Miss Wangero's hands and dumped them into Maggie's lap. Maggie just sat there on my bed with her mouth open.

"Take one or two of the others," I said to Dee.

But she turned without a word and went out to Hakim-a-barber.

"You just don't understand," she said, as Maggie and I came out to the car.

"What don't I understand?" I wanted to know.

"Your heritage," she said. And then she turned to Maggie, kissed her, and said, "You ought to try to make something of yourself, too,

Maggie. It's really a new day for us. But from the way you and Mama still live you'd never know it."

She put on some sunglasses that hid everything above the tip of her nose and her chin.

Maggie smiled; maybe at the sunglasses. But a real smile, not scared. After we watched the car dust settle I asked Maggie to bring me a dip of snuff. And then the two of us sat there just enjoying, until it was time to go in the house and go to bed.

Nineteen Thirty-Seven

By EDWIDGE DANTICAT

My Madonna cried. A miniature teardrop traveled down her white porcelain face, like dew on the tip of early morning grass. When I saw the tear I thought, surely, that my mother had died.

I sat motionless observing the Madonna the whole day. It did not shed another tear. I remained in the rocking chair until it was night-fall, my bones aching from the thought of another trip to the prison in Port-au-Prince. But, of course, I had to go.

The roads to the city were covered with sharp pebbles only half buried in the thick dust. I chose to go barefoot, as my mother had al-ways done on her visits to the Massacre River, the river separating Haiti from the Spanish-speaking country that she had never allowed me to name because I had been born on the night that El Generalis-simo, Dios Trujillo, the honorable chief of state, had ordered the mas-sacre of all Haitians living there.

The sun was just rising when I got to the capital. The first city person I saw was an old woman carrying a jar full of leeches. Her gaze was glued to the Madonna tucked under my arm.

"May I see it?" she asked.

I held out the small statue that had been owned by my family ever since it was given to my great-great-great-grandmother Défilé by a French Man who had kept her as a slave.

The old woman's index finger trembled as it moved toward the Madonna's head. She closed her eyes at the moment of contact, her wrists shaking.

"Where are you from?" she asked. She had layers of "respectable" wrinkles on her face, the kind my mother might also have one day, if she has a chance to survive.

"I am from Ville Rose," I said, "the city of painters and poets, the coffee city, with beaches where the sand is either black or white, but never mixed together, where the fields are endless and sometimes the cows are yellow like cornmeal."

The woman put the jar of leeches under her arm to keep them out of the sun.

"You're here to see a prisoner?" she asked.

"Yes."

"I know where you can buy some very good food for this person."

She led me by the hand to a small alley where a girl was selling fried pork and plantains wrapped in brown paper. I bought some meat for my mother after asking the cook to fry it once more and then sprinkle it with spiced cabbage.

The yellow prison building was like a fort, as large and strong as in the days when it was used by the American marines who had built it. The Americans taught us how to build prisons. By the end of the 1915 occupation, the police in the city really knew how to hold human beings trapped in cages, even women like Manman who was accused of having wings of flame.

The prison yard was as quiet as a cave when a young Haitian guard escorted me there to wait. The smell of the fried pork mixed with that of urine and excrement was almost unbearable. I sat on a pile of bricks, trying to keep the Madonna from sliding through my fingers. I dug my buttocks farther into the bricks, hoping perhaps that my body might sink down to the ground and disappear before my mother emerged as a ghost to greet me.

The other prisoners had not yet woken up. All the better, for I did not want to see them, these bone-thin women with shorn heads, carrying clumps of their hair in their bare hands, as they sought the few rays of sunshine that they were allowed each day.

My mother had grown even thinner since the last time I had seen her. Her face looked like the gray of a late evening sky. These days, her skin barely clung to her bones, falling in layers, flaps, on her face and neck. The prison guards watched her more closely because they thought that the wrinkles resulted from her taking off her skin at night and then putting it back on in a hurry, before sunrise. This was why Manman's sentence had been extended to life. And when she died, her remains were to be burnt in the prison yard, to prevent her spirit from wandering into any young innocent bodies.

I held out the fried pork and plantains to her. She uncovered the food and took a peek before grimacing, as though the sight of the meat nauseated her. Still, she took it and put it in a deep pocket in a very loose fitting white dress that she had made herself from the cloth that I had brought her on my last visit.

I said nothing. Ever since the morning of her arrest, I had not been able to say anything to her. It was as though I became mute the moment I stepped into the prison yard. Sometimes I wanted to speak, yet I was not able to open my mouth or raise my tongue. I wondered if she saw my struggle in my eyes.

She pointed at the Madonna in my hands, opening her arms to receive it. I quickly handed her the statue. She smiled. Her teeth were a dark red, as though caked with blood from the initial beating during her arrest. At times, she seemed happier to see the Madonna than she was to see me.

She rubbed the space under the Madonna's eyes, then tasted her fingertips, the way a person tests for salt in salt water.

"Has she cried?" Her voice was hoarse from lack of use. With every visit, it seemed to get worse and worse. I was afraid that one day, like me, she would not be able to say anything at all.

I nodded, raising my index finger to show that the Madonna had cried a single tear. She pressed the statue against her chest as if to reward the Madonna and then, suddenly, broke down and began sobbing herself.

I reached over and patted her back, the way one burps a baby. She continued to sob until a guard came and nudged her, poking the barrel of his rifle into her side. She raised her head, keeping the Madonna lodged against her chest as she forced a brave smile.

"They have not treated me badly," she said. She smoothed her hands over her bald head, from her forehead to the back of her neck. The guards shaved her head every week. And before the women went to sleep, the guards made them throw tin cups of cold water at one another so that their bodies would not be able to muster up enough heat to grow those wings made of flames, fly away in the middle of the night, slip into the slumber of innocent children and steal their breath.

Manman pulled the meat and plantains out of her pocket and started eating a piece to fill the silence. Her normal ration of food in the prison was bread and water, which is why she was losing weight so rapidly.

"Sometimes the food you bring me, it lasts for months at a time," she said. "I chew it and swallow my saliva, then I put it away and then chew it again. It lasts a very long time this way."

A few of the other women prisoners walked out into the yard, their chins nearly touching their chests, their shaved heads sunk low on bowed necks. Some had large boils on their heads. One, drawn by the fresh smell of fried pork, came to sit near us and began pulling the scabs from the bruises on her scalp, a line of blood dripping down her back.

All of these women were here for the same reason. They were said to have been seen at night rising from the ground like birds on fire. A loved one, a friend, or a neighbor had accused them of causing the death of a child. A few other people agreeing with these stories was all that was needed to have them arrested. And sometimes even killed.

I remembered so clearly the day Manman was arrested. We were new to the city and had been sleeping on a cot at a friend's house. The friend had a sick baby who was suffering with colic. Every once in a while, Manman would wake up to look after the child when the mother was so tired that she no longer heard her son's cries.

One morning when I woke up, Manman was gone. There was

the sound of a crowd outside. When I rushed out I saw a group of people taking my mother away. Her face was bleeding from the pounding blows of rocks and sticks and the fists of strangers. She was being pulled along by two policemen, each tugging at one of her arms as she dragged her feet. The woman we had been staying with carried her dead son by the legs. The policemen made no efforts to stop the mob that was beating my mother.

"*Lougarou*, witch, criminal!" they shouted.

I dashed into the street, trying to free Manman from the crowd. I wasn't even able to get near her.

I followed her cries to the prison. Her face was swollen to three times the size that it had been. She had to drag herself across the clay floor on her belly when I saw her in the prison cell. She was like a snake, someone with no bones left in her body. I was there watching when they shaved her head for the first time. At first I thought they were doing it so that the open gashes on her scalp could heal. Later, when I saw all the other women in the yard, I realized that they wanted to make them look like crows, like men.

Now, Manman sat with the Madonna pressed against her chest, her eyes staring ahead, as though she was looking into the future. She had never talked very much about the future. She had always believed more in the past.

When I was five years old, we went on a pilgrimage to the Massacre River, which I had expected to be still crimson with blood, but which was as clear as any water that I had ever seen. Manman had taken my hand and pushed it into the river, no farther than my wrist. When we dipped our hands, I thought that the dead would reach out and haul us in, but only our own faces stared back at us, one indistinguishable from the other.

With our hands in the water, Manman spoke to the sun. "Here is my child, Josephine. We were saved from the tomb of this river when she was still in my womb. You spared us both, her and me, from this river where I lost my mother."

My mother had escaped El Generalissimo's soldiers, leaving her own mother behind. From the Haitian side of the river, she could still see the soldiers chopping up her mother's body and throwing it into the river along with many others.

We went to the river many times as I was growing up. Every year my mother would invite a few more women who had also lost their mothers there.

Until we moved to the city, we went to the river every year on the first of November. The women would all dress in white. My mother would hold my hand tightly as we walked toward the water. We were all daughters of that river, which had taken our mothers from us. Our mothers were the ashes and we were the light. Our mothers were the embers and we were the sparks. Our mothers were the flames and we were the blaze. We came from the bottom of that river where the blood never stops flowing, where my mother's dive toward life—her swim among all those bodies slaughtered in flight—gave her those wings of flames. The river was the place where it had all begun.

"At least I gave birth to my daughter on the night that my mother was taken from me," she would say. "At least you came out at the right moment to take my mother's place."

Now in the prison yard, my mother was trying to avoid the eyes of the guard peering down at her.

"One day I will tell you the secret of how the Madonna cries," she said.

I reached over and touched the scabs on her fingers. She handed me back the Madonna.

I know how the Madonna cries. I have watched from hiding how my mother plans weeks in advance for it to happen. She would put a thin layer of wax and oil in the hollow space of the Madonna's eyes and when the wax melted, the oil would roll down the little face shedding a more perfect tear than either she or I could ever cry.

"You go. Let me watch you leave," she said, sitting stiffly.

I kissed her on the cheek and tried to embrace her, but she quickly pushed me away.

"You will please visit me again soon," she said.

I nodded my head yes.

"Let your flight be joyful," she said, "and mine too."

I nodded and then ran out of the yard, fleeing before I could flood the front of my dress with my tears. There had been too much crying already.

Manman had a cough the next time I visited her. She sat in a corner of the yard, and as she trembled in the sun, she clung to the Madonna.

"The sun can no longer warm God's creatures," she said. "What has this world come to when the sun can no longer warm God's creatures?"

I wanted to wrap my body around hers, but I knew she would not let me.

"God only knows what I have got under my skin from being here. I may die of tuberculosis, or perhaps there are worms right now eating me inside."

When I went again, I decided that I would talk. Even if the words made no sense, I would try to say something to her. But before I could even say hello, she was crying. When I handed her the Madonna, she did not want to take it. The guard was looking directly at us. Manman still had a fever that made her body tremble. Her eyes had the look of delirium.

"Keep the Madonna when I am gone," she said. "When I am completely gone, maybe you will have someone to take my place. Maybe you will have a person. Maybe you will have some *flesh* to console you. But if you don't, you will always have the Madonna."

"Manman, did you fly?" I asked her.

She did not even blink at my implied accusation.

"Oh, now you talk," she said, "when I am nearly gone. Perhaps you don't remember. All the women who came with us to the river, they could go to the moon and back if that is what they wanted."

A week later, almost to the same day, an old woman stopped by my house in Ville Rose on her way to Port-au-Prince. She came in the middle of the night, wearing the same white dress that the women usually wore on their trips to dip their hands in the river.

"Sister," the old woman said from the doorway. "I have come for you."

"I don't know you," I said.

"You do know me," she said. "My name is Jacqueline. I have been to the river with you."

I had been by the river with many people. I remembered a Jacqueline who went on the trips with us, but I was not sure this was the same woman. If she were really from the river, she would know. She would know all the things that my mother had said to the sun as we sat with our hands dipped in the water, questioning each other, making up codes and disciplines by which we could always know who the other daughters of the river were.

"Who are you?" I asked her.

"I am a child of that place," she answered. "I come from that long trail of blood."

"Where are you going?"

"I am walking into the dawn."

"Who are you?"

"I am the first daughter of the first star."

"Where do you drink when you're thirsty?"

"I drink the tears from the Madonna's eyes."

"And if not there?"

"I drink the dew."

"And if you can't find dew?"

"I drink from the rain before it falls."

"If you can't drink there?"

"I drink from the turtle's hide."

"How did you find your way to me?"

"By the light of the mermaid's comb."

"Where does your mother come from?"

"Thunderbolts, lightning, and all things that soar."

"Who are you?"

"I am the flame and the spark by which my mother lived."

"Where do you come from?"

"I come from the puddle of that river."

"Speak to me."

"You hear my mother who speaks through me. She is the shadow that follows my shadow. The flame at the tip of my candle. The ripple in the stream where I wash my face. Yes. I will eat my tongue if ever I whisper that name, the name of that place across the river that took my mother from me."

I knew then that she had been with us, for she knew all the answers to the questions I asked.

"I think you do know who I am," she said, staring deeply into the pupils of my eyes. "I know who *you* are. You are Josephine. And your mother knew how to make the Madonna cry."

I let Jacqueline into the house. I offered her a seat in the rocking chair, gave her a piece of hard bread and a cup of cold coffee.

"Sister, I do not want to be the one to tell you," she said, "but your mother is dead. If she is not dead now, then she will be when we get to Port-au-Prince. Her blood calls to me from the ground. Will you go with me to see her? Let us go to see her."

We took a mule for most of the trip, Jacqueline was not strong enough to make the whole journey on foot. I brought the Madonna with me, and Jacqueline took a small bundle with some black rags in it.

When we got to the city, we went directly to the prison gates.

Jacqueline whispered Manman's name to a guard and waited for a response.

"She will be ready for burning this afternoon," the guard said.

My blood froze inside me. I lowered my head as the news sank in.

"Surely, it is not that much a surprise," Jacqueline said, stroking my shoulder. She had become rejuvenated, as though strengthened by the correctness of her prediction.

"We only want to visit her cell," Jacqueline said to the guard. "We hope to take her personal things away."

The guard seemed too tired to argue, or perhaps he saw in Jacqueline's face traces of some long-dead female relative whom he had not done enough to please while she was still alive.

He took us to the cell where my mother had spent the last year. Jacqueline entered first, and then I followed. The room felt damp, the clay breaking into small muddy chunks under our feet.

I inhaled deeply to keep my lungs from aching. Jacqueline said nothing as she carefully walked around the women who sat like statues in different corners of the cell. There were six of them. They kept their arms close to their bodies, like angels hiding their wings. In the middle of the cell was an arrangement of sand and pebbles in the shape of a cross for my mother. Each woman was either wearing or holding something that had belonged to her.

One of them clutched a pillow as she stared at the Madonna. The woman was wearing my mother's dress, the large white dress that had become like a tent on Manman.

I walked over to her and asked. "What happened?"

"Beaten down in the middle of the yard," she whispered.

"Like a dog," said another woman.

"Her skin, it was too loose," said the woman wearing my mother's dress. "They said prison could not cure her."

The woman reached inside my mother's dress pocket and pulled out a handful of chewed pork and handed it to me. I motioned her hand away.

"No no, I would rather not."

She then gave me the pillow, my mother's pillow. It was open, half filled with my mother's hair. Each time they shaved her head, my mother had kept the hair for her pillow. I hugged the pillow against my chest, feeling some of the hair rising in clouds of dark dust into my nostrils.

Jacqueline took a long piece of black cloth out of her bundle and wrapped it around her belly.

"Sister," she said, "life is never lost, another one always comes up to replace the last. Will you come watch when they burn the body?"

"What would be the use?" I said.

"They will make these women watch, and we can keep them company."

When Jacqueline took my hand, her fingers felt balmy and warm against the lifelines in my palm. For a brief second, I saw nothing but black. And then I saw the crystal glow of the river as we had seen it every year when my mother dipped my hand in it.

"I would go," I said, "if I knew the truth, whether a woman can fly."

"Why did you not ever ask your mother," Jacqueline said, "if she knew how to fly?"

Then the story came back to me as my mother had often told it. On that day so long ago, in the year nineteen hundred and thirty-seven, in the Massacre River, my mother did fly. Weighted down by my body inside hers, she leaped from Dominican soil into the water, and out again on the Haitian side of the river. She glowed red when she came out, blood clinging to her skin, which at that moment looked as though it were in flames.

In the prison yard, I held the Madonna tightly against my chest, so close that I could smell my mother's scent on the statue. When Jacqueline and I stepped out into the yard to wait for the burning, I raised my head toward the sun thinking, One day I may just see my mother there.

"Let her flight be joyful," I said to Jacqueline. "And mine and yours too."

Dream Song:
A Mother's Interior World

The writers here explore the music of a mother's inner life, the sometimes seemingly vacant and repetitive tune, hummed to the accompaniment of endless domestic chores, contains the progression of which symphonies are made. Mothers are, inherently, creative spirits, shaping the world with the tools at their disposal: rags, leftovers, even the spit used to polish other people's crystal stairs. Mothers suffer, as creative spirits often do, questioning the value of their art, always measuring themselves against an unattainable standard of perfection, yearning for the freedom and means to render masterpieces. But they discover the joys hidden in the folds of everyday life, and the power of witnessing their children's spirits take flight. Although they are not always aware of it, motherhood ripens them to life.

Daystar

BY RITA DOVE

She wanted a little room for thinking:
But she saw diapers steaming on the line,
A doll slumped behind the door.

So she lugged a chair behind the garage
To sit out the children's naps.

Sometimes there were things to watch—
The pinched armor of a vanished cricket,
A floating maple leaf. Other days
She stared until she was assured
When she closed her eyes
She'd see only her own vivid blood.

She had an hour, at best, before Liza appeared
Pouting from the top of the stairs.
And just *what* was mother doing
Out back with the field mice? Why,
building a palace. Later
that night when Thomas rolled over and
lurched into her, she would open her eyes
and think of the place that was hers
for an hour—where
she was nothing,
pure nothing, in the middle of the day.

Mother

BY ANDREA LEE

*I*n the summer my mother got up just after sunrise, so that when she called Matthew and me for breakfast, the house was filled with sounds and smells of her industrious mornings. Odors of frying scrapple or codfish cakes drifted up the back stairs, mingling sometimes with the sharp scent of mustard greens she was cooking for dinner that night. Up the laundry chute from the cellar floated whiffs of steamy air and the churning sound of the washing machine. From the dining room, where she liked to sit ironing and chatting on the telephone, came the fragrance of hot clean clothes and the sound of her voice: cheerful, resonant, reverberating a little weirdly through the high-ceilinged rooms, as if she were sitting happily at the bottom of a well.

My father left early in the morning to visit parishioners or to attend church board meetings. Once the door had closed behind him, the house entered what I thought of as its natural state—that of the place on earth that most purely reflected my mother. It was a big suburban house, handsomer than most, built of fieldstone in a common, vaguely Georgian design; it was set among really magnificent azaleas in a garden whose too-small size gave the house a faintly incongruous look, like a dowager in a short skirt. The house seemed little different from any other in my neighborhood, but to me, in my early-acquired role as a detective, a spy, a snooper into dark corners, there were about it undeniable hints of mystery. The many closets had crooked shapes that suggested secret passages; in the basement, the walls of the wine cellar—its racks filled by our teetotaling family with old galoshes and rusty roller skates—gave a suspicious hollow sound when rapped; and on the front doorbell, almost obliterated by the pressure of many fingers, was printed a small crescent moon.

The house stayed cool on breathless summer days when tar oozed in the streets outside, the heat excluded by thick walls and drawn shades, and the dim rooms animated by a spirit of order and abundance. When I came dawdling down to breakfast, long after Matthew had eaten and gone plunging off on his balloon-tired Schwinn, I usually found my mother busy in the kitchen, perhaps shelling peas, or stringing beans, or peeling a basket of peaches for preserves. She would fix me with her lively, sarcastic eyes and say, "Here comes Miss Sarah, the cow's tail. What, pray tell, were you doing all that time upstairs?"

"Getting dressed."

What I'd been doing, in fact—what I did every summer morning—was reading. Lounging voluptuously in my underpants on the cool bare expanse of my bed, while flies banged against the screen and greenish sunlight glowed through the shades, I would read with the kind of ferocious appetite that belongs only to garden shrews, bookish children and other small creatures who need double their weight in nourishment daily. With impartial gluttony I plunged into fairy tales, adult novels, murder mysteries, poetry, and magazines while my mother moved about downstairs. The sense of her presence, of, even, a sort of tacit complicity, was always a background at these chaotic feasts of the imagination.

"You were reading," Mama would say calmly when I stood before her in the kitchen. "You must learn not to tell obvious lies. Did you make up your bed?"

"I forgot."

"Well, you're not going outside until you've done something to that room of yours. It looks like a hooraw's nest. Your place is set at the table, and the cantaloupe is over there—we've had such delicious cantaloupe this week! Scrape out the seeds and cut yourself a slice. No—wait a minute, come here. I want to show you how to cut up a chicken."

Each time she did this I would wail with disgust, but I had to watch. The chicken was a pimply yellow-white, with purplish shad-ows and a cavernous front opening; my mother would set her big knife to it, baring her teeth in an ogress's grin that made fun of my squeamishness. "You saw along the backbone like this—watch care-fully; it takes a strong arm—and then you *crack* the whole thing open!"

In her hands the cave would burst apart, exposing its secrets to the light of day, and with another few strokes of the knife would be transformed into ordinary meat, our uncooked dinner.

It was easy for me to think of my mother in connection with caves, with anything in the world, in fact, that was dimly lit and fan-tastic. Sometimes she would rivet Matthew and me with a tale from her childhood: how, at nine years old, walking home through the cobblestone streets of Philadelphia with a package of ice cream from the drugstore, she had slipped and fallen down a storm drain acci-dentally left uncovered by workmen. No one was around to help her; she dropped the ice cream she was carrying (something that made a deep impression on my brother and me) and managed to cling to the edge and hoist herself out of the hole. The image of the little girl—who was to become my mother—hanging in perilous darkness was one that haunted me; sometimes it showed up in my dreams.

Perhaps her near-fatal tumble underground was responsible for my mother's lasting attraction to the bizarre side of life. Beneath a sometimes prudish exterior, she quivered with excitement in the same way her children did over newspaper accounts of trunk murders, for-eign earthquakes, Siamese twins, Mafia graves in the New Jersey pine barrens. When she commented on these subjects, she attempted a firm neutrality of tone but gave herself away in the heightened pitch of her voice and in a little breathy catch that broke the rhythm of each sen-tence she spoke. This was the voice she used to whisper shattering bits of gossip over the phone. "When Mr. Tillet died," I heard her say once, with that telltale intake of breath, "the funeral parlor did such a poor job that his daughter had to *wire her own father together!*"

My mother, Grace Renfrew Phillips, had been brought up with all the fussy little airs and graces of middle-class colored girls born around the time of World War I. There was about her an endearing air of a provincial maiden striving for sophistication, a sweet affectation of culture that reminded me, when I was older, of Emma Bovary. She and her cluster of pretty, light-skinned sisters grew up in a red-brick house with marble steps in South Philadelphia. They all played the piano, knew a bit of French and yards of Wordsworth, and expected to become social workers, elementary-school teachers, or simply good wives to suitable young men from their own background—sober young doctors, clergymen, and postal administrators, not too dark of complexion. Gracie Renfrew fit the pattern, but at the same time dismayed her family by attending Communist Party meetings, joining a theater group, and going off to a Quaker work camp.

When she married my father, the prescribed young minister, my mother had become, inevitably, a schoolteacher—a beautiful one. She was full-faced, full-bodied, with an indestructible olive skin and an extraordinary forehead—high, with two handsome hollows over the temples. She had a bright, perverse gaze, accentuated by a slight squint in her left eye, and a quite unusual physical strength. She swam miles every summer at the swim club, and at the small Quaker school, where I was a student and she taught sixth grade, it was common to see her jumping rope with the girls, her large bosom bobbing and a triumphant, rather disdainful smile on her face. Her pupils adored her, probably because her nature held a touch of the barbarism that all children admire; she would quell misbehavior, for instance, by threatening in a soft, convincing voice to pull off the erring student's ears and fry them for supper.

At home Mama was a housekeeper in the grand old style that disdains convenience, worships thrift, and condones extravagance only in the form of massive Sunday dinners, which, like acts of God, leave family members stunned and reeling. Her kitchen, a long, dark inconvenient room joined to a crooked pantry, was entirely unlike the cheerful kitchens I saw on television, where mothers who looked like June Cleaver unwrapped food done up in cellophane. This kitchen had more the feeling of a workshop, a laboratory in which the imperfect riches of nature were investigated and finally transformed into something near sublimity. The sink and stove were cluttered with works in progress: hot plum jelly dripping into a bowl through cheesecloth; chocolate syrup bubbling in a saucepan; string beans and ham bones hissing in the pressure cooker; cooling rice puddings flavored with almond and vanilla; cooked apples waiting to be forced through a sieve to make applesauce; in a vat, a brownish, aromatic mix for root beer.

The instruments my mother used were a motley assemblage of blackened cast-iron pots, rusty-handled beaters, graters, strainers, and an array of mixing bowls that included the cheapest plastic variety as well as tall, archaic-looking stoneware tubs inherited from my grandmother, who had herself been a legendary cook. Mama guarded these ugly tools with jealous solicitude, suspicious of any new introductions, and she moved in her kitchen with the modest agility of a master craftsman.

Like any genuine passion, her love of food embraced every aspect of the subject. She read cookbooks like novels, and made a businesslike note in her appointment book of the date that Wanamaker's received its yearly shipment of chocolate-covered strawberries. Matthew and I learned from her a sort of culinary history of her side of the family: our grandfather, for instance, always asked for calf brains scrambled with his eggs on weekend mornings before he went out hunting. Grandma Renfrew, a sharp-tongued beauty from North Carolina, loved to drink clabbered milk, and was so insistent about the purity of food that once when Aunt Lily had served her margarine instead of butter, she had refused to eat at Lily's table again for a year. My mother's sole memory of her mother's mother, a Meherrin Indian called Molly, was of the withered dark-faced woman scraping an apple in the corner of the kitchen, and sucking the pulp between her toothless jaws.

Mama took most pleasure in the raw materials that became meals. She enjoyed the symmetry, the unalterable rules, and also the freaks and vagaries that nature brought to her kitchen. She showed me with equal pleasure the handsome shape of a fish backbone; the little green gallbladder in the middle of the chicken liver; and the double-yolked eggs, the triple cherries, the peculiar worm in a cob of corn. As she enjoyed most the follies, the bizarre twists of human nature and ex-perience, so also she had a particular fondness for the odd organs and connective tissues that others disdained. "Gristle is delectable," she would exclaim as Matthew and I groaned. "The best part of the cow!"

I was a rather lazy and dunderheaded apprentice to my mother. She could be snappish and tyrannical, but I hung around the kitchen anyway, in quest of scrapings of batter, and because I liked to listen to her. She loved words, not as my father the minister did, for their cer-emonial qualities, but with an off-handed playfulness that resulted in a combination of wit and nonsense. In her mischeievous brain, the broad country imagery of her Virginia-bred mother mingled with the remains of a lady-like education that had classical pretensions. When she was annoyed at Matthew and me, we were "pestilential Pestalozzis"; we were also, from time to time, as deaf as adders, as dumb as oysters, as woolly as sheep's backs; we occasionally thrashed around like horses with the colic. At odd moments she addressed recitation to the family cat, whom she disliked; her favorite selections were versions of "O Captain! My Captain!" ("O Cat! My Cat! Our fearful trip is done . . .") and Cicero's address to Catiline ("How long, Cat, will you abuse our patience? . . .").

On summer evenings, after the dinner dishes had been washed and as the remains of the iced tea stood growing tepid in the pitcher, my mother, dreamy and disheveled, finally would emerge from the kitchen. "Look at me," she'd murmur, wandering into the living room and patting her hair in the mirror over the piano. "I look like a Wild Man of Borneo."

She would change into a pair of oxfords and take a walk with me, or with a neighbor. At that time of day June bugs hurled themselves against the screens of the house, and my father, covered with mosquito repellent and smoking cigarette after cigarette, sat reading under the maple tree. In the diffuse light after sunset, the shadows around the perfectly ordinary houses up and down the street made the unambitious details of their designs—turrets, round Victorian towers, vague half-timbering—seem for once dramatic. All the backyards of the town seemed to have melted into one darkening common where packs of kids yelled faintly and fought their last battles before bedtime. Cars pulled out of driveways and headed for movie theaters or the shopping centers along the Pike, and the air smelled like honeysuckle and onion grass. When Mama and I walked together, we would wander up and down the long blocks until the streetlights came on.

One evening during the summer that I was six years old, we stopped to visit a neighboring family in which something sad and shocking had happened the previous winter. The father, a district judge named Roland Barber, had driven one gray afternoon to the marshland outside the airport and there had shot himself. Judge Barber, a short, grave, brown-skinned man with a curiously muted voice, had been a member of my father's congregation and had served with him on the board of the NAACP. His suicide, with hints of further-reaching scandal, sent a tremendous shock through the staid circles of my parents' friends, a shock that reached down even into the deep waters that normally insulated Matthew and me from adult life. For a few weeks after the suicide we held long grisly discussions on arcane, even acrobatic ways to do away with oneself.

The house in which Mrs. Barber continued to live with her teenage daughter was little different from our house, or any other in our neighborhood: a brick Colonial with myrtle and ivy planted around it instead of grass, and a long backyard that sloped down to a vegetable garden. I knew the Barbers' yard well, because there was an oak tree near the vegetable garden, with a swing in it that neighborhood kids were allowed to use. On the evening my mother and I came to visit, the daylight was fading, and the windows of the house were dark. It seemed that no one was home, but in the summers in our town, people often waited a long time in the evening before turning on lamps. It occurred to me as we walked up the driveway that the house itself seemed to be in mourning, with its melancholy row of blue spruces by the fence; I gave way, with a feeling that was almost like ecstasy, to a sudden shudder. Mama rubbed my goose-pimply arms. "We'll just stay a minute," she said.

My mother was carrying a recipe for peach cobbler. It was intended for Mrs. Barber, a bony woman who had fascinated me even before her husband's death, because she wore a very thick pair of elasticized stockings. However, after we'd knocked and waited for a while, the front door was finally opened by Phyllis, the Barber's sixteen-year-old daughter. Mama, who had taught Phyllis, sometimes referred to her as "the fair and brainless"; I had seen her plenty of times at the swim club, pretty and somewhat fat-faced, drawing the stares of the men to her plump legs in Bermuda shorts. That night, though it was only about eight o'clock, she opened the door in a light summer bathrobe and peered out at us without turning on the porch lights.

"Hello, Mrs. Phillips. Hi, Sarah," she said in a low, hesitant voice. She came out onto the dark steps as she spoke, and let the screen door bang behind her. She explained that her mother wasn't there, and that she had been taking a shower when the bell rang; she radiated a fresh scent of soap and shampoo. When my mother asked her how she was feeling, she answered in the same hesitant tone, "All right."

I looked at her with a kind of awe. It was the first time I had seen her since I had heard the news about Judge Barber, and the first time I had ever stood right in front of anyone associated with an event that had caused such a convulsion in the adult world. In the light-colored robe, with her wet hair—which normally she wore flipped up at the ends and pulled back with a band, like other high-school girls in the neighborhood—combed back from her forehead, she had a mysterious, imposing look that I never would have suspected of her. I immediately ascribed it—as I was ascribing the ordinary shadow of the summer twilight around the doorway—to the extraordinary thing that had happened to her. Her face seemed indefinably swollen, whether with tears or temper, and she kept her top lip tightly clenched as she talked to my mother. She looked beautiful to me, like a dream or an illustration from a book, and as I stared at her, I felt intensely interested and agitated.

In a few minutes Phyllis went back inside. My mother and I, as we had done many times before, walked quietly up the Barbers' driveway and through the backyard to the swing in the oak tree. Mama stopped to pick a few tomatoes from the overloaded plants in the Barbers' vegetable garden, and I helped her, though my second tomato was a rotten one that squashed in my fingers.

It was completely dark by then. Lightning bugs flashed their cold green semaphores across the backyards of the neighborhood, and a near-tropical din of rasping, creaking, buzzing night insects had broken out in the trees around us. I walked over and sat down in the oak-tree swing, and Mama, pausing occasionally to slap at mosquitoes, gave me a few good pushes, so that I flew high out of the leaves, toward the night sky.

I couldn't see her, but I felt her hands against my back; that was enough. There are moments when the sympathy between mother and child becomes again almost what it was at the very first. At that instant I could discern in my mother, as clearly as if she had told me of it, the same almost romantic agitation that I felt. It was an excitement rooted in her fascination with grotesque anecdotes, but it went beyond that. While my mother pushed me in the swing, it seemed as if we were conducting, without words, a troubling yet oddly exhilarating dialogue about pain and loss.

In a few minutes I dragged my sneakered feet in a patch of dust to stop the swing. The light of a television had gone on inside the Barber house, and I imagined fat, pretty Phyllis Barber carefully rolling her hair on curlers, alone in front of the screen. I grabbed my mother's hand and said, "It's very sad, isn't it?"

We took a shortcut home, and by the time we got there, it was time for me to scrub my grimy arms and legs and go to bed. Mama went immediately to the refrigerator and got out an uncooked roast of pork, which she stood contemplating as if it were the clue to something. She smelled of sage and dried mustard when she came upstairs to kiss Matthew and me good night.

Slip and Fall

BY CECELIE S. BERRY

The usual hubbub occupied the house on that cold January morning. Christmas was over and splinters of tinsel winked from dusty corners. My sons, Sam, who was 8, and Spenser, who was 6, were speedskating in their footed pajamas across the hardwood floor. From the kitchen, I hollered for them to turn off the cartoons and get dressed for school. A listen: More laughter as they crashed and fell. Unless I grew two sizes larger, burst out of my shirt and turned green, they'd ignore me. I was too tired for that performance and before me, I had, literally, a full plate.

Sam's birthday cake consisted of two lemon-flavored sheet cakes stacked on top of each other with raspberries in the middle, coated in vanilla icing. It was an ungainly confection, and I worried it: centering the layers, patching the frosting, rehearsing a plan of slicing so that each portion would be just right.

I made a mental note: Don't obsess.

Sam's late-December birthday made the holiday season a marathon. That day was the final event in the triple-header birthday celebration that is now the norm: The party with friends at a migraine-inducing play joint, a family party with a bust-the-bank present and—the morning's finale—the class party. It was ridiculous, absurdly excessive. I shook my head as I spelled out "SAM!" in raspberries.

Seconds later, he slid to a halt beside me. "It doesn't say 'Happy Birthday'."

" 'Happy Birthday' is implied in the exclamation mark."

He gazed at it and then me in utter dismay. Daggers-in-the-eyes I can take, eye-rolling, I'm immune, but Utter Dismay, the horrifying realization dawning in his oceanic gaze that Mom is a bonehead . . .

I shook it off. "Everybody knows it's your birthday. Why would I bring in a cake if it weren't your birthday?"

That got him.

From the living room, Spenser began to play the piano. "Ode to Joy."

"It's not time to PRACTICE. And that's TOO FAST!"

"What about candles?" Sam asked.

"Fire hazard." I pushed passed him, sculpted a cake dome out of aluminum foil, and began to design a strategy for transporting the cake in the station wagon. There was no way to secure it in the back, it might tip over on the front seat, I couldn't trust the children to carry it, so I'd put it on the floor on the passenger's side—a tight squeeze. The juice and cups in the back. It would take two trips in to school, a long walk in the cold, unless I risked parking in the handicapped zone. I'd already paid the $100 fine twice, and been warned: Next time; 90 days community service. A reverie: I could stay in a halfway house, it might be clean and quiet, with convicts, yes, but adults, and only work 9–5.

Hang on, I urged, but the cheerleader inside me gave way to the rebel: Why do I have to do break my neck to make them happy? Just tell Sam: You've got a wonderful life. Be grateful, damn it.

I threw on my old down jacket, slapped open the kitchen cabinets and shoved nine stray birthday candles into my pocket. How do perfect children become perfectionists?

"It's you," Mother says when I complain. "You've made them this way."

No it was you, I want to say, *you started it. You handed me the baton and I ran with it and now I want to stop running. It's all your fault.*

I want to say that, but even now, I don't dare.

I took a deep breath, and yelled, "Get Dressed." I ran outside, turned the ignition, pulled the parking brake, opened the hatch and the passenger door. Up and down the street, denuded Christmas trees quivered in the wind. Ours had rolled off the curb, and I made a mental note to drag it up later. Back in the house, I picked up the cake and headed to the car, slapping the screen door open with my hip. I crossed the front porch, stepped down, and realized that something was missing, that stabilizer of human folly, friction. I heard the surreptitious whisk of one foot then the other, registered an inopportune leaning and made a mental note that I was going to. . . .

I fought like a marlin. The foil flew away, but my fingers clawed into the cake and I hung on until the top step cracked against my spine. The cake and I landed side by side in the pachysandra.

I stared at the sky and it stared back. In the distance, the branches of an ancient maple arched in the sky, impatient black etchings framed in a celestial shell: An egg hatching. Reduced to no more movement than my skittering eyeballs, I grasped those branches with my soul. In moments when I am both free and tethered, suspended in time and beyond it, a vision of those tender, inscrutable interstices, returns.

The lush silence was pierced by a distant, syncopated squealing: Me. Trying to breathe.

The air had been knocked clean out of me. Raw instinct forced me to keep heaving, but nothing came in or out. On the ground, the snow melded to me, warming to my form. I made a mental note to give in to death and stop making that horrible noise. To depart with frosting on my lips, the scent of lemon teasing my nostrils. I could do worse.

Get up. You're not going to die. A voice said. I thought perhaps it was God, but it was just me, the one who never says die. She's inside all of us, the Kellys and the Hilarys, the black girls with perfect manners masking irrepressible fight. She-who-never-says-die keeps us going when the doors are slammed in our faces and our hearts seem irreparably broken. I always thought that she existed to guide me through the labyrinth of proving myself into the land of Being Somebody, a person of consequence. I had no idea that it would take all those gallons of water choked on in synchronized swimming and all the falls off the balance beam and all the wrong notes played, musical and otherwise, to help me survive becoming a Nobody; in other words, a stay-at-home mother.

The school bus rumbled past, the air filled with exhaust and I realized, as I have again and again while raising my children and with immeasurable bitterness, that no one was coming to save me. I would have to save myself.

It's all you, girlfriend. So get up. I tried, and flopped over face down into the cake, which muffled a groan.

Try harder.

The children came running out the screen door, reaching for me. I rasped: "Don't TOUCH me." They reared, yelping with panic. I pushed myself into a kneeling position and then pulled myself up on the stair rail. Walking hurt. Breathing hurt. Driving would hurt, but I'd be damned if they weren't going to school.

In the car, Spenser bawled me out. "Why did you have to make that stupid cake? I hate your cakes, they never taste good." I knew he was scared, but I wasn't in the mood. At their school, I pulled over. "Get out."

Sam called tearfully, "Bye mom, I hope you're not crippled." Together they ran into the building. Stooped by overstuffed backpacks and encased in down, they looked like astronauts traversing the moon.

Mountaintop Hospital was about five minutes away, and I drove slowly, hoping not to pass out on the way. I discovered that day that it is impossible to breathe without moving. Checking my blind spot made my head spin. I made a mental note that since I was not arriving in an ambulance, I'd have to use visitors parking, a good five hundred feet from the emergency room entrance. It would serve them right if I didn't make it. Reaching for the parking ticket sent fresh dispatches of pain through my shoulders. My mind whirred around the possible prognoses: a collapsed lung, spinal trauma, collateral heart damage.

The parking garage was dark and wet like a womb. Or a tomb. There's a reason why they rhyme. I laughed darkly. I pulled out my cell phone and called my husband Scott's voice mail, my tone heavy with the accusation that this was all his fault. He was in some warm conference room, with gourmet cookies and fresh cappuccino, being Mr. Fabulous Negro, while I was homesteading the prairie.

I leaned back, closed my eyes, and pulled the darkness around me. In the car, I sort through things, a habit I picked up early. Often when I was young, mom and I would pull into the garage at home, and remain there talking for hours. In the house, certain things couldn't be said, and in public, face had to be kept, but in the gray intermission of the garage, the truth sometimes came out.

There, one day, we lingered after Mom had driven me to a job interview. Thanks to piano lessons (Mom's idea) and typing in summer school (Mom's idea) I could type uncommonly fast, and I'd been hired by a local corporation as a temporary secretary for the summer. I must have been about sixteen.

Suddenly, my mother blurted, "You're so lucky. I wish I could get a job." She draped herself across the steering wheel, and cried.

I was dumbstruck. My mother had not had a paying job in all the years I'd been alive. She had never expressed a desire to work—to us anyway—and seemed insulted if anyone suggested it, as if they were saying that by raising her children she was wasting her life.

My sisters and brother and I never took her being at home to mean that she wasn't capable. Mother was not just capable, Mother was fierce. She could slay shopgirls with a look, make school superintendents cower. We depended upon her judgment, yearned for her respect. That she harbored self-doubt or uncertainty was inconceivable.

The emergency waiting area was deserted, televisions hovered from corner perches like sleeping crows, discarded tabloids lounged on empty seats. I limped to the intake office and knocked on the frosted window. A bird-like white woman with dreadlocks, bright blue eyes, and facial eczema slid back the window. Her name tag read "Ginnie" and I told her what had happened. She appraised my lemon-scented, icing-flecked face and hair and said, "Yup, it's treacherous out there." She photocopied my insurance card, and handed me a clipboard.

I tried to sound officious. "I would like to be X-rayed. There's something wrong with my spine, or my lungs or my heart. I might need to be monitored for a couple of days." Or a week. Or life.

I filled out the form, lingering as always over the section marked "Employment." It's best to write "lawyer," the threat of legal action being the best insurance, but I couldn't bring myself to do it. I hated being a lawyer; I hated the law, with all its conventions and rationales. *Res Ipsa Loquitur:* the thing speaks for itself. That's not true. Everything requires interpretation, perspective.

Writing "housewife," is always good for a few moments of being stared at like a leper. When I told one white neighbor that I'd stopped working at a job after Spenser was born she repeated, dazed "You don't have a job . . . Are you *sure?*"

But how to fill in the blank? "Sometime writer," "missed-the-boat career woman?" My identities are fractured due to the Great Hiatus of Motherhood

How I remember the comments from my Harvard Law School classmates, when I stayed home with the children for good.

"Well you've gone from dinks ("double-income-no-kids") to sinks."

"What a waste of a fine education."

And from my own sister: "Now you'll never be a Power Couple."

The most unforgiving, the most appalled were Them. That's

what I call them. Them. You know, the giant radioactive worker ants from the B-movie of the same name who consume everything in their path, the slaves of achievement, the newly minted black professionals in hot pursuit of the Glamorous Life. I was kept totally in the loop when it came to the latest accomplishments of Them, even if they had to be invented.

I remember when we moved to the New Jersey suburbs, Sam was two and Spenser, a newborn. I received a housewarming present, a food processor, from a woman—one of Them—who had been a lawyer with my husband's law firm. In her note she informed me that she'd just joined the legal department of some movie studio, implying that she would soon be the next Louis B. Mayer. I took the food processor out to the circular driveway, set it in the exact middle then rolled over it with the station wagon until it was confetti. Then came the tears, and my husband asked the question that makes every young mother want to scream: He said: "What's wrong?"

"What's *wrong*? That woman is an idiot compared to me."

"It's just contract review and negotiation," he said calmly. "You'd get bored and quit in no time."

"That's not the point. By the time she's done telling tales, she'll be up for the director's prize at Cannes. And people will think that she's interesting. They'll think that she matters. And nobody thinks that about me."

I'd like to say that it was just that moment of searing envy. But it went on for years, day-to-day, the sound and the fury of my fractured identity.

Ginnie pulled me up on the computer. She looked concerned. "You've been here before." Indeed. Though most mothers become emergency room regulars because of their children, I am an E. R. habitue in my own right.

There was the time I'd sliced open my hand. The children were

2 and 4 then, home from their half-day of Montessori and I'd started drinking rum and diet Cokes with lunch. By 5:00 I needed to eat to hide the ill effects, so I tried to slice a bagel in half with a butcher knife and nearly lost a thumb.

A few months later, Spenser poked me in the eye during a pre-dawn game of chase and I had to wear an eyepatch for a week.

Then when they started school full days, I broke my ankle running for the New York train.

I planned my pregnancies, and, as Mother had warned me, I didn't have to try twice. But motherhood proved hazardous. It seemed that when I became a mother, I became accident prone; all I did was slip and fall.

I was ushered into the emergency room's inner sanctum, where the sick people lay, leaned, and drifted through the hallways sur-rounding the nurse's station like abandoned rafts in a stagnant stream. There was a white couple in their fifties, the woman, her arm band-aged, lay on a gurney, the man in a Totes hat and scarf, held a *Times* in one hand, stroked her forehead with the other. They shared a joke. I glanced at them and turned away quickly. Watching people in love was torture then.

A black woman, her thick gray Shirley Temple ringlets alert be-neath a maroon skullcap, smiled at me. Beneath the brisket of her knee, her legs swelled into elephantine slabs. Her socks, having surrendered the fight, fell limp about her ankles and moles the size of igloos rode her legs. She reminded me of one of my father's patients, whom I had met the one time he'd taken me on a house call in a vain effort to interest me in medicine. (Mom's idea.) Deep in the Eastside ghetto of Cleveland where he grew up. I sat in this woman's apartment amidst circumstances so depleted that I felt by comparison overgrown, a giant-girl, come down the Beanstalk. I wore white gloves, a navy tam, and a double-breasted navy blue coat with gold buttons perfect for games of "rich man, poor man." Glittering on the breast pocket was a coat of arms of unknown origin. Mother had special-ordered the ensemble, one for each of us, three girls and a boy, from Best & Co. While the woman's sister, the only person she had left on earth, lay dying of heart failure in the next room, she plied me with pie. "Are you sure you won't help yourself?" she asked repeatedly with rising anxiety, as if my having that pie could ward off the inevitable. I wanted to yell at her to go into the other room, to take that pie out of my face, but I was respectful of my elders. And, too, I was scared that if I made any sudden move, I might slide yet again down the beanstalk to a world even more decrepit. She thought I wouldn't eat the pie because I was too good for her. But I didn't eat it because I wasn't good enough.

The clock ticked heavily above the nurse's station. By now, Sam was in Social Studies, Spenser in Art. I was sweating. Nobody was helping me. My eyes drifted to the one black nurse, flipping charts, dispensing instructions. Roberta. She seemed happy.

Maybe I would have been happy in health care, I mused. I had wanted to be a nurse when I was a child. "Nurses just change bedpans," Mother corrected, "what you want is to be a doctor."

Mother.

I sighed.

She didn't want us to fall into the trap that so many black girls do, casting themselves always in supporting roles, settling too early. She and Dad taught us to aim high and about that, I have no regrets. Their expectations were an endorsement that I needed all of my life.

And yet, there comes a time when what a child wants—no matter how humble—has to be good enough for the parent. Achievement is important; but it will never be more important than love—love of what you do, of who you are, of those closest to you. Most people don't really believe this love is itself an accomplishment—the most important one of all—and that it can be "won" through homemaking, being a parent who is *there*. My mother didn't believe it, although she wanted to. I have come to believe it, though I fought it as long as I could.

When Sam was a baby, I would sit at work, filled with ulcerous bile, and wonder what that "woman-from-God-knows-where"— Mother's always had a way with words—was doing with my child. I would tear through the subways, a single thought, desperately whirring: "I've got to get home." The nannies came and went like bowling pins. Until recently, the boys' favorite bedtime stories were the circumstances of their firings. They'd yawn sleepily and say, "Mom, tell us again why you fired Gertrude or Jenny or Lorraine." And I'd whisper as they drifted off: she let you watch MTV; she gave you too many ice cream sandwiches; she said: "my bad" and I said: "you're out." It made them happy to think that nobody measured up to taking care of them. That meant, though, that I had to. And I wasn't sure I could. So I kept tripping and slipping and cutting and falling, in between bouts of doing my best.

The cost of stay-at-home motherhood has been my sure-footedness, but the cost of leaving my children was perpetual psychic torment, the kind you have in the infamous dream when you arrive at school and gradually realize that you forgot your clothes. Only in my case, I'd arrive suited for work and realize every day that I had forgotten my heart.

"You're the slip and fall?"

Dr. McDougal stroked his mustache, fiddled with his tie, fingered his pockets. A nervous wreck. "Rough morning, eh? You're having trouble breathing?"

I repeated my litany of injuries.

"Okay, come with me." I followed him around the corner to a small, cold examining room. He pointed to a blue gown, which I took to mean that I was to put it on, and said "Be back in a minute."

I knew he was lying, but I didn't care. I took off my sweater and bra and was oddly comforted by the stretch marks dribbling down my breasts, and the sight of my enormous all-terrain boots making hooves of my feet. I imagined myself half-woman–half-beast, a hybrid creature from the mythology of an undiscovered tribe.

Roberta bustled in and sent me a quizzical look.

"Just taking stock." Embarrassed, I quickly donned the blue gown and she propped my back against the X-ray machine.

"I need you to take a deep breath," she said.

I breathed.

"No, bigger."

I tried again. "It hurts."

"Deeper."

I tried. She came from around the machine, put her hands on her hips and said, "Girl, can't you breathe any deeper than that? Now, *inhale*."

I closed my eyes tightly and little shoots of pain spurt out behind my lids. I inhaled. The X-ray buzzed.

"Good job," Roberta smiled.

She escorted me to a darkened side-hall, where I was told to lay on a gurney and wait. The only light came from the screensaver of a single computer with the words "LiveWell" twirling into the cyber darkness. Like a comet, the phrase fell apart as it hurtled away, shedding layer after layer, then it rebounded from its destination, twisting, boomeranging, cutting a new path with its return, rebuilding itself to its initial vigor. I watched the screen for some time, until a familiar voice said, "*Go home.*"

At the outpatient desk, I announced my intention to leave. I was handed a clipboard and signed a release. Dr. McDougal came by and informed me, unnecessarily, that my X-ray was fine. He scribbled a prescription for painkillers and rushed off. Ginnie reviewed my exit instructions. Tylenol was recommended, she said.

I showed her the prescription the doctor had given me.

"I don't know why he gave you that—it's effective, but highly addictive." She conferred with Roberta, who looked at me heavily, "You don't need that."

I promised to stick with Tylenol, stuck the prescription deep in my pocket, and made a mental note to have it filled, just in case.

The Christmas trees were gone by the time I drove up the street. The squirrels danced across our lawn, chuckling at me. I climbed the front stairs tentatively, gripping everything in reach. I was digging for my keys when the front door opened. It was Scott. My husband.

"What are you doing here?" I demanded, both six-shooters drawn.

"I came home from work to see how you were."

And . . . holstered. "Sorry," I mumbled. He helped me upstairs and I undressed and got into bed.

"I'm going to the store, do you need anything?"

"There's a prescription in my pocket. I got it from the doctor."

He nodded and left. I closed my eyes.

"Oh and Scott?"

He came to the door.

"Can you get two pints of raspberries, two cans of whipped vanilla icing, and two lemon cake mixes, with the pudding in the mix. It's no good without the pudding in the mix."

He smiled. "Are you sure? Sam'll get over it, you know."

"I know, but I'm sure." From bed, I could just make out the top of the maple tree in the distance. Amazing, the way its most delicate branches radiated outward, defining the contour of the whole. But slowly, it faded from view. Snow began to fall, sweetly at first, then bountifully and, finally, with holy abandon, as if the falling itself were enough.

"Scott?" I called. "I'm glad you're home."

The wagon pulled out of the driveway and I made a mental note to tell him later. I sighed, and glanced at the clock: Sam was in gym, Spenser, language arts. They'd be home soon. Opportunity knocked; it was now or never. I settled in, closed my eyes and slept.

An Unnatural Woman

BY MARTHA SOUTHGATE

I am standing by the sink, chopping parsley and putting butter into pasta. Behind me, my son, Nate, sits writing a story; he asks me to carefully spell out each word. He is almost eight. My daughter, Ruby, who is four, plays with a few small plastic dinosaurs on the rug in the dining room, talking to herself in a quiet voice. My husband is not home from work yet. My voice is patient and even as I spell. I haven't worked on my new novel in a month and a half—haven't worked on it continuously and thoughtfully in six months. As I move the knife over the parsley, I think, briefly, of turning the knife to my wrist, a messy end. Or maybe I'll walk out the door and never return, seamlessly gone, leaving behind the children, the cold pasta and chopped parsley. For a moment, I am tantalized by the idea that my disappearance from this scene would be easier than trying to keep going as an artist, a mother and a wife.

You may ask: How could you think such a thing? You have two beautiful children, a loving husband and family, a home, two published books. How could you think of leaving them? How could you think you'd be happier without them? At one time, I would have asked those questions myself. I'm less judgmental now. I know how even the simplest request from the most beautiful children, the most patient husband, can feel like an imposition when you never feel like you have enough money, time or ease.

In his essay, "Fires," Raymond Carver writes about being a young parent and a writer: "There were good times back there, of course; certain grown-up pleasures and satisfactions that only parents have access to. But I'd take poison before I'd go through that time again." When I read those words in a bookstore, I sagged against the shelf, my eyes filled with tears. *That's exactly how I feel*, I thought. That the person who had articulated my feelings was a white man, a brilliant writer who revolutionized the short story form, and a recovering alcoholic who left his first wife, were not lost on me. Only a white man whose place was established, and who had nothing to lose, could write with such brutal honesty. For a woman, especially a black woman, to talk so is almost unimaginable. I sweat even as I type these words.

A woman loves her children. That is a given in our society, reinforced at every conceivable turn. And a black woman is the mother to the world. Look at our history—all the babies we've raised. Our own and other people's. By necessity or by choice. A black mother's love is supposed to be uncomplicated, Aretha Franklin-like, it moves mountains. Some of us have always known the picture to be more nuanced than that—as in the scene in Toni Morrison's *Sula* when Hannah Peace asks her mother if she ever loved them and is met with an angry tirade that ends, ". . . what you talkin' 'bout did I love you girl I stayed alive for you can't you get that through your thick head or what is that between your ears, heifer?" That's a kind of love—but not the kind we talk about or celebrate.

Gradually, I have realized that I have to write to live. I'm like Sula—or would be if I hadn't found my way to words. "Had she paints, or clay, or knew the discipline of the dance, or strings; had she anything to engage her tremendous curiosity and gift for metaphor, she might have exchanged the restlessness and preoccupation with whim for an activity that provided her with all she yearned for. And like any artist with no art form, she became dangerous."

I am a writer, but I also have chosen to have children. And there's the rub. I'm 41 years old and I love my children, enormously. I'm a fairly good parent, but it's not easy for me. It's not easy for anyone, but I find it harder than most. Family life—taking care of others, the bump and rub of a group—I've never been comfortable with it. My children's needs intrude on my need for solitude, reflection, selfishness, time to be. I resent it. I try not to let my resentment affect my parenting, but I must be honest. As I become more serious about my work as an artist, I am less patient with chauffeuring and PTA meetings and all the minutiae that fragment a mother's day.

Carver wrote about that, too, how the little things can seem like torture, how the laundromat can be a kind of hell, how all the chat about how you should enjoy these years crumbles to nothing in the face of them. That seems like another thing that only a man would have stated so baldly, so without remorse. But there's something to that—getting to the nut of it, the ugly truth of how children intrude on an artist's life, how all writers are profoundly selfish in our consuming search for transcendence. Why do you think we can't stay married? Why do you think we drink so much?

Well. That's a cliché. In fact, I don't drink to excess (people in my family did but that's another story) and I love my husband. But we writers are scarred, and searching. Our search isn't compatible with family life, but we must pursue it to the end.

I didn't always imagine myself a mother or a writer. Both things came to me rather late in life, a surprise. I was always told I wrote well but never considered fiction writing as a career until I was 30 and found myself truly interested in some characters I was making up. Interested enough to tell their story even though no one else might want to hear it. I remember, before I had children, sitting at my keyboard, writing what would later turn out to be a novel but was then, frankly, a mess. I loved it. I was possessed by a desire to know where my characters' lives would lead. I needed silence to do it.

Kids are loud. I am constantly shocked by the din my two small children make, their brown bodies colliding, shouting, shrieking, embracing each other. And the fighting. More often than I'd like, I use a sharp tone with them, or I sound exasperated. Sometimes, I'm not sure what they've done to frustrate me so. I only know that I feel overwhelmed, and fatigued by their persistent needs and desires, their mere existence.

I have had a few stays at artist's colonies, the Virginia Center for the Creative Arts (VCCA) and the MacDowell Colony in New Hampshire. They are bastions of calm where writers and visual artists can get away from the demands of daily life and be pampered and free to concentrate on their work. The first time I went away to VCCA, Nate was just two, Ruby not even conceived. I didn't miss Nate much. I thought sometimes of his soft, *café au lait* skin, the fuzziness of his hair. I knew I wouldn't want to be away forever. But I was in a fever of creating and no one could stop me. At VCCA, I was the only parent of a young child. The other artists looked befuddled as I explained why I would stay only two weeks instead of the customary month.

"Wow, you have a two-year-old," people would say, astonished. I, too, was astonished: Astonished that I could leave and have such a good time; astonished that my husband and son could manage and even thrive without me. Other mothers who've visited artists' colonies talk of loneliness, missing their children so much that they couldn't work. I worked like a demon, made some dear friends, and went out one night to a feed-cap bar in the rural Virginia town, drank too much and came home giggling like a teen caught out after curfew. At the end of my stay, I returned to Brooklyn, reluctant but restored, with 50 new pages. Being away was a gift, an invaluable jewel. I envied all those childless artists their freedom.

The best part of my stay at MacDowell was the night I went with a fellow writer to see a movie with no negotiation, no discussion, no need for a sitter. Just free to go. The way single people are. Boy, that felt good.

Those memories should make the moments by the pasta bowl more bearable, but still the knife entices, the door beckons. But freedom is not all there is, in anyone's life. People without children struggle just as mightily to create as parents. In some ways, I've been forced into a kind of efficiency, a seriousness that I might never have achieved without becoming a mother. I know that writers can find every way under the sun to avoid writing and I can't blame my kids for every day I piddle away. My suicidal dreams, my fantasies of self-obliteration have everything to do with parts of my heart I hope my children will never know—and nothing to do with them.

They have given me great gifts, even as they constrain me. Labor was a gift with both of them—18 hours into a 30-hour-long labor with my son Nate, I realized that there was nothing I could do—it wouldn't be done until it was done. I couldn't type it into a Palm Pilot, to be rescheduled at my convenience. I just had to ride the wave until it was finished—a highly useful lesson for a novelist to learn.

From Nate, I have learned the virtue of attentiveness. On the subway or the bus, during any emotional encounter, he is all eyes and ears, silent and watchful, like a deer by a creek. It is all internal—he does not always share his thoughts, but he misses nothing. All of life fascinates him.

From Ruby, I learn language anew. Once, when I commented on something her assistant teacher did, she misheard me and responded indignantly, "Jackie's not the singing teacher, she's the washing teacher." The one who helps with handwashing and lunch and nap, these fine arts. One day, when I chased her around the playground, she scooted up the jungle gym, laughing and shouting to me, "Climb inside the poetry!" Who knows what she thought she was saying, but she offered me some words to live by.

Truth to tell, hard though it is, there is a certain usefulness to being forced to stop thinking of oneself all the time, to have to stop living in one's head. There is a certain usefulness in having to take care of someone else, to love and be loved so thoroughly, to learn how to hang onto oneself and one's work in the face of constant pressure not to. When I think of leaving, I think of the doorknob cool inside my hand, the comforting swing of the door towards me. I never think of the moments, days, years after—the devastation I would feel, the ache of not being able to feel those hard little heads under my hands. I suppose that's why my leaving remains a fantasy—it never goes beyond imagining. And I suppose that's how I know I have become a mother for good.

The best writing, the best art, shows us the world—either a character's inner world or the world as the writer sees it. My children force me, not as often as I should, sometimes resentfully or with exasperation, to look at the world. "Look, Mommy," calls Ruby, "there's music in the bench." We are coming from my son's flute lesson at the local music school. She points out a brick, embedded in a park bench, too low for me to see without crouching, in which someone has painstakingly carved a staff of tiny musical notes. Music resides in strange places. Music I might never have heard had I not had children.

When Wild Southern Women
Raise Daughters

BY EVELYN COLEMAN

I am a radical woman. When all my friends were baking home-made cookies, volunteering at PTA meetings, driving their children here and there like taxi drivers, I was too busy to do it for my own two girls. Either that, or I was too stupid, selfish or, according to many people who knew me, just plain too immature.

I worked two or three jobs, did the Bump at nightclubs every weekend—yes, I'm that old—and after a failed marriage, dated and married as often as I could. I usually saw my children to sleep and hit the road. I hugged them a lot, kissed them a bunch and left them with my family, what most folks considered way too much.

I grew up in the South with a checkered Yankee-influenced past. My mother was a teacher from a small Southern town, my father a mystic from New Jersey. I grew up next door to my grandmother with my mother's relatives in practically every house on the street. Until I was fifteen I was the only girl in this wonderful family. None of them understood me, but they gave me a sense of nurturing and love that could not be shaken. But I believe it was, in part, due to their complete acceptance of me that I didn't grow up—that coupled with the fact that almost every woman in my father's family didn't grow up until they were past thirty.

So when I had my daughters, I was twenty-years-old chronologically, but mentally, I was still fifteen. And like many women in my father's family, my top priority was having sex, then having a boyfriend or husband, and lastly, to my mother's embarrassment, figuring out how to raise my daughters. I hate to admit this, and my girls don't even remember it, thank God, but at the time that was just *me*.

I moved around a lot from city to city, dragged them with me, and, while I worked or partied, I often left them in the care of friends, like the Taylors in Winston-Salem, North Carolina, who could see "I didn't have sense enough to take care of my own children." In fact, I moved my kids so much that when they were around twelve and thirteen and found themselves in the same school they'd attended the year before, they called me frantic that they'd been dropped off at the wrong school.

I courted more men than I can remember and that's the honest truth. Some would say I was a loose woman, but I had a different philosophy about sex, shaped by an avant-garde father's understanding and knowledge. I must admit I am not ashamed of it. Of course, there was no AIDS epidemic back then.

Don't get me wrong, I tried to keep my daughters from danger, shielded them from situations where strange men could take advantage, and I exposed them to many exciting cultural experiences. But I continued on with my hectic, often unbelievably complex life.

When I discovered that my daughters were interested in sex, I told them what my father told me: Anyone touches you without your permission, you tell, we will believe you, and there is no way it's your fault; sex and love are not the same thing; always use your own prophylactics; the longer you wait the better it will be, mainly because you'll know what the heck you're doing; and masturbation is not only the best substitute for sex but the best training seminar on how a man can please you. Oh, and always try to get satisfied first.

Doomsayers always told me that if I didn't become a better mother, meaning put my kids' desires first, something terrible was going to happen to them. I reasoned at the time, right or wrong, that I didn't think it wise to "give up yourself" to raise children. I needed to mother within the parameters of my life. There were things I wanted to do, and I did them.

I allowed my daughters' space to be who they were because, to me, that had more to do with good parenting than putting plates on a table at six o'clock. My youngest hated school. I myself had been in love with school until I went to college. I couldn't understand her dislike of elementary school. I mean, who runs away in the first grade? However, I understood her passionate creativity. I talked to her teachers, making it plain that as long as she learned how to read and write, I wasn't planning on freaking out along with them. This girl was flaky as all get out, but a talented artist and a logical thinker.

My eldest daughter loved school and made excellent grades but couldn't find her way out of a paper fortress. Her logic just didn't seem to work. But she was loving, kind and nurturing, the qualities valued most in my family.

I taught them to meditate or trance out so they could explore the miracle of the mind without drugs. I challenged them to make friends who were different from them, not just in race, culture and ethnicity but beliefs. I encouraged them to seek peace rather than a fight, but never let anyone walk over you. I made rules and changed them when they didn't make sense anymore. I allowed that a junky room was not a reflection of one's character or a roadmap of one's destiny. Even kids have days when they don't want to do anything but chill. And my daughters grew into polite, kind girls, respectful of their family, elders and friends.

Then came a surprise, but not one I hadn't expected. Almost overnight, the two of them became rebellious hellions. Now, as a teen I'd been way past insane, I mean certifiable-for-white-coated-men-to-take-away. Given a different family, I would have been locked up or medicated at the very least.

I tried to help my daughters through this stage by allowing them to find themselves, to make mistakes. I nurtured their freedom of verbal expression. (No profanity or disrespect, just tell me what you're honestly feeling) After a while, anytime I displeased them, they demanded to go live with their father.

When I divorced their father I created the same relationship with him that chickens have with roosters. A chicken may let a rooster jump on her back, but once she's perched on the egg, the rooster can go. We'd had a rough marriage with me getting the brunt of the pain, both physical and mental. All I knew was: I could not imagine a child's life without a father, if he were living. Two things struck me: One, I didn't believe my ex could ever support two families, hell he'd barely been able to support one; and two, in his own peculiar way, this man loved my children and they loved him. So I sacrificed. I never asked him for child support and I let him pick up the girls anytime he wanted them to visit. In the long run, the sacrifice was worth it. Eventually, we became good friends. He often provided me with financial as well as emotional support whenever I reached a crisis in my life. So during one of their teenage *coups d'état,* I let them go live with him.

It didn't take long before their father was calling me asking the same question I'd begun to ask myself, "Who are these people?"

So my Ex and I harmonized our style of parenting, recognizing the differences in both girl's personalities, yelling at them to straighten the heck up, and then reminding them that we'd already climbed that "crystal stair." And we recalled together that we, too, had been stark raving, irresponsible nuts as young people.

By the time I was thirty-four and finally reaching some semblance of maturity, my motto as a mother was simple, "As long as you don't do drugs or have all your teeth pulled out of your head, go for it. Any mistake you make can be corrected." This, from a woman married four times, doesn't seem all that unorthodox. I loved my daughters unconditionally just as my family had loved me. I told them often that I loved them, kissed and hugged them daily, and every now and then, gave them a lecture.

When my oldest daughter was out of high school and refusing to go to college or to work, I put her out of my house. Yep, packed her stuff and sat it outside and locked my door. The one thing my kids never saw me do is "not work." I always kept a job to feed, clothe and shelter them. Plus, I liked and respected work. Working to me was a given, not something you chose.

A few minutes after learning she couldn't come back in she went to a phone booth and called me. "Mom, you're going to make me have to do something I don't want to do."

"Like what?" I asked her.

"You're going to make me have to become a prostitute."

I burst into laughter. "Please, prostitutes work. They do not *sit* on the corner, they stand on the corner and then walk back and forth all night. Do you really think I believe you would do that? And the first man who drove up to you while you were resting on the curb, and heard your Freddy Kruger-ish 'What?' would just drive away. Sweety, let me assure you, if you can swing that job, you'll be working."

I hung up and cried. To be honest, I was not afraid of my strong-willed, steely-eyed oldest becoming a prostitute or dancing naked on a stage. There was no doubt in my mind that she would spit on anybody who thought she would so much as smile for a dollar. But I was torn: afraid of the experiences that might go with life on the street; and, at the same time, terrified that if I didn't practice tough love at this point in her life, she'd never be able to survive. I wanted her to grow up. To understand that every action has a consequence and if you're too bad and bold about it, life will knock you on your butt. It hurt me to teach her this lesson since I'd learned it myself the hard way. But sometimes, for some bullheaded people, the hard way is the only way.

My youngest daughter was another story. She would gladly give her love and affection away if she thought the person was down and out and she could save them. She struggled with her idiosyncrasies, her hermitic ways, her love of art, martyrdom and men. Yet, somewhere along the line she developed into one of the wisest young women I've ever met.

When my daughters reached thirty, as it should be for women in our family, they focused, turned their lives in the direction they wished to go and are now both dancing to their own beat, creating with their lives what the great visual artist, Aminah Lynn Robinson, calls a "symphonic poem." I am proud of the women both my children became—no thanks to me. I understand I don't deserve all the credit for who they are since they were always on the way to "being."

They don't recall all my nights shaking on the dance floor because most of the time when I left they were asleep.

They don't remember most of the men who were in my life, and the ones they do they think of fondly.

The funny thing is, to the dismay of all my critics, the only thing my children remember is that I was a "good mother." They talk about me to their friends and I'm tempted look around to see if they haven't mistaken me for someone else.

They know that it isn't acceptable to stay in a bad marriage, a bad job or any unrewarding situation. They know that because they never saw their mother do it.

They think of me as a hard-working woman who always followed my own path. They understand hard work often requires starting at the bottom and working your way to the top.

They know that you never let anyone take your body unless the next step they take is on the way to jail. "No" means: you better get your damn hands off me.

They witnessed that you never give up your life for somebody else. God granted us free will for a reason. I have never allowed gender to frame who I am, or what I wanted. I loved men but if I'd loved women I would not have kept it a secret. I brought my daughters up to accept the choices of love all people make. I wanted my daughters to grow up to acknowledge the male and female of our Creator and to understand that God abides in all of us. We are spirit and spirit has no gender.

Truth be told, I wanted to be the best mother I could be to them, but I wasn't willing to sacrifice myself. I worked hard to show them I loved them in my own way. I forced them at times to move on, to allow things to happen with expectation and not fear. I believed in them as individual spirits even from the start. And I wanted them to honor the spirit within themselves. I believed that the only way they could do that was to see me honoring my own.

I have known parents who sacrificed everything for their children and still had to set their visits by a prison clock. I have known parents who never realized their children were not clones of themselves, manifested on earth to carry out their dreams and desires. I have known people that, in the face of their child choosing a same sex relationship, gave them up, yet claimed to believe in the spirit of God. I have known women who, in their effort to teach their girls about family, have taught them that abuse and marriage go hand and hand. And mothers who teach their daughters that sex is for procreation and anything else makes it dirty. I could not have been like those parents and didn't want to be a "traditional" self-sacrificing, life-denying Mother for my daughters. Hell, I'm married to a wonderful man now and I don't even own pots and pans.

I cannot say I didn't have many times when I admonished myself for inadequate parenting and my inability to stick with a man who raised his voice even once. Or, moments when I didn't think I should at least try to become a Leave It to Beaver mother, like many of my friends. But on days I doubted myself I always returned to the poem "Children" in Kahlil Gibran's *The Prophet*. He writes, "Your children are not your children. They are the sons and daughters of Life's longing for itself." I would read that passage over and over for strength and inspiration. It helped me remain firm despite my doubts that my daughters would be all right as long as I loved, honored and nurtured their true spirits.

I have grown confident through the years that the greatest gifts we mothers can give our daughters is freedom from our own small minds and fears, liberation from the pressure to conform, a joyful sexuality, and good vibrators. Wild Women of the World—rejoice!

Unmasking Step-Motherhood

BY DEBORAH ROBERTS

O ne hot summer afternoon, as I padded around my kitchen preparing lunch, Leila, my three-and-a-half year old, joyously peddled around me on her tricycle. As usual, she was full of observations. "My friend, Claire, the one from ballet class, isn't very nice anymore," she reported. "She hits me and she's jealous," Leila proclaimed.

When I asked why she thought Claire was jealous of her, Leila scrunched her face and said, "I'm not sure." Her pace slowed and she made graceful figure-eights across the floor, circling me in ever-tightening loops.

Suddenly, the subject switched to death. Leila had been fascinated with the meaning and power of death since her cherished paternal grandfather died just a few months before.

"Is your mom dead?" she asked, coyly, for she knew the answer.

"No, sweetie, you remember we visited Grandma Ruth last year down in Georgia where she lives."

"Nana is daddy's mom, right?" she followed up.

"That's right" I answered over my shoulder, as I combed the refrigerator for her favorite cheese slices.

"And are you Courtney's mom?"

I hadn't seen that coming. "No. You've met Courtney's mom before, I'm her step-mom."

"Are you serious?" Leila's pigtails danced. "You're NOT kidding."

"Of course not."

Leila's disbelief sprang from her understanding that step-moms are mean, wicked creatures who live to torment sweet-tempered children like Cinderella or Snow White. After we had read the classic fairytales and watched the videotapes, Leila equated the role of step-mother with evil. How could her mom be part of a class of inherently wicked creatures?"

Then came the familiar pangs of my self-doubt: Did Leila feel threatened by Courtney? Was either girl unsure of her cherished place in our hearts? How many "I love you-s" does it take before they can believe?

Later it dawned on me. In her questions that morning Leila was exploring the association between jealousy and death, expressing, if indirectly, her desire to have family roles be specific and concrete. In attempting to establish who belonged to whom and what title they had, Leila was trying to define a framework that would distinguish family members from dangerous, destructive outsiders, and to affirm her place in that architecture. Her concern was not with actual death, but the emotional death of being insecure in intimate relationships, not knowing who cares for whom, not feeling one's place in the family structure to be unique. She teased these issues like a kitten with a ball of string, playfully, but instinctively, I sensed that what she wanted—and needed—was clarity.

I buttered the bread, and set it sizzling in the pan. "Leila, 'step-mother' is just a way of saying that I'm sort of *like* Courtney's mother. There are lots of step-mothers in the world and we act as mothers to kids like Courtney when we're with them, but that's it." She rode up to me and held my gaze, silently demanding elaboration. "I mean, Courtney has her own mother, to whom she is also very, very special. And I sort of help her, like, like—"

Like what? I searched for an analogy a three-year-old might grasp: a handmaiden? a fairy godmother? An aunt like Leila's Aunt Alisa? A career in communications can't help you talk to a three-year-old who reads fluently between the lines. A quick decision: Better not take the fairy-tale allusions too far. To do so might affirm the notion that good and evil are static character traits in a situation where everyone makes mistakes, including me.

"I'm Courtney's mom's helper," I announced brightly—and firmly. "Now would you be my good helper and set the table?" Leila grinned, satisfied. I flipped the grilled cheese and felt relieved to close a sensitive subject.

Our discussion left me thinking about Courtney, Leila and the six-week summer visit then underway. Things were peaceful; the girls at ease with one another. But while we had come a long way, I suspected we still had some distance to go in securing the fragile, evolving structure of our family.

Courtney was only five when Al, her father, and I first met, and it was a disaster. We had begun to date in the midst of a difficult separation from his wife of seven years. The split was devastating for Courtney who was deeply attached to her father. One winter day, in an effort to do something fun, Al arranged for us to go to a children's show on Broadway. I was nervous about meeting this little girl who was struggling to cope with the painful changes in her life. When I arrived at the theater, Courtney shyly gazed up at me and then hid her face behind her father's coat. I leaned down to say hello, but she emerged only to offer a cool stare. I remember thinking: This is going to be fun.

Throughout the performance, which included mimes and magicians, Courtney never broke a smile. And she never looked at her father or me. She was in shutdown, blind and mute to the festival of amusements Al had provided—an unhappy child.

Afterward, we went back to Al's apartment to visit and have dinner. Still, there was no sign of pleasure from that round, angelic face. Courtney's long, raven pigtails swayed as she announced that she wanted to watch cartoons in her room. Spotting an opportunity for us to talk, Al consented. He explained that Courtney was usually bubbly and fun. "She's having a tough time," he said, in part to spare my feelings. Then Courtney emerged from her bedroom. I turned expectantly, hoping that she wanted to join us. Instead, she threw out a tiny grenade. "When is she going home?" she demanded to know. I was crushed. Al, whom I had expected to come to my defense by chiding his rude child, said nothing. He seemed paralyzed, confused as to which side to take.

"I'll be going now," I announced to silence. After a moment, he asked me to stay, but by then I was outraged. I grabbed my coat and left in a huff. How could a grown man allow a little child to insult his girlfriend?

Later, Al called and apologized. He realized that he should have said something to Courtney, but it was difficult. He felt badly for his little girl, who was trying to figure out this new life, new relationships. I understood his dilemma, but, perhaps selfishly, I wondered, "What about me and my feelings?"

That question has come up a number of times over the last ten years as Courtney and I have tried to figure out where we fit, if we fit. When her dad and I became engaged and began looking for a new apartment, she hated every place that I loved. After the wedding, when we began a new life together, she often made it a point to call up her mother during her weekends with us to say, within earshot of me, how much she missed her and couldn't wait to get home. When I bought her surprise gifts after returning from business trips, she often received them with little more than a tepid thank you.

Each time I felt that we made progress, that we were something of a family, somehow Courtney reminded me that we weren't. More specifically, she made me feel that I was an intruder on her territory— an illegitimate contender for Al's love and attention. We each tugged at Al in a constant effort to force him to choose. If we disagreed over a movie, a dinner, anything, we each expected him to prove his allegiance. One Sunday afternoon, when it was time to take Courtney back home to her mother, she pleaded to stay longer, even though her Dad and I had dinner plans. Al was torn. Whom should he disappoint? I won that time. But looking at Al's pained face made for a hollow victory.

Three years into our marriage, things had settled a bit and Al and I welcomed our daughter Leila into our home. Courtney was quiet on the subject of her little sister, but seemed intrigued by this tiny, albeit demanding, creature. She was afraid to pick her up, but gradually grew to like and even protect her. As Leila began to walk and run, Courtney, terrified by her sister's fearlessness, often shouted for her to stop as Leila raced up the sidewalk outside our apartment building. Sometimes, she even grabbed Leila's arm, fearing that Leila would dart into traffic.

On weekends, when Courtney came for a visit, she often volunteered to accompany me if I needed to take Leila on an errand with me. She'd entertain her drooling sister as I mailed a package at the post office or paid the cashier at the grocery store. It warmed my heart to see Courtney begin to care about her sister, but I was cautious. It seemed that my hopes had been raised so often only to be dashed, I didn't know if I dared to believe that we could become a real family.

Time passed, and as Courtney prepared to celebrate her thirteenth birthday, she began to feel that her mom and dad didn't understand her friends, her taste for super-low-cut jeans or her obsession with rap music. Since her parents were in their forties and I was still in my thirties, somehow I was cool—or, at least, cool-er. Occasionally, she came to me with a problem about girls at school or secretly shared intelligence with me on a boy she liked. It felt good to be trusted by this young girl who reminded me so much of myself as a frightened, insecure teenager. Memories of me as an acne-scarred, gawky adolescent came flooding back. How tough it was, struggling to be popular and yearning for a boy who never noticed me. I'll never forget the confusion I felt and the distance that I felt from my parents.

For years, I had struggled to be a mother to Courtney, but that only served to confuse her. After all, she had a mom. And any time I got too close to co-opting that role, it made for friction. Courtney couldn't invite a new mother into her life without feeling like a traitor to her mom. Nor could she shut me out without putting distance between Al and her. My job was to find an alternative relationship. To be a mother-figure when needed, but mostly to be a friend and confidante. That was the connection that Courtney could understand. Gradually, Leila has come to understand it too.

For ten years now we've been hammering away at this family, making sense and order out of the chaos of jealousy and competition that could have destroyed us. It has taken some time, longer than the fairy tales promise. There continue to be difficult periods, times when I desperately want to walk away from it all and I'm sure that Courtney feels that way too. Then she walks through the door for her next weekend visit and Leila lights up. I watch the two girls as they race toward each other and fall into a warm embrace. In those moments, I realize that we have actually done it. We are indeed a family after all.

The Complex Mathematics of Mothering

BY AJ VERDELLE

i

Motherhood and time are cart and horse. So much about a driving future that we mothers career, trying to cook meatballs, while the team gallops on. The time before us seems full even when it has not yet come.

I hear a low rumble, the words repeat: Future, Future. Like a drum call, a low percussion, a near surreal elongation of time ahead.

The math of mothering is all about this: time and weights. How old is she? How big is she? What is she doing, now?

ii

My daughter bestows upon me this unique condition: hovering, planning, training, wonder. Nine times the wonder. I wonder whether her shoes still fit, whether her winter clothes are ready for Goodwill, whether her giraffe coat will stand as high fashion outerwear for one more season. I wonder if it's time to start interviewing for kindergarten. I wonder about her tomorrows. The requirements, big and little, that will come along. I touch on these curiosities gently, lightly, while I decide which issues will soon be present-tense, which matters get drawn into today in some way. Perhaps it's time to iron her lavender linen pedal pushers. Perhaps this is the moment to make more mac & cheese. Perhaps I should make a schools trip—the Village, the Upper East Side. Take out a membership at the Natural History Museum. Refresh her barrettes.

iii

Mostly anything I eventually do has to appear first on one of my lists. This is how a task qualifies for my attention, it shows up on a list and gets looked at thereupon. As you might expect, my daughter was once referenced listwise. Not that her name, or her babyhood, was ever a list line-item. But there was a time in my life, let's call it pregestation, when you could sum some list items which would add to our child: Take folic acid. Continue basal temperature. Find doula possibilities. Prenatal yoga. Visit Truro birthing center.

As you might imagine, I applaud the word, *Voilà*.

iv

Childhood draws up a past it does not know, just as deftly as it makes neon of the ever coming future. My daughter's childhood, for example, is embedded (what a word for our time) in the childhoods we parents have known. We know our parents' music, their politics, the prejudices, the causes for improving the world. We champion what they teach us to.

When I was writing my first novel, and trying, ever gently, to shape my young girl heroine, to make her plausible, I realized that we all, growing up, are *dated* to the knowledge our parents had to share. The first songs we know are the crooners our parents loved. I knew as much about Sam Cooke and Nat King Cole and Nina Simone and Nancy Wilson as I did about Parliament and their crazy antics. Scores later (as in now) my daughter could give a whit about Parliament. Our little girl sings Ella, and Louis Armstrong and the theme song to Little Bill. Music makes a history for each one of us, and our parents are our tour guides. I'll never forget discovering how much math there is in music. *Half notes quarter notes six four time.* Music gave me respect and love for math. You can't shake a stick at a triplet.

As a mother, my teaching job is to situate all the referents I can see and name in time. To assemble and identify referents as appropriate. To accomplish the monumental act of sorting—through both the noise and the music of life. To say, *Yes, this is deserving.* To say, *This is what the past has wrought.* To say, *Yes this is important. Take this with you to your present tense.*

v

Repeating oneself is annoying, but repetition is also a form of time management. Yet another thing that no one could have told me in advance. Now that my daughter and I have language between us, I have to repeat myself as a matter of routine. As part of the contract a mother signs in Delivery, when she goes from plan to purpose, when she goes from future tense to now. Once baby-making goes from heaven through oven to kitchen, repetition is forever in the recipe cards.

Women have, of course, had babies for time immemorial. This repetition is perpetual, truly cosmic. Pregnancy grants you membership into an ancient, knowing line of queens. There is a ferocious community of wise women who can knowingly and with surety handle pre-linguistic bundles of warm, working parts.

Parents for time immemorial have waited for babies to roll over, to drool. Moses, Tutankhamen, or my little girl—we mothers watch them in the reeds to see when they raise their heads.

Now that my daughter and I have language between us, my *words* are repetitive—and this violates the economy of the business I'm in. For as much as I repeat myself, these words should be poetry—they should rise and be elliptical, be musical, be metric—to account for all the time they occupy in my surrounding air. *Put your doll baby back in the basket, sweetie, put your doll baby back in the basket. One, two shoes, Pumpkin, one two shoes. Come along, Rubicon, it's time to go now, Vamanos, mija, vamonos ahora.* All my repetitions are punctuated by commas, endearments, sometimes contain other languages. Why bother with a period when you know what's coming next, when both my child and I know that I'm just about to say what I said again.

There was a sad refrain when I was young and in school. *We think she's bored*, the administrations, one after the other, said to my mother. Usually occasioned a sigh. When absolutely necessary, my mother would hunt down a new school for me, but mostly she just hoped I'd find a good book to read, and that I'd continue to focus on piano practice and homework. I obliged, except when I was acting out. Then the narrative of my school days took stunning plot twists.

Our little girl has barely begun her school day narrative. She goes to nursery three mornings a week. When you ask her what she did in school, she invariably answers, *Play*. It's a cute and accurate answer. So you can imagine my surprise when I went to pick her up one day, and not only was she not in the "circle" for the second day in a row, but her teacher whispered to me, "We think she's bored." Although I felt faint enough to blurt out anything, I did not say, *But she's two years old*. I did not say, *You've got to be kidding*. I did not question what they planned to do. I simply sat down, and was reminded of the truth she comes by honestly. School always fit me like a dress from a prior season.

Marking the seasons, sizing a dress, knowing how often to vary the Circle rhyme—all of these are numbers. Math lies in wait, and grins.

vi

Starting out in life ultimately became one of the key repetitive phrases on my childhood. People start out in life differentially, I learned. Accidents of birth, situations of health, dispensations of money, available teaching, character education, the communication of a moral sensibility. Values. Neighborhood. Soon comes, school. All of these, and your ancestors (living especially, but dead as well), factor into what amounts to your start in life. America, I was told, does her best to equalize our differential starts. It would be years—true future tense—before I could understand these American assertions.

Decades before I would have learned enough to weigh the American assertions for their truth.

vii

Kids choose each other—for friends, for teams, for enemies, for partners in the inevitable crimes. From a mass of kids, their chosen associations—two by two by two—can reduce a morass to a couple of posses. They form groups, car pool size. We parents would much rather see our children with kids who are compatible and engaged in something, than to see our kids alone or poorly matched.

In this way, we parents see pairing, collecting, as a kind of multiplication. A few good kids can make my child a better person, a more social being, a child who can have fun with others. A few happy activities can make my child more fulfilled, more skilled athletically, more aware of how games are played, exposed to sportsmanship. A few other good parents can reinforce what I'm teaching her, show her we're not Martians on earth.

But from the child's perspective, pairing is division. Making the crowd manageable, making the sea tame. *These, Mama, are the friends I can name. Can she come to my birthday party? Can he come to my Green House?*

viii

Many times, as I consider Time, I wonder about this joke I've heard, which is really solely punchline. There is this barroom sign: Free Beer Tomorrow. That's the joke. Why doesn't this tomorrow-never-comes referent work with other kinds of objects, or people, or goals? There is nothing inherently particular about beer, so why does it make sense, but not for say, Homework Help. Homework Help Tomorrow is not funny, it is cruel.

The tomorrows I face are eventualities, kinds of promises. Here are some of the promises waving in this mother's future. My daughter will grow out of her shoes. One day the tomorrow when her foot is the next size, will become today and will require a search on my part for the ever-fewer Stride Rite sales locations. I am nostalgic for Stride Rite from the many shoe shopping trips that populated my own ancient childhood. My daughter loves Michael Jordan sneakers and Ghanaian flip-flops. Stride Rite does not necessarily impress her, she can buy shoes anywhere.

The photographs I have of her first Stride Rite visit, her face is wide and pumpkin-looking. She had yet to grow in teeth. This was in November, in a year when she was small. The hat she wore had ear flaps and tied, all neat and fleece, beneath her chin.

I believe that on average, I dress her too warmly.

Tomorrows become todays at a rapid pace in this my life full of future. This I promise. I also promise that kindergarten will come. Well before that, places in kindergarten will fill. I will worry over this, this I also promise. Any advance work helps. I promise this too. Her lavender linen pedal pushers, for example. When it's time to wear them, they should be hanging, there. It is best to be left only with hair to brush, barrettes to arrange, *teeth to clean*.

ix

When I have to account for how time is spent, when I have to rethink my daughter's early years, I will think of the time she spent training and feeding us. We parents were hungry for her to tell us what next, we were eager to taste, and give kisses to, whatever new appetite she devised. As a parent, I am ever willing to stand with the stopwatch, the popsickle stick tally, and announce: This is what skill we're practicing now: dressingyourself, matching colors, naming shapes, tyingshoes, swimming, coloringoutsidethelines, paintingwithoutlines, notscreamingindoors, keeping your balance, honoringyourmothers. This is the same strategy for the motherhood childhood partnership the world over. (Plus or minus some material comforts—like, the presence of war, the abundance or scarcity of foods and medicines, the availability of national infrastructure, a history of stolen resources.) I'll coach, you train. You coach, I'll train. We role-play with our children, shifting postures all the time.

Each of us will remind the other that the races and the trials and the sessions we spend debriefing together add up. There *is* an equation involving the number of days we each will live, and the usually uncounted and unnamed skills we practice together. *Watch me sightread this score to mothering, Daughter. Watch me foresee a future for you.*

x

We celebrate when we paint with two hands, one, two. We have not yet learned to show off three fingers, even though we are certain as fully-set jello that we are indeed three years old. I can't even imagine how many times I've counted to ten and to twenty and sometimes to fifty, in English and Spanish, aloud, and under my breath. I have counted the hours until bedtime, as subtraction. This, in mathematics, is called a remainder. But as I've mentioned, our daughter is a sum.

Numbers are, after all, one of a child's major frontiers of formal learning. How many times have I repeated one arm, two arms? For every coat she puts on when she is awake, for every *camisa*, for every undershirt cool mornings require. Every time the Count starts seeking the Number of the Day, standing goofy before his pipe organ, on Sesame Street. We are counting every thing in our household—fava beans, puzzle pieces, shoes and arms of shirts. Pencils, pelotas, pinatas, purple pairs of pants. Windows, doors, fortune cookies. The number of steps to the top. This counting repetition will be endless, I can tell; infinite—like numbers have been forever.

xi

Do you see how/that this plus this plus this plus this sums to our little girl? Do you see our daughter there? Isn't she the finest little sum you've ever seen?

xii

All this mathematics, this numerical mumbo mambo, clouds up the chalkboard, the chalk held long way, and scraped to flat, we mothers note the careful arrows, the parentheses, the straight, flat, repetitive equal signs. O, the causality we try to teach. We try to define the zero sum games, to point out odds you can't win, to describe winning formulas for what we hoped we'd win, what we want you to try to win, now. We mothers are happy to stand still and see you work with chalk and board. However inaccurate, however incorrect, we are thrilled to see you start to write. We are surprised, and reflective, about how tall you have grown. We are bursting with pride about the math you know. We add what tips we have for you, after we have watched you get the answer, or partial credit. We have hope that the mathematics of the life we live will not go over your head. We have hope that we will not leave you before we have taught you sums and currency, procreation and creation, fractions and recreation, when it's time to rest.

Time and money, and weights and measures and odds and logic and quarter and half notes, all these notions add up, to math.

And so I instruct my daughter, in words that are elastic and that I hope stretch to meet her age, her understanding. *Consider the sums that have produced you. Look at your ancestral numbers: birth dates, longitude, height in the present tense, length at birth. Sixty million and more. Consider the equations that birthed you. Observe their couplings, trios, simultaneity. Notice their parentheticals. Read between the lines. Do not be afraid of the numbers in life. Add, subtract, divide, pair, multiply. Live the mathematics of music. I will stand and watch you. We, your parents, will be your witness. One, two, we watch you.*

Goin' Round the Bend

BY MELBA NEWSOME

*W*henever the phone rings late at night or very early in the morning, I tremble. Good news never comes at that hour. So when the sound rattled me from sleep early one morning ten years ago, I picked up the receiver with shaking hands.

"Mama passed." My brother's voice sounded hoarse and ragged from crying.

"Thank God," I said. There was a long silence. "It's, ok, really, it is," I told him, hoping he'd believe it as strongly as I did. I hung up, then I cried with the relief of knowing her lifetime of suffering was finally over.

Somewhere around 1955—two years before I was born—my mother stepped through the door that separates reality from delusion. There are a dozen theories about what prompted her emotional collapse but I doubt anyone truly knows what trauma pushed her beyond the pale.

I envy my brothers because they knew her B.C.—before craziness—when she took pride in the house and doted on them and held hands with my Dad. I don't recall precisely when I realized she lived in another world or that she was unlike other moms but I have vivid memories of the shame I felt at having a mother who was so different. All I wanted was a mother who blended and my mother was not the blending kind.

When I was young, we lived in a small rural town in Arkansas, which was both a good thing and a bad thing. Everyone knew Mama and watched out for her, yet those same people took a kind of perverse pleasure in letting us know that they knew "Miss Hattie don't have good sense."

Three months before my brother's pre-dawn call, I received another one—this time during the safe period of day—after the telemarketers but before the 11 o'clock news—and answered without hesitation.

"Hey," said my sister Debra. I hadn't heard from her in a while. We were in a tiff, the kind that, as children, we would have settled before bedtime. But it seems that, as our ability to recall such banalities as names and dates fades, the recollection of any slight or difference of opinion between us endures. Our silence had stretched on for months.

"Ma has cancer," she said. "Of the pancreas."

"That's terminal," I said. I have no idea why I said that or even how I knew. Our conversation lasted only a few minutes as we discussed the details of our mother's diagnosis, Although we never addressed our estrangement, I knew it wouldn't last much longer. Debra was my only sister; we two girls were born when Ma had nearly given up after having four boys in a row. Our rift would heal but Ma wasn't so lucky. After a lifetime of trips to the edge of madness only to be dragged back toward sanity, she had used up her cache of last-minute reprieves.

Since the first time she went round the bend, cracked her plate, stopped putting both oars in the water (we've used so many euphemisms), my mother's life was one long psychotic episode interrupted by brief periods of sanity. When she was medicated, she laughed, sat down with us as a family and engaged in long, insightful conversations. Life was good. Once when I was home from college, Ma, Daddy and I went to town together. As we stood on Main Street, arm-in-arm, peering through the department store window, my friends passed by, honked at us and waved. We waved back. Being with my parents like that—something I had craved all of my life— thrilled me.

But like all the other times, it didn't last. The war for my mother's mind was a series of bruising battles that stretched on for 35 years with no decisive victory. She hated the medication because, she said, it made everything go into slow motion and fogged her brain. She once told me it was like wading through molasses. Funny. To us, it was the only time her mind was clear and absolutely the only time she ever admitted she was sick. A few good months would pass until she convinced herself she could get by with less medication. Soon she wouldn't take it at all.

I always knew when she was being sucked back into her illness. She'd withdraw from us physically and emotionally, preferring instead to spend time with the voices that convinced her that she was being persecuted and we couldn't be trusted. It was like watching a little child fall through the ice and we had to reach her to pull her out. She was both pleading and defiant as we dragged her to the doctors. She would swear she'd get better, tell us she was sorry and life would be good again—until the next time.

Ten minutes after I hung up with Debra, the phone rang again. This time it was Mama.

"Melba, they say it's cancer," she told me, her voice plaintive. I heard her breathing, almost gasping for air as she waited for me to tell her something different.

"Well, you've got your God with you, right?" I chose my words carefully, emphasizing, 'your God' because mine was caught up in a tangle of unanswered questions.

"Yeah, you're right about that," she laughed weakly.

My earliest memory of my mother was associated with both pain and comforting. I was a three-year-old with a terrible earache and she was my tireless caretaker, rocking me in an old wooden rocking chair all night long. Despite her sickness, she eased my pain many times; other times, she caused it. I know I did the same for her.

Sick or well, I loved my mother dearly but I hated what the sickness did to her life and to mine. We lived off-kilter, either in the middle of an episode or waiting anxiously for the next one. By the time I reached junior high, I was in constant fear that her demons would manifest themselves in a way guaranteed to humiliate me, as they often did.

Some of my friends understood what was going on and were kind enough to be complicit in my denial. Once, my best friend, Vanessa, spent the night and my mother launched into an early morning tirade. When she stepped outside, Dad locked the storm door behind her to "give her a minute to cool off." Bad idea. The brief quiet was shattered by the sound of breaking glass. Mama had picked up a rock, smashed the window and opened the door herself. Vanessa and I continued eating, pretending that the back porch wasn't covered with glass.

Our lives had taken so many turns by the time Ma was diagnosed with cancer. In hopes of finding better medical care, my parents had traded the rural south for the bleak southside of Chicago where they could be near my brothers and their doctors. Two years before my mother's diagnosis, my father had succumbed to the diabetes and strokes that claimed his sharp, witty mind as well as his body.

Despite their tortured relationship, none of us ever doubted that my parents loved each other, but they were caught up in circumstances that made their love impossible to express. After Dad's death, Ma's grief seemed to eat her alive. Always too thin, she grew even more frail and drawn. My brothers' doctors in Chicago couldn't find anything wrong, so they prescribed vitamins.

That's when my sister stepped in and took Mama back to New Jersey with her and pressured doctors until they told her what she needed to know but didn't really want to hear: Mama was dying.

That summer was surreal. Time both stood still and rushed by in a whirl of telephone calls, plane trips, medical tests and consultations. Extended despair was interspersed with brief periods of hope. Amid the chaos, my mother spoke as rationally as any time I can remember.

"I want to get well," she told us, half-scared and half-resolved.

"But if I don't, promise me you won't let me linger." We promised. And somewhere along the way, Debra and I made our peace.

Unlike the cancer diagnosis, we never got an official name for Ma's mental problems. Maybe she was schizophrenic; maybe she wasn't, but something was terribly wrong. Ma talked to herself, which I understand is fine. But she also answered herself, which I understand is not. She locked herself in a closet praying fervently as if she needed to be forgiven for all the world's sins. Sometimes she fussed for days on end and not even necessarily at anyone. It was a cross between a Spalding Gray monologue (an endless stream of recitations with no pause for a response) and a Dennis Miller rant (angry, over-the-top, irrational and vitriolic). The drone of her enraged voice became the background music of my childhood.

She rarely acknowledged there was a problem. It was always someone else who was crazy and needed to be locked away in the nut house. In the next breath she'd comment, "you can always tell if someone is crazy because they're always talking about somebody else's sense." The irony was completely lost on her.

As an adult, I realized that my mother's ailment had not only changed her life but mine as well. When I was growing up, I always heard how much I was like my mother, a comparison that both pleased and concerned me. She was considered pretty and I liked knowing that I resembled her physically, but worried that our similarities didn't end there. I worried that the madness in her lay dormant in me. I often wondered if my characteristic intensity was a fuse waiting to explode into insanity. Lately, I have found comfort in the notion that every family has something or someone in the family closet.

In the late summer months of my mother's last year, Debra complied with Mama's wish not to let her die in New Jersey and took her back to Chicago. She enrolled her in a hospice which placed a premium on dying with dignity. At check-in, but before she could sign the "do not resuscitate" clause, Mama collapsed. The emergency medical technicians broke her teeth when they jammed the tube down her throat so that she could breathe. They cracked her ribs when they pounded her 70-year-old, 80-pound frame to restart her worn out heart. They saved her life—only to put her through two more surgeries, to drip pain-dulling morphine into her veins. Her limbs became swollen and disfigured as her organs shut down.

During the weeks that seemed like months, Debra and I took turns sleeping on the hospital floor as she drifted in and out of consciousness, her communication with us limited to a nod or a blink. When she ceased to wake at all, doctors said it was just a matter of time. How much time they couldn't say. The machines breathed for her, keeping her alive—although that wasn't the word that came to my mind.

My brothers dealt with her condition in what I later thought of as a uniquely male fashion—they didn't. Instead, they washed their cars and painted their houses. And they refused to make any decisions. I never questioned their caring, just the way they chose to show it.

"You know this isn't what Mama wanted," I said.

"I'm not ready," said one. The correlation between his readiness and Mama's right to die escaped me.

I had been disillusioned with my parents' religion long before, angry with a God who seemed to do unkind things to kind people. But I held one belief that never wavered: there are far worse things than death. Mama's life was hardly charmed. In fact, the majority of it was pure hell. And if my family believed a fraction of what they shouted in church every Sunday, then Mama's heaven was just around the corner.

But we couldn't agree. My sister and I on one side, my brothers on the other and Ma in the middle. After a while, doctors removed her from ICU–breathing machines, morphine drip, and all. Later, when they said she'd be sent back to a nursing home, I caught a plane back to Los Angeles. Mama hated nursing homes.

The next morning the call came from my brother. "Thank you, God," I said, trying to recall the last time I had uttered those words.

I felt that Mama had waited for us to do the right thing, and grant her one wish not to linger. When we proved ourselves too weak, she became her own Genie. At last, she took responsibility for her own life in her death.

That night, I dreamed of visiting Mama in the funeral home. But instead of finding her in a coffin, she sat in a chair wearing a pink dress, looking 20 years younger.

"Ma, what are you doing here?" I asked, bending down to hug her. "We came to bury you."

"Child, I'm fine," she said flashing her chipped tooth smile. "Just fine."

And for the first time in my life, I knew she was. Maybe it's simply a denial of the possibilities, but I think I'm fine, too.

Torch Song for Mother and Child

Motherhood can be tragic, unfulfilling, or unfulfilled, and thus we lend an ear to the torch song, the song of unrequited, star-crossed love.

Mothers who harm, abuse, or neglect their offspring are frequently in the news, always provoking shock and repulsion, but the emotional underpinnings that make for such tragedy are rarely reported, and need examining. In this section, fiction goes where journalism dares not tread in exploring the harm mothers can do.

Infertility is a challenge experienced by many women, and the injustice of it weighs mightily on those who have much to give. Abortion, still controversial, is an option exercised by those who are determined to maximize their own life potential on their own terms. It is a choice that resuscitates one's freedom, but exacts its own price for years afterward.

Although motherhood can be, for some, an unparalleled opportunity for happiness, for others it means a loss of control, a regimen of self-denial, a submission to domination by nature and man. Motherhood's disappointments and desperation are plumbed herein.

the lost baby poem

BY LUCILLE CLIFTON

the time I dropped your almost body down
down to meet the waters under the city
and run one with the sewage to the sea
what did i know about waters rushing back
what did i know about drowning
or being drowned

you would have been born into winter
in the year of the disconnected gas
and no car   we would have made the thin
walk over genesee hill into the canada wind
to watch you slip like ice into strangers' hands
you would have fallen naked as snow into winter
if you were here I could tell you these
and some other things

if i am ever less than a mountain
for your definite brothers and sisters
let the rivers pour over my head
let the sea take me for a spiller
of seas   let black men call me stranger
always   for your never named sake

later i'll say
i spent my life
Loving a great man

later
my life will accuse me
of various treasons

not black enough
too black
eyes closed when they should have been open
eyes open when they should have been closed

will accuse me for unborn babies
and dead trees

later
when i defend again and again
with this love
my life will keep silent
listening to
my body breaking

1972

Many Rivers to Cross

BY JUNE JORDAN

*W*hen my mother killed herself, I was looking for a job. That was fifteen years ago. I had no money and no food. On the pleasure side, I was down to my last pack of Pall Malls plus half a bottle of J & B. I needed to find work because I needed to be able fully to support myself and my eight-year-old son, very fast. My plan was to raise enough big bucks so that I could take an okay apartment inside an acceptable public school district, by September. That deadline left me less than three months to turn my fortunes right side up.

It seemed that I had everything to do at once. Somehow, I must move all of our things, mostly books and toys, out of the housing project before the rent fell due, again. I must do this without letting my neighbors know because destitution and divorce added up to personal shame, and failure. Those same neighbors had looked upon my husband and me as an ideal young couple, in many ways; inseparable, doting, ambitious. They had kept me busy and laughing in the hard weeks following my husband's departure for graduate school in Chicago; they had been the ones to remember him warmly through teasing remarks and questions all that long year that I remained alone, waiting for his return while I became the "temporary" sole breadwinner of our peculiar long-distance family by telephone. They had been the ones who kindly stopped the teasing and the queries when the year ended and my husband, the father of my child, did not come back. They never asked me and I never told them what that meant, altogether. I don't think I really knew.

I could see how my husband would proceed more or less naturally from graduate school to a professional occupation of his choice, just as he had shifted rather easily from me, his wife, to another man's wife—another woman. What I could not see was how I should go forward, now, in any natural, coherent way. As a mother without a husband, as a poet without a publisher, a freelance journalist without assignment, a city planner without a contract, it seemed to me that several incontestable and conflicting necessities had suddenly eliminated the whole realm of choice from my life.

My husband and I agreed that he would have the divorce that he wanted, and I would have the child. This ordinary settlement is, as millions of women will testify, as absurd as saying, "I'll give you a call, you handle everything else." At any rate, as my lawyer explained, the law was the same as the law today; the courts would surely award me a reasonable amount of the father's income as child support, but the courts would also insist that they could not enforce their own decree. In other words, according to the law, what a father owes to his child is not serious compared to what a man owes to the bank for a car, or a vacation. Hence, as they say, it is extremely regrettable but nonetheless true that the courts cannot garnish a father's salary, nor freeze his account, nor seize his property on behalf of his children, in our society. Apparently this is because a child is not a car or a couch or a boat. (I would suppose this is the very best available definition of the difference between an American child and a car.)

Anyway, I wanted to get out of the projects as quickly as possible. But I was going to need help because I couldn't bend down and I couldn't carry anything heavy and I couldn't let my parents know about these problems because I didn't want to fight with them about the reasons behind the problems—which was the same reason I couldn't walk around or sit up straight to read or write without vomiting and acute abdominal pain. My parents would have evaluated that reason as a terrible secret compounded by a terrible crime; once again an unmarried woman, I had, nevertheless, become pregnant. What's more I had tried to interrupt this pregnancy even though this particular effort required not only one but a total of three abortions—each of them illegal and amazingly expensive, as well as, evidently, some-what poorly executed.

My mother, against my father's furious rejections of me and what he viewed as my failure, offered what she could; she had no money herself but there was space in the old brownstone of my childhood. I would live with them during the summer while I pursued my crash schedule for cash, and she would spend as much time with Christo-pher, her only and beloved grandchild, as her worsening but partially undiagnosed illness allowed.

After she suffered a stroke, her serenely imposing figure had shrunk into an unevenly balanced, starved shell of chronic disorder. In the last two years, her physical condition had forced her retirement from nursing, and she spent most of her days on a makeshift cot pushed against the wall of the dining room next to the kitchen. She could do very few things for herself, besides snack on crackers, or pour ready-made juice into a cup and then drink it.

In June, 1966, I moved from the projects into my parents' house with the help of a woman named Mrs. Hazel Griffin. Since my teens, she had been my hairdresser. Every day, all day, she stood on her feet, washing and straightening hair in her crowded shop, the Arch of Beauty. Mrs. Griffin had never been married, had never finished high school, and she ran the Arch of Beauty with an imperturbable and contagious sense of success. She had a daughter as old as I who worked alongside her mother, coddling customer fantasy into confi-dence. Gradually, Mrs. Griffin and I became close; as my own mother became more and more bedridden and demoralized, Mrs. Griffin ex-tended herself—dropping by my parents' house to make dinner for them, or calling me to wish me good luck on a special freelance ven-ture, and so forth. It was Mrs. Griffin who packed me up, so to speak, and carried me and the boxes back to Brooklyn, back to the house of my parents. It was Mrs. Griffin who ignored my father standing hate-ful at the top of the stone steps of the house and not saying a word of thanks and not once relieving her of a single load she wrestled up the stairs and past him. My father hated Mrs. Griffin because he was proud and because she was a stranger of mercy. My father hated Mrs. Griffin because he was like that sometimes: hateful and crazy.

My father alternated between weeping bouts of self-pity and storm explosions of wrath against the gods apparently determined to ruin him. These were his alternating reactions to my mother's increasing enfeeblement, her stoic depression. I think he was scared; who would take care of him? Would she get well again and make everything all right again?

This is how we organized the brownstone; I fixed a room for my son on the top floor of the house. I slept on the parlor floor in the front room. My father slept on the same floor, in the back. My mother stayed downstairs.

About a week after moving in, my mother asked me about the progress of my plans. I told her things were not terrific but that there were two different planning jobs I hoped to secure within a few days. One of them involved a study of new towns in Sweden and the other one involved an analysis of the social consequences of a huge hydroelectric dam under construction in Ghana. My mother stared at me uncomprehendingly and then urged me to look for work in the local post office. We bitterly argued about what she dismissed as my "highfalutin'" ideas and, I believe, that was the last substantial conversation between us.

From my first memory of him, my father had always worked at the post office. His favorite was the night shift, which brought him home usually between three and four o'clock in the morning.

It was hot. I finally fell asleep that night, a few nights after the argument between my mother and myself. She seemed to be rallying; that afternoon, she and my son had spent a long time in the backyard, oblivious to the heat and the mosquitoes. They were both tired but peaceful when they noisily re-entered the house, holding hands awkwardly.

But someone was knocking at the door to my room. Why should

I wake up? It would be impossible to fall asleep again. It was so hot. The knocking continued. I switched on the light by the bed: 3:30 A.M. It must be my father. Furious, I pulled on a pair of shorts and a t-shirt. "What do you want? What's the matter?" I asked him through the door. Had he gone berserk? What could he have to talk about at that ridiculous hour?

"OK, all right," I said, rubbing my eyes awake as I stepped to the door and opened it. "What?"

To my surprise, my father stood there looking very uncertain.

"It's your mother," he told me, in a burly, formal voice. "I think she's dead, but I'm not sure." He was avoiding my eyes.

"What do you mean," I answered.

"I want you to go downstairs and figure it out."

I could not believe what he was saying to me. "You want me to figure out if my mother is dead or alive?"

"I can't tell! I don't know!!" he shouted angrily.

"Jesus Christ," I muttered, angry and beside myself.

I turned and glanced about my room, wondering if I could find anything to carry with me on this mission; what do you use to determine a life or death? I couldn't see anything obvious that might be useful.

"I'll wait up here," my father said. "You call up and let me know."

I could not believe it; a man married to a woman more than forty years and he can't tell if she's alive or dead and he wakes up his kid and tells her, "You figure it out."

I was at the bottom of the stairs. I halted just outside the dining room where my mother slept. Suppose she really was dead? Suppose my father was not just being crazy and hateful? "Naw," I shook my head and confidently entered the room.

"Momma?" I called, aloud. At the edge of the cot, my mother was leaning forward, one arm braced to hoist her body up. She was trying to stand up! I rushed over. "Wait. Here, I'll help you!" I said.

And I reached out my hands to give her a lift. The body of my mother was stiff. She was not yet cold, but she was stiff. Maybe I had come downstairs just in time! I tried to loosen her arms, to change her position, to ease her into lying down.

"Momma!" I kept saying. "Momma, listen to me! It's OK. I'm here and everything. Just relax. Relax! Give me a hand, now. I'm trying to help you lie down!"

Her body did not relax. She did not answer me. But she was not cold. Her eyes were not shut.

From upstairs my father was yelling, "Is she dead? Is she dead?"

"No!" I screamed at him. "No! She's not dead!"

At this, my father tore down the stairs and into the room. Then he braked.

"Milly?" he called out, tentative. Then he shouted at me and banged around the walls. "You damn fool. Don't you see now she's gone. Now she's gone!" We began to argue.

"She's alive! Call the doctor!"

"No!"

"Yes!"

At last my father left the room to call the doctor.

I straightened up. I felt completely exhausted from trying to gain a response from my mother. There she was, stiff on the edge of her bed, just about to stand up. Her lips were set, determined she would manage it, but by herself. I could not help. Her eyes fixed on some point below the floor.

"Momma!" I shook her hard as I could to rouse her into focus. Now she fell back on the cot, but frozen and in the wrong position. It hit me that she might be dead. She might be dead.

My father reappeared at the door. He would not come any closer. "Dr. Davis says he will come. And he call the police."

The police? Would they know if my mother was dead or alive? Who would know?

I went to the phone and called my aunt. "Come quick," I said. "My father thinks Momma has died but she's here but she's stiff."

Soon the house was weird and ugly and crowded and I thought I was losing my mind.

Three white policemen stood around telling me my mother was dead. "How do you know?" I asked, and they shrugged and then they repeated themselves. And the doctor never came. But my aunt came and my uncle and they said she was dead.

After a conference with the cops, my aunt disappeared and when she came back she held a bottle in one of her hands. She and the police whispered together some more. Then one of the cops said, "Don't worry about it. We won't say anything." My aunt signalled me to follow her into the hallway where she let me understand that, in fact, my mother had committed suicide.

I broke away from my aunt and ran to the telephone. I called a friend of mine, a woman who talked back loud to me so that I could realize my growing hysteria, and check it. Then I called my cousin Valerie who lived in Harlem; she woke up instantly and urged me to come right away.

I hurried to the top floor and stood my sleeping son on his feet. I wanted to get him out of this house of death more than I ever wanted anything. He could not stand by himself so I carried him down the two flights to the street and laid him on the backseat and then took off.

At Valerie's, my son continued to sleep, so we put him to bed, closed the door, and talked. My cousin made me eat eggs, drink whiskey, and shower. She would take care of Christopher, she said. I should go back and deal with the situation in Brooklyn.

When I arrived, the house was absolutely full of women from the church dressed as though they were going to Sunday communion. It seemed to me they were, every one of them, wearing hats and gloves and drinking coffee and solemnly addressing invitations to a funeral and I could not find my mother anywhere and I could not find an empty spot in the house where I could sit down and smoke a cigarette.

My mother was dead.

Feeling completely out of place, I headed for the front door, ready to leave. My father grabbed my shoulder from behind and forcibly spun me around.

"You see this," he smiled, waving a large document in the air. "This am insurance paper for you!" He waved it into my face. "Your mother, she left you insurance, see?"

I watched him.

"But I 'gwine burn it in the furnace before I give it you to t'row away on trash!"

"Is that money?" I demanded. "Did my mother leave me money?"

"Eh-heh!" he laughed. "And you don't get it from me. Not today, not tomorrow. Not until I dead and buried!"

My father grabbed for my arm and I swung away from him. He hit me on my head and I hit back. We were fighting.

Suddenly, the ladies from the church bustled about and pushed, horrified, between us. This was a sin, they said, for a father and a child to fight in the house of the dead and the mother not yet in the ground! Such a good woman she was, they said. She was a good woman, a good woman, they all agreed. Out of respect for the memory of this good woman, in deference to my mother who had committed suicide, the ladies shook their hats and insisted we should not fight; I should not fight with my father.

Utterly disgusted and disoriented, I went back to Harlem. By the time I reached my cousin's place I had begun to bleed, heavily. Valerie said I was hemorrhaging so she called up her boyfriend and the two of them hobbled me into Harlem Hospital.

I don't know how long I remained unconscious, but when I opened my eyes I found myself on the women's ward, with an intravenous setup feeding into my arm. After a while, Valerie showed up. Christopher was fine, she told me; my friends were taking turns with him. Whatever I did, I should not admit I'd had an abortion or I'd get her into trouble, and myself into trouble. Just play dumb and rest. I'd have to stay on the ward for several days. My mother's funeral was tomorrow afternoon. What did I want her to tell people to explain why I wouldn't be there? She meant, what lie?

I thought about it and I decided I had nothing to say; If I couldn't tell the truth then the hell with it.

I lay in that bed at Harlem Hospital, thinking and sleeping. I wanted to get well.

I wanted to be strong. I never wanted to be weak again as long as I lived. I thought about my mother and her suicide and I thought about how my father could not tell whether she was dead or alive.

I wanted to get well and what I wanted to do as soon as I was strong again, actually, what I wanted to do was I wanted to live my life so that people would know unmistakably that I am alive, so that when I finally die people will know the difference for sure between my living and my death.

And I thought about the idea of my mother as a good woman and I rejected that, because I don't see why it's a good thing when you give up, or when you cooperate with those who hate you or when you polish and iron and mend and endlessly mollify for the sake of the people who love the way that you kill yourself day by day silently.

And I think all of this is really about women and work. Certainly this is all about me as a woman and my life work. I mean I am not sure my mother's suicide was something extraordinary. Perhaps most women must deal with a similar inheritance, the legacy of a woman whose death you cannot possibly pinpoint because she died so many, many times and because, even before she became your mother, the life of that woman was taken; I say it was taken away.

And really it was to honor my mother that I did fight with my father, that man who could not tell the living from the dead.

And really it is to honor Mrs. Hazel Griffin and my cousin Valerie and all the women I love, including myself, that I am working for the courage to admit the truth that Bertolt Brecht has written; he says, "It takes courage to say that the good were defeated not because they were good, but because they were weak."

I cherish the mercy and the grace of women's work. But I know there is new work that we must undertake as well: that new work will make defeat detestable to us. That new women's work will mean we will not die trying to stand up: we will live that way: standing up.

I came too late to help my mother to her feet.

By way of everlasting thanks to all of the women who have helped me to stay alive I am working never to be late again.

Mother, Unconceived

BY ERIN AUBRY KAPLAN

Before I write any story, I must first say that the story isn't over. I don't have children, but I could because it's still possible. I'm 39. I have ovaries and a womb that still wait, as they have been waiting since I was thirteen or so, at least that's the way I've imagined it. They wait with incredible patience and wonderful equanimity—they could wait for the rest of their active lives, and not mind at all or cause me any grief. I could never utilize the creation potential, resurrected every month with Sisphyean precision, and not suffer any consequences for my laziness or irresolution or rare good sense.

I'm still trying to figure out what keeps me well above the baby fray. I may sit and puzzle this out forever and let the time and the last of the blood slip away to menopause and then, only then, will I breathe a sigh of relief and feel in my marrow that I've done the right thing. I will confirm what I've felt all along, what I felt as a small, hard seed at thirteen and later as full-flowered righteousness. Right? Maybe. I'm almost certain.

But is almost good enough, sure enough? Is there reasonable doubt to this thing? If so, I'm unconvictable, a free woman made free by the murk of desire and doubt, and if not—well, I'm a free woman still. And so the problem.

Not having children cannot be this easy. Culture has long had it that black women are empathy made flesh (also attitude made flesh, but that's another essay entirely), nurturers by nature or by default, cooks nearly from birth. We are founts of blind encouragement, bricklayers of discipline, the most inimitable babysitters and line-leaders you ever saw without even trying. We harbor steely resolve in our sleep. We have been firewalls for trouble of all kinds—

mistreatment of black men, popular unease with black people period—and if we aren't mothers, we have had extensive experience in
raising younger siblings and looking after various play sisters and
brothers.

Not me. I was fourth in a family of five and had no one to look
after for a long time; another sister was born when I was six. By then,
people recognized my tendency to isolation and deep thought, noted
my lack of smiles, and no one brought babies around for me to model
motherhood on. I didn't cook, or pretend to; my mother loved me
but kept me out of the kitchen. I read, imagined, watched other people. When my sister Heather was born I was briefly surprised, but too
young and too used to a house full of bodies to feel resentful. I did
look after Heather somewhat, took her out in her stroller in the afternoon, but in the end we became friends, confidantes with the
same odd tastes in music and other pastimes. I felt sororal, not maternal toward her; in fact, it was she who most often provided me with
emotional support during a fitful but sustained depression that has
only significantly lifted in the last few years.

Heather had the pragmatism and circumspection I seemed to lack
entirely, and that I thought all mothers must have. Where she plotted
and executed a career in law—getting scholarships, passing the California bar on the first try—I was getting blown off course, wanting
to write but puttering around half-heartedly as an actor and substitute teacher. Of course, she got married before me, and had a baby
two years ago, an event I was deeply afraid would change our easy
dynamic forever. I felt very guilty about this fear, which I thought
selfish and all the evidence I needed that I was unsuited to motherhood; women were at least supposed to regard each other's pregnancies as good news, circle the wagons of procreational instinct.

Black women are thought of as especially guided by such in-
stincts, the least likely to wonder aloud whether they want babies at
all even if a pregnancy is unintended. We have grown skilled at accepting our lot, and pregnancy is no different; for us, it is not choice

but charge. And people like seeing us with kids because it completes a picture that is skewed without them, almost unsettling—a woman will always battle the notion that minus kids she is 'less than,' but a black woman battles that, plus the notion that she is failing socially, culturally, historically. Black women have little individual *she* to work with, despite decades of feminist dogma that has become a very accepted part of American sociological discourse. Those of us who are black and who have doubts about baby are still very much on the outside.

So the problem, and the solution, is, as I've already said, that I *do* have a choice. It is covert, doesn't quite feel like mine, but I have exercised it. I have had more abortions than I care to reveal here. My black female friends, mostly careerists, were accepting but vaguely admonishing, and assured me that one day I would go through with it (in a couple of instances, they insisted on it, and while I thought it was none of their business, I didn't disagree because it felt like they were speaking to something higher, greater, than my individual wants. So I said nothing.) I am not at all happy about those abortions; choice does not mean happiness, merely options. I feel disquieted, uneasy, like a black woman steering clear of troubles is committing a criminal act. I even get faint stabs of that unease when I indulge in other luxuries of choice that seem far more innocuous, like impulse shopping or going to movies when I want or sitting alone; I think, I have little right to live this way. Even the fact that I work as a de facto black advocacy journalist does little to assuage the feeling that I'm treading a forbidden path of least resistance. I'm cheating a god I don't even believe in, quite.

And yet. I admire mothers, beginning with my own, who inhabited her role comfortably, but freely admitted she would have done something different had she not had the five of us. I admire my younger sister, who became a mother but hardly lost herself, or us, in the process: We still do dinner at least once a week, often with my nephew in tow. I love Julian, as I do all five of my other nieces and nephews, but loving them has not so far translated into wanting kids of my own. I like being the mentor, the reinforcement rather than the enforcer, the figure who can assert opinions but doesn't have to render judgment. Though I enjoy the inevitable moments of vicarious motherhood: giving Julian a bottle or a bath, sternly telling him 'no,' offering my teenage niece advice on what to wear because she's asked me for it.

But my sisters, the mothers, are constantly living two lives, or three, in my own mother's case, five: I can barely live one to maximum effect. In some ways that's a poor excuse, a Twenty-First century argument for the luxury of solitude and personal space that American culture epitomizes, but that black history and its large-scale struggles have never been able to afford. Despite the unprecedented black affluence in the country, perhaps I have no right to assume such freedom. Yet it defines all Americans, and if I don't claim it, I am further diminished as such, and our progress is universally compromised. Reconciling the cult of individualism with the needs of the collective is the millennial version of what DuBois defined one hundred years ago as the plague of double-consciousness—being black and being American at once. We have not quite pulled ourselves together and still largely shuttle between the two, but in ways now that DuBois could not have imagined. Straddling the notion of motherhood, with its self-evident rewards and cultural imperatives, and the nirvana of American self-fulfillment is but one of those ways.

Social theories notwithstanding, I am mostly uncertain: I don't know. I am not convinced of having children, but I sustain anxiety that maybe I'm not convinced for the wrong reasons, like the fact that raising a child is a big damn inconvenience. Or because when it's all over and my ovaries fall silent, I might feel incomplete, not psychically so much as experientially; part of me is afraid that not having a baby will wind up feeling like the small but nagging regret I have for not going out to see the Pope the one time he came to town in the mid-1980s. That's not a good reason to have a child, but it's an American one, a rationale driven by convenience and consumerism. (If I had gone to see the pope, I could have picked up some limited-edition souvenirs of his visit.) And as our consumerist ethos shifts from the acquisition of things to the acquisition of experience—you don't buy Nikes so much as you pay for the feeling of *being* Michael Jordan—the whole proposition of "acquiring" babies takes on its own unsettling dimensions.

Maybe this is where I have rare good sense, and my lifelong wariness of doing what everybody else is doing will stand me in good stead. My husband is leaving the whole enterprise in my incapable hands; he is not interested in having kids, never has been, but he says, if I absolutely must, he will probably go along. Since I tend to think everything out of existence or action—my American right, my cultural fallibility—I can see where this is headed. We've only been married a year and I'm contemplating all the things we haven't done together, all the things I haven't written, but not all the children we could have.

I have answered my own question, I know. I answered it long ago. I suppose I answered it in the beginning of this convoluted letter to myself. In the end, the only answer I have lies in uncertainty. *Thinking* that my answer may be the wrong one, that I may be abusing more than respecting my ectopic freedom, fuels anxiety but also an odd comfort. It leaves me in the middle of a labor that I will likely try with words, not with any issuance of my womb. The injustices, and the joys, that I inherited from the ages will be strictly mine to nurture.

Good Night Moon

BY FELICIA WARD

It's my birthday. I feel ambushed by their stares. Every thought scatters—ricochets from unmade beds to unwashed dishes and back again to my children, one-two-three, kneeling between wall and bed. Their frosting-smeared faces are as obscene to me as a baboon's bright blue ass and just as unexpected.

I keep not hitting them. I keep not hearing crunch of bones; keep not seeing leather shoes welting skin. I look into those familiar eyes, and I want to give in to the way I feel about them. Relent to mothering, the way one finally gives into a virus; adjusting to clogged airways, mucous and phlegm.

I want the fever of memory to break, so we can breathe again.

Last year, as a birthday surprise, my husband arranged for the aunts to take our children, and spirited me away for a long weekend. Ninety minutes after we left our house in Berkeley, we were at my mother-in-law's place. A small house overlooking Austin Creek.

We were on a peace-keeping mission. My husband wanted to save our marriage. For a change, I indulged his every wish. We spent the first morning of a three-day weekend sharing the same deck chair, our legs intertwined. I even let Gus play with my hair.

"Honey," he said, "I'm experiencing déjà vu all over again."

To humor him, I tilted my head back and planted a dry kiss on his throat. Content, he worked his way over every square inch of my head, oiling my scalp, and twisting my thick dark wool into locks.

"Look," Gus said, pointing up at the sky, "a portent."

The rising sun hit a stand of redwood trees, and turned the bark bone white. A breeze, as gentle as a newborn's breath, agitated the branches. "What's important?" I asked.

"Portent. An omen, a sign."

"I know what a portent is, Gus. Don't patronize me."

"I'm not. Honey, look . . . right there . . . all silvery . . . see?"

A clump of clouds gave way, and I could see long silken threads floating across blue sky.

"Baby spiders," I said, disappointed, "ballooning to escape cannibalistic mothers."

"Like in *Charlotte's Web*?"

"Exactly."

I have three children: boy-boy-girl.

I call my oldest son my "prodrome" baby. He's the result of a vulvar tingle; followed by a not unpleasant swelling, that in my case, masqueraded as lust. Members of my husband's latte crowd called Herpes, the "Spanish fly" of the 80s. More potent than oysters and Champagne, it was epidemic among his friends. My husband used to call this explanation my Herpes defense. Whatever. One hundred hours of labor made me a mother, a mama, a mommy, forever.

I breast-fed Ben, blood and milk. Not intentionally. I didn't have a clue how to toughen up my tits; get them ready for a toothless carnivore.

Ask the aunts. That's what Gus said.

I told him no, they're as sterile as mules.

Your doctor then, he said.

Ding-ding-ding, I pretended to clang his head like a bell to remind him: HMO remember. They've already pamphleted me to death.

End of conversation.

Our second son is the result of ordinary lust. He loved to suck. My husband, the English professor, preferred I say "suckle." I only wish I could have vacuum-suctioned Miles to his bologna-colored paps.

Now my daughter, Rachel, was a dream. She developed an allergy to her mama's milk. She read my mind. I wish the other two had considered that option.

Fatherhood has always suited Gus. He loves his sons, but he's wild about Rachel. Completely smitten. When other men crowed about their son's perfect little penis, delighted in the first time, undiapered, the little whizzer pumped daddy full in his face with pee, my husband went on and on about his daughter's "internal maternal devices."

"Can you believe it?" he says, to a banquet table full of his academic cronies, "my baby girl's uterus is about the size of a garlic clove. Her ovaries, the same circumference around as a sweet pea."

"You mean a black-eyed pea, don't you?" his department chair says.

All conversation stopped. There was no clink of crystal against dentures. No pink-lipsticked faculty wives, dabbing at the corners of their smiles with white linen napkins. Everyone turned to look at me, nine long noses wrinkling, like they'd discovered a bad smell in the house. The glass of Merlot in my hand tipped, just a millimeter too far, and dribbled wine onto the tablecloth. My husband didn't notice the stain creeping over to his side of the table.

"Right," he says, his blue eyes shining, "just think, she's only four years old and my daughter has all the eggs she'll ever need."

"Thank goodness," his department chair says, winking at his wife.

What I had to do next—the words I used to punctuate every single blow—made that the last meal I ever shared with my untenured husband.

All winter, from December to March, I moved my things from my husband's house to my father's. I didn't want help. I wanted the dumb numbing repetitive motion of punching collapsed cardboard into boxes. The satisfying ache of sore muscles. The physical exhaustion that comes from carrying 57 boxes up and down three flights of stairs.

On the last day of the move, the students I'd hired to haul furniture got lost. I told them to look for the brown shingle house with the stunted "Juliet" balcony, and the orange gingerbread trim.

They pulled up to the front door five minutes later.

When they were gone, I stood at the kitchen sink and watched a weary stream of ants pour through a crack in the kitchen window.

I pinched one dead.

My father would be home soon. "One hard knock," he'd probably say about the divorce, "that don't make you no tree."

I don't know what that means either. I've spent half my life trying to figure that man out. I was five years old when he sent me to live with his sisters: The Aunts. The first time I saw them, all I could think was, what big eyes they had; what long white teeth. When they couldn't resist planting wet kisses on my cheeks, I asked them why they looked like walnuts and smelled like Spam.

Aunt Sis stayed Aunt Baby's hand; caught it by the wrist in mid-flight. Under her breath, Aunt Baby said, "I ought to slap her to kingdom come."

Aunt Sis said, "Not tonight you don't."

I'll never forgive them for not taking me and my children in.

Right at the breakfast table, with all three of my children looking her straight in the mouth, Aunt Sis says, "You been with us two weeks. You need to go on home, Honey. Your daddy's house can't take nothing away from you it ain't already took."

I could hear my spine straightening. The vertebrae clicking into place.

"We'll keep your doggone chirren here with us," Aunt Baby said, "'til you can get your things moved in. I know your daddy's house is going to be a tight fit, but we old now. You can see that. And mind you, if you hear the rustle of love, you get on back to Russ."

"Gus."

"Gus, go on back to him."

———

I pinched another ant dead . . . then another. I regretted it later. I understood their urgency. But I couldn't stop. I wasn't going to shoot myself. I'm not sure how much time passed before I gave it up. There were just too many, and they had a smell.

At eight o'clock my father came in with take-out. Wonton soup. Sweet and sour. Chow mein with crispy noodles. My favorites, he reminded me.

I couldn't eat. I did crack open my fortune cookie. It read, "You have a good sense of humor." I guess I do. For the first time in 30 years I spent the night in my father's house.

I slept like the dead.

Saturday morning, I woke to cold winter light. A quiet house, empty of children. My father said he'd bring them here, around seven o'clock, along with two birthday cakes. Chocolate for me. Lemon cake, with Cookie Monster–blue frosting for Rachel.

I forced myself out of bed to do the routine. Pee. Wash. Check out the face for changes. Pillow tracks, as deep as tribal markings criss-crossed both cheeks. I looked soft and rumpled. Nothing like myself. I got back in bed.

By noon, I was as numb as a rock from too much sleep.

By two o'clock I was as lonely as God on the fifth day; before he created Adam; before Eve was a twinkle in his eye.

By three, I needed my children's sounds. In this house, I can't be a mother without them.

I couldn't face unpacking, so I wandered from room to room trying out chairs; opening and closing cupboards; and nibbling from a tube of raw cookie dough I found in the fridge. I saved rifling through my father's bedroom closets for last. I didn't find a thing. No letters in his 50-year-old chiffarobe. No newspaper clippings in a shoe box. No death certificates under the mattress.

There was one photograph. Me and the X. A mall pose excreting matrimonial bliss. I turned it face down and walked back to the living room.

The best thing about this house is the view. Sitting at the living room window you get water, hills, sky and block after block of one- and two-story houses marching down to the San Francisco Bay.

Getting this house was the equivalent of winning the lottery for my parents. Nate and Nola Choyce were part of the great migration north, from Louisiana and Texas, in the 40s. Him a longshoreman at the naval shipyards; her a cook at the university. Colored people living in high cotton. They should have had it made. They were the reason I could sit there, and watch the darkening sky.

Winter sunsets here are rudely beautiful. Shameless. At five o'clock the sun collapsed into the bay, leaving deep violet hills, aqua blue water and clouds as outrageously pink as the G-string on a drag queen. Three minutes, and it was over—everything faded to black.

I left the window to turn on a lamp.

When I came back, I could see the glow of street lights, and my face mirrored in the glass. I don't know why I look like I do. My X used to say that no matter how angry I got, I always managed to look serene. The aunts swear I look like a dark-skinned Jackie-O. They don't say pre Onassis, but post grim tragedy. They do say I have her same wide set eyes. Ditto, the Mona Lisa smile. The dark clothes. They don't mention the secrets either. That's our primary kinship. I should be stark raving mad. I'm not.

I'm a 34-year-old black woman, alive at the end of the 20th Century and passing for sane. Believe me, that's saying something. I am not one to fall apart. I heard my father say that to one of the detectives, 30 years ago. He said, "My little girl, Honey, she's not going to fall apart."

And I'm not.

I understand the colored tradition of preferring truth over facts. I have a completely unsentimental view of what happened in this house. Aunt Baby and Aunt Sis painted very particular and peculiar pictures of our family history.

Aunt Baby's the one who told me, "Your mama's heart was as numb as a foot in a too-tight shoe."

Aunt Sis backed her up, saying, "I believe it was her raisin-hearted ways that led her to stray."

"Your mama had everything going for her," Aunt Baby said, "she was as pretty as Dorothy Dandridge, as smart as Eleanor Roosevelt—"

"She had feet like Harriet Tubman," Aunt Sis said, "Hard and callused, not at all tender."

They didn't mention my mother's daughters. I learned to steel myself against feeling anything for them. What happened is neither here nor there. As my father would say, "There are worse things than losing your mother."

Now, I'll be the first one to Amen that because, it's being a mother that stains my linen. My children smell like the spare change my father used to keep in his pockets. The warm penny he doled out every day.

That's how my children smell when they've been playing outside all day—like warm, copper pennies. And if they stand too close, if I get that smell, it brings back the sound of my mother tearing rags to stuff in the windows. Then the whole day long that's all I get, the sound of tearing—and I can't shake it, unless I sleep—and when I sleep I get one dream: *It's March 15, 1965. My fifth birthday. I'm in the big bed I share with my sisters. I wake up first. When I open my eyes, there's a red-and-white dress floating above my head, hiding my mother's face. She's standing over me twisting the dress back and forth in the early morning light, admiring it, checking and re-checking the seams for loose threads, the buttons the lace trim. It's perfect. White organdy with a red-checked apron. There are tiny red polka dots on the puffy sleeves and the hem is a waterfall of flounces.*

I am a big girl. Smart.

I don't believe her when she says we're going back to Texas.

That's the only dream I ever dream. It's easy enough to manage if I can keep a little distance, a cushion of air, between me and my children. It's not like they need lap time anymore. Not even Rachel. I tell you, my daughter's a dream.

I understand why my folks chose California. There were all these things not to be afraid of. Tornadoes. Hurricanes. Rednecks. Not where you could see them. I love raising my kids here. My children are safe from just about everything and everyone but me. That's something I can't ever guarantee. My mother ended it all, for herself and three daughters. In one fell swoop—whoosh—they were gone.

Why?

I don't have the be-all, end-all answer to that, but I do keep a running list. I started it when I became a mother. I've listed "forks in the trash can" at least 17 times.

Last night after dinner, I fished two forks out of the trash can; dunked them in the dishwater, and towel dried my hands. I didn't hurry. I put the leftovers away and tied up the trash. Then I left the kitchen for the living room. I could hear the television, and the sound of my father snoring. I didn't rush. Before I reached my children, I wanted to let my breathing return to normal. That takes time. It's not like I've mastered the "three maternal powers." That's what the X and I called them. It was a game we played. He understood my history.

When I got to the living room, I waited in the doorway. I could see my father sprawled in front of the television, the fingers of both hands tucked inside the waistband of his trousers. He's like me. Sleeps like the dead. It would take dynamite to rouse him. The aunts say we're both lucky to be alive. I've never been able to decide whether that's a curse or a blessing.

Rachel was using her granddad as a headrest. Our Siamese cat, my share of the community property, leg gracefully extended was licking his pedigree. Ben and Miles were in a tug-of-war over a bag of chips. I didn't try to stop them. I wanted to see who'd win, who's stronger. It wasn't much of a contest. Ben gave in first. I still didn't say a word. I wanted them to sense my presence on their own. That's maternal power number one.

The living room was smothered with furniture. Three coffee tables stacked waist high. Two side chairs. My father's 30-year-old Barcalounger, permanently stuck in recline. Two couches, one mossy green, and one gold. I couldn't even see my mother's piano, for the nubby orange love seat propped against the wall.

The sight of my life squeezed inside that room deflated every power I even thought I had. The kids didn't notice me at all. Before I could regain my full strength, Rachel, savoring momentary possession of the remote control, flipped through every channel twice. "The Simpsons" flashed on and off. "Seinfeld." Moesha on the WB—then back to Bart. When I saw Ben's head begin to pull in my direction, I made my words sting, like a wet towel on naked skin.

"Get to bed," I said, "Now!"

They were not impressed.

The boys whined in unison. Drawn out grating phantom-of-the-opera chords. All the organ keys flattened at once. Pathetic and miserable. "Ma-a-a," my Ben says, "our shows ain't off yet."

"You see this?" I took a deep breath before I held up a fork and added, "Guess where I found it?"

Rachel's head swiveled back and forth searching my face first, then Ben's. Her old woman's eyes taking everything in. I could feel the second power surging through me. The power to make them obey. The hairs on the back of my neck were standing on end.

The boys got up from the floor, mouths zipped shut, eyes focused on the floor. Rachel, on the other hand, decided to rub the cat; long hard strokes in the wrong direction. Anyone but a four-year-old could tell by the eye the cat had shut, and the other eye it had half-opened, that any minute, it was going to rip her to shreds. I reached over and pushed the thing off her lap. It curled itself around my legs, complaining in that eerie human-child sounding yeowl that only Siamese cats have.

I took the remote control away from Rachel, and aimed it at the TV. That's when Miles said, "Don't turn it off ma, it'll make you sad."

That completely broke the spell. I tried to cover by pointing down the hall. Both boys slunk out of the room. Apparently, they hadn't noticed the depletion of my powers. On the other hand, baby sister made me usher her out, with a swat on her behind. Clear evidence my powers had evaporated.

Rachel took her own sweet time, back pressed against the wall, to slide down the entire length of the hallway, scooting inch by inch, just as slowly as she could possibly make herself go.

She stopped at the open bedroom door and demanded, "Lights!"

I flicked them on, and used the third maternal power. I resisted the urge to kick her into the room. Instead, I distracted myself with petroleum based toddler detritus. It was scattered from one end of the room we shared to the other. I picked up Pocohontas Barbie by the head, Little Mermaid Barbie by the leg, and I kicked Tickle-Me-Elmo to my daughter's side of the room.

Rachel ignored me, until she heard Tickle-Me-Elmo giggling. Then she shucked off her slippers with tight little kicks, straight into the air. She barely missed my face. Luckily for both of us, she chose that moment to transform herself into a frog. She hopped the rest of the way to her bed, and landed with her tail end pointed up at me. I lifted the covers so she could get underneath. Then I said, "Kiss mommy good night."

"No kiss," she said, "story."

I was relieved. I didn't want to touch her. How many times, I wondered, did it take before a mother gave in and pushed a pillow over that dimpled face. I made a mental note to add slipper kicking to my list.

Just then, rapid-fire belching erupted from the boys' room—

followed by muffled laughter. "Choose a book," I said, holding up one finger, "I'll be right back."

Standing outside my old bedroom door, I stopped. I'm not one for surprises, not really. I coughed to signal, "Mommy's coming."

Unfortunately, when I opened the door, I forgot my own strength, let it get away from me. The damned thing swung open and kept on going. I didn't want to, but I looked. When I pulled the door back, a new layer of plaster crumbled to the floor. Where knob meets wall a huge receptive hole, about the size of a newborn baby's head, was at least two inches deeper.

My father. He refuses to make any changes in this house. He will not paint. He won't remove my mother's 26 pillbox hats, or her sherbet colored suits. Nada. Nothing. Not even a $1.99 doorstop.

I turned around to face my boys. They were too frightened to blink. I stared right back. I didn't apologize. It was late. I abandoned the maternal powers for fast, mean "mamalese."

"Lie down. Shut up. Go to sleep."

They obeyed. I tucked blankets under chins, took a deep breath and planted kisses near cheeks. The folds of Miles' neck smelled like warm pennies. I studied his face. He's my link to the maternal line. The aunts say my children are watered down. Too much white blood they say. I don't know about that, but Miles has my mother's eyes. Her fuzzy, soft around the hairline, nappy in the back, brick red hair. Her fawn-colored skin. He's not dark like me.

Love will obliterate him.

That's what I think when I see him laying there with his thumb inside his mouth. The little finger of the same hand feathering the tip of his nose. Every nerve ending reduced to this single pleasure. "It's mommy," his mouth full of thumb reassures. Pathetic.

I walked to the door and heard rustling. When I turned around, Ben had raised himself up on one elbow to blow me a kiss. I shot him one back, and he smiled. I pitched my voice low to say, "Don't make me come back in here."

Miles paused mid-suck. The sappy smile on Ben's face disappeared.

I closed the door behind me thinking, I don't care what anybody says. By the time I was seven years old, I already knew about the poorhouse, atomic bombs, assassinations, napalm, polio, the Klan. I'd seen Buddhist monks go up in flames. I understood the need to self immolate. I'd seen those little Texas girls, cotton wadded in blinded eyes. I understood that some folks' anger was explosive. Others had hate that seared to the bone. And of course, I had my own mother. I wanted my children to know fear.

Fear couldn't hurt them. In fact, they might need it some day.

Walking back down the hall, my naked feet on hardwood floors made a heavy slapping sound. The same sound my mother's feet made, when she went room to room collecting daughters. By the time I reached Rachel, I had a briny taste in my mouth.

Baby sister was wide awake, a thin book clutched in her hands. A gift from my imagination-stunted mother-in-law. She's responsible for all the Birkenstocked–parent approved, dull as water, culturally appropriate pulp, masquerading as children's literature my daughter owns.

I try to balance the Disney-Barney-Blue Dog palaver she rains on my children with fairy tales. The Brothers Grimm. Hans Christian Anderson. Ice Queens. Bloody red shoes. The possibility of being baked and eaten alive. The classics. I'd place Grimm in every home, like the Gideons do with the Bible.

The last hours of my childhood: the sirens; the breaking glass; my sisters' faces; and my mother's as dull as unfired clay—they'll always be what they were. That's something I can't ever change. But fairy tales were my trail of bread crumbs. My way out of the forest. I will always thank my mother for that. There was no other savior in this house.

My boys may have already chosen the weakest of survival weapons. Ben wants to please others. Miles (according to the aunts) was weaned too soon. But I think, maybe, Rachel has a chance. My youngest child is a lot like me. She plays hide and seek as if it was a war game, as if her life depended on it.

I perched on the edge of Rachel's bed and pretended to read the words printed in her new book. I didn't get very far before she stopped me.

"Mommy," she said, her right eyebrow cocked, "what's oncet-upon?"

"Everything that came before right now," I say.

My answer seemed to satisfy her, so I read on, hiding witches and trolls in that story-book bunny's darkening room, until I heard soft breathing.

It's our birthday. I wake to laughter floating through the house. Rachel's bed is empty. Good. Her Grandpa Nate must have banana pancakes on the griddle. I lay there with closed eyes and listen. From the sound of their laughter, my children are drunk on the Sunday sweetness of doing nothing. I swing both feet out of bed and the soft nappy body of Elmo giggles.

I place my full weight on him, but he won't stop. My children do. Their sounds are abruptly cut off, like someone has hands over their mouths. I shove Elmo under my pillow, to shut him up; and my children's sounds start to rise and fall again. I bounce up-and-down on the bed, to make it creak, and their sounds die down completely.

There's no use putting it off. I shrug on my robe, and search for them.

It doesn't take long to find them. They're in the living room, all three sitting in a tight circle, painting each other's faces blue with frosting. When I step inside the room they scatter.

Miles crawls over to the orange love seat on all fours, and slips behind it.

Ben wedges himself underneath the coffee tables.

Rachel thinks we're playing a game. She tags my leg, and calls out, "You're it!" before she scoots under the extended footrest of the Barcalounger. When I see her tuck herself into a tight ball, so that she is hidden in the cavity of my father's chair, my hiding place, I hiss, "What-the-hell-are-you-doing?"

My rage is biblical.

I reach down and pull Rachel out by both feet. I drag her over to Miles' hiding place; and yank him out by the arm. Then I haul them both to the center of the room. I get close enough to the stacked coffee tables, to hold Ben down with my foot.

"Answer me," I say, measuring each breath, "what-the-hell-are-you-doing?"

Everything is ceremonially quiet.

I don't hear any screams. There is no crying.

I can't tell if they are mute with fear, or if I am deaf with rage.

"Wait here," I say, "don't move an inch."

I leave them to rummage through my still-packed boxes, but I can't find what I need. I check the hall closet. My father has cleared it out to make room for us. I try the kitchen: drawers; under the sink; inside the broom closet. I walk back to the living room with the extension cord dangling from my hand.

No children.

Only Puss 'n Boots, with frosting-spackled whiskers.

I restrain myself. I don't kick him to kingdom come.

The door to the boys' room is closed.

I put my ear against it and listen.

When I can only hear myself breathing, I turn the knob.

The door swings open with a whoosh of air. I hold on to it this time, and don't let go until the knob is nesting in that hole like a baby in its cradle.

My children are huddled together. Miles is shivering like he's cold. Ben has the hiccups. Rachel has her thumb in her mouth.

I keep the three of them in my line of sight and sneak a look down at my hands. There's no streak of red beneath my nails. No crimped skin. The uncoiled extension cord is limp.

I look at my feet. There's no sign that the earth spins beneath me.

I look back up at my children's fear-struck faces.

There is no evidence that I will ever learn what part of my nature to temper.

Mother's House

BY TANANARIVE DUE

*G*randmother's dead," my cousin Muncko called to say. "She died this morning."

It was 7 A.M. on Christmas day.

I'd last seen my grandmother at Thanksgiving, when she had brought a pot of collard greens to dinner at my parents' house in Miami. When I told her I wouldn't be back in Miami until April, her eyes widened as if to say, *But I might not be here in April.* I'd talked to her on the telephone a week before she died. I was pregnant with my first baby, so I'm sure we talked about that. I'm sure we both said *I love you.* I only wish I could remember.

There was no answer when I tried to call my mother's house. Next, I called her cell phone. Mom was carrying her phone and answered it accidentally, though she had not heard it ring. She was walking into her mother's bedroom, seeing the body for the first time. The phone was too far for her to hear my voice. She probably didn't realize it was in her hand.

Are you sure she's not moving? I thought I saw her lips move, I heard her say, desperate for the paramedics to be wrong.

I sat helplessly thousands of miles away, hearing my mother cry.

During the 1960s, my grandmother was deathly afraid for her children.

In 1960, while my mother and her sister were in college at Florida A&M University, they made history. Rather than paying a fine, they were among five students who spent 49 days in jail for sitting-in at a Woolworth lunch counter in Tallahassee, becoming the nation's first "jail-in." Throughout the 1960s, the sisters were jailed several times, and they met with violence.

Years later, my grandmother told me that every time the phone rang late at night, she still feared terrible news about her children. But she was not a fearful woman. She was strongwilled and sassy, wearing colorful clothes perfectly matched with hats, jewelry and perfume—her favorite, Giorgio. I often borrowed my grandmother's clothes. When I was a child, my grandmother and mother were often mistaken for sisters.

My grandmother lived ten minutes from our family almost as long as I can remember. In family photographs, we were Mom, Dad, Tananarive, Johnita, Lydia—and Mother, as we called our grandmother. We loved our paternal grandmother in Indianapolis, but Mother was a member of the immediate family. She was our emergency contact on field trip forms, trusted babysitter, and safe haven.

Mother had cared for her own mother, who was deaf, for most of her adult life, until my great-grandmother died in 1973. Having been a long-time caretaker, Mother had high expectations when her health began to fail. She refused to give up her house and accept my mother's offer to move in with her, but Mother expected Mom to be constantly available to take her to doctor's appointments or to run errands. Mom and Aunt Priscilla both lived close to Mother in Southwest Dade County in Miami, but the burden wore on Mom.

Finally, my mother put her foot down. Mother *would* move in with her and Dad, and they would live in a large house in Quincy, where Mom was born, in upstate Florida. A month before she died, I took Mother to a Chinese buffet restaurant she loved. She walked gingerly because she had broken her hip that summer, but her resilience astounded me yet again.

"Listen, I'm realistic, Tananariva," Mother told me. "I know I can't live on my own forever. But I need time."

Then Christmas came. She died in her bed. In *her* house.

Eighteen months after Mother died, a buyer made a serious offer for her house. Her death became real yet again. Mother's house had to be cleared out and cleaned for new people.

Much of the task fell on my mother's shoulders. My uncle lived in Georgia, and hadn't returned since the funeral. My aunt was in Miami, but didn't handle the family's business matters. My father's back was bothering him.

Mom is the strongest woman I know. She put her life at risk in the 1960s, and she fought like a tiger to raise her three daughters. She could have been a field commander during World War II, but I could not imagine Mom cleaning out Mother's house alone.

My two sisters and I discussed the problem; Lydia in Dallas, Johnita in New York and me in Washington state. Johnita and Lydia, both attorneys, had obligations and couldn't make a trip soon. I was pregnant. I'd miscarried my first baby during a book tour soon after Mother's death, and I had vowed not to travel during the first three months of my new pregnancy. Under the circumstances, I felt Mom wouldn't want me to come; she would treat me with kid gloves.

Soon, nature solved my dilemma: I had another miscarriage—after eight weeks, as before. I buried my grief. In my quest for answers, I told myself: *Well, maybe it was supposed to happen this way so I can help Mom clean out Mother's house.*

Mother had been Mom's best friend, just as Mom is mine. My friend needed me.

We'd been a circle, the three of us: Mother, Mom and me. Neither of my sisters had come back to live in Miami after college, but I got a position at *The Miami Herald* and stayed for ten years. Mom and I had spent years collaborating on a mother-daughter memoir about the impact of the civil rights movement on our family, traveling together doing research, recording interviews, writing and editing. I was beginning to think I would always live in Miami, never far from Mom.

Then, I fell in love with a man who lived in Washington State. As excited as I was about getting married, leaving home was a big step, and it was hard on me. But not nearly as hard as it was on my mother. I was her daughter, but now, suddenly, I was also a wife and a stepmother to a 12-year-old girl, Nicki. When I left home, I was so accustomed to sharing hotel rooms with Mom that for the first few weeks I lived with my husband, I often mistook the person sleeping beside me for her.

After my second miscarriage, I knew it wasn't time for me to be a mother yet. I would be a daughter instead. Since Mother's death, Miami had not felt like home. I hadn't set foot inside Mother's house since the funeral, and I dreaded going back, but the miscarriage was my emotional anesthesia. I was numb. Besides, I was going home to *Mom*, the person I wanted to be with most after losing a baby. It was a kind of homecoming, even if it was the saddest kind.

I know why Mother didn't want to leave her house.

Mother's three-bedroom house sat amid a tangle of tropical plants in the front yard. And orange trees bearing fruit. And palm fronds and bougainvilleas with fuchsia and pale orange blossoms swathing the rear. The house was built in the 1950s, pure concrete, white with turquoise trim and broad, Florida-style metal shutters. She'd converted it to two bedrooms to have more closet space. It had a dining room addition that was once a carport, a screened-in front porch, and a screened, covered back patio that seemed to double its size. Mother had spent nearly forty years making her house exactly what she wanted it to be.

When Mom and I arrived for our first day of work, I could almost *see* Mother sitting in the shade of her front porch with her Miami Herald and Miami Times newspapers spread at her feet, drinking ice-water from the green water jar she kept in her refrigerator. *Don't forget to latch the gate*, I could almost hear her call to me.

Inside the house, we had our work cut out for us.

The living room had been stripped of the African artwork and bric-a-brac that had crowded every shelf as long as I could remember: her Louis Armstrong doll, her Michael Jackson doll, her brown-skinned praying angels, her ceramic cats and dogs. Rodin's *Thinker*. With Mother gone, her house seemed full of orphaned things with no one to tell their history. The house was still full, but empty.

All around me, I could only see what was missing.

Mom got annoyed when I suggested throwing anything away. She wanted to treat everything her mother had owned with care, but I feared that forty years' worth of things were going to be carted straight to her house. There was almost nothing my grandmother didn't keep. She had old telephones and television sets that no longer worked. Bags of shoes she hadn't worn in decades. Stacks of newspapers, many of them with stories I'd written over the years. Figurines of cats and dogs everywhere. And clothes, clothes, clothes.

In later years, whenever I'd visited Mother, she'd tried to show me the overflowing racks of clothes in her bedroom. *Maybe something will fit you*, she always said. *Some other time*, I promised. I had missed the point: Mother loved her clothes, and she wanted them to have a good home when she was gone. "I remember Mother wearing this," Mom pulled out a polyester pantsuit that probably hadn't seen light since 1972. She folded it and put it aside, not planning to wear it herself, but unable to give it away.

Still, some things had to go. Bags for Goodwill and other charities were filled. The debate over throwing anything away became a ritual repeated countless times over the week.

"Someone might want it," Mom would say.

"It's a *cracked* ice-tray." Or a tattered robe. Or something we couldn't even identify.

"You'd be surprised at what people would want."

I wanted to feel less numb. I *wanted* more tears to flow. But what I wanted most was to finish.

By the week's end, Mom and I were worn out from lifting, moving and remembering. We'd hired a man to help us move discarded items to the trash pile, which had become a small mountain despite my mother's deliberations. On the back patio, we found two large tin containers, so old that Mom couldn't pry off their lids.

"You'll probably just want to throw those away," the hired man told Mom.

I rolled my eyes. Good luck with *that* argument, I thought.

She was so tired that she almost agreed, but my mother insisted on opening the tins. Our helper pried them open. Inside, my mother found papers, envelopes addressed by her own hand. The letters were postmarked from 1960. Sent from jail.

Tell Granny to write me . . . If you get me an [Easter] dress before we come home, make sure we can take it back. I think I have gained a few pounds. I'm not sure. I don't even know what color I want—just make sure it's slenderizing. Write as often as you can. Give me Junior's address. I want to tell him we are in jail. He will laugh himself to death. . . . P.S. Are you coming up for Easter? Let me know. . . . Bring your sharpest clothes. I have been doing a lot of bragging about you and the rest of the family.

So long ago, I thought. Mother had been a young, stylish woman, practically a teenager, the belle of the ball. I had not been born.

So much had yet to happen.

Those letters were like a portal to a different time that was worse in some ways, but better in others. Worse because segregation was still the law of the land, and the painful trials of the civil rights movement lay ahead. But better, too. In 1960, Mom had more than forty years left to share her thoughts and feelings with Mother.

More than forty years of laughter and irritation, counsel and assurance.

When will it be my turn? I wondered as I watched Mom enjoy her reunion with Mother through the 42-year-old letter.

How many years would I have before it was my turn to clean my mother's house and rediscover that same letter?

And would I ever have a child of my own who would come and discover mine?

Linda Devine's Daughters

BY CAROLYN FERRELL

I

*F*inish them pears and go get the girls. Don't let them give you any *lip*, she said, thrusting the pear plate in my face. There was no way she'd let anyone simply sit in her kitchen and *not eat*, even if that person had committed a mortal sin. An empty stomach was an innocent. And an evil heart—well, the heart was an innocent, too. She didn't know that I'd had the procedure a good month ago and could barely stand the sight of food. The concentrated look on her face was her mother's in life, hard and ineluctable; now her hands worked like demons to knead the frozen sausage down in the pan. The smell of soul food, normally so lovable, now made the puke rise in my throat. She'd been working like this since dawn, when preparation for Miss Amy's wake breakfast had gotten underway: kneading and sawing and occasionally glancing at me doing my job on the other side of the kitchen. Maybe glaring, I couldn't really tell. She was under the impression that her daughters were frightening me.

Mae opened the kitchen curtain; some time ago, she'd sent Winsome and Essie down the lane, to see what the clouds were doing. The sky threatened rain, in that undramatic way I always remembered about eastern North Carolina in July: water but no water, heat pouring down from the heavens in large, green sheets of weather, but never enough rain, never enough moisture. Nothing to drench thirsts. Nothing to calm children or animals or sinners. I wiped the sweat from my neck with a dishrag and continued.

My job was to stack the white Corelle plates. In an hour all manner of relatives whom I hadn't seen in ages and who lived on this road—Foster Road, Auntsville, N.C.—would be stopping by on empty stomachs and breaking bread over Miss Amy. She'd died this past Saturday, as old as the first buildings made in town. I had to lay out the knives and forks next to the white Corelle plates. I had to make sure no flies sat on the flowered napkins. Later I would be in charge of keeping the children away from the best food and reattaching the fly papers to the ceiling. People would be coming, and then I'd also have to pretend I recalled all the stories they told, and I would have to laugh or cry. I would not tell any of these people that what I remembered most about Miss Amy was her temper: that she would whip you for just about anything, take down a smooth piece of branch and tan your behind if you were too bad or too good or had too many thoughts in your head, or were too raw. I wouldn't tell this to anyone at the wake breakfast. I'd laugh or cry and pass the food on the white Corelle plates. Afterward it would be on to the Jones Hill Tabernacle for funeral services, where we'd all say good-bye to Miss Amy with empty mouths.

—*Eat yourself some pears. You feel sick, then try the cherries. Miss Amy's best from last year. They say cherries are good for cleaning you out.*

Outside and inside, the sun was already unbearable. My breasts floated under my tee shirt like lilies in a pond. In a corner by the stove, underneath the daisy clock, Rufus, Mae's brother, was watching me until I watched him back. Many years ago, during eighth grade summer vacation, he had shown me the exact way in which a hickey breaks the blood vessels to express true love. I lowered my eyes to the linoleum which, the night before, Mae had massacred into cleanliness using a pad of steel wool. Rufus left the kitchen. The wake breakfast was down to the letter of Miss Amy's breakfasts in life: scrambled eggs and fried eggs and slab bacon; a fry pan full of sausage, cut fresh from the frozen roll and now tender in its own grease; a blue casserole dish chock full of famous hot pork barbecue. Miss Amy's last harvest of butterbeans glistened like diamonds in the bowl. Fruit lay on doilied platters. And bread was plenty: cornbread burnt at the edges or dinner rolls split down the center. To drink was ice water and cans of cola.

I looked out the screen door, which now rapped against its frame with the gathering storm wind, and saw Rufus again, this time waiting outside in the path. He gave me a thumbs up, as if I'd done something remarkable. His hair had already gone gray, but his eyes still carried the same fire. Once, Rufus made my world move. That was back in the eighth grade, when I loved him till my heart swelled like a water moccasin's deadly bite.

Things were different now, twenty-seven years later. These days my stomach carried on in loose spin cycles, expelling four-week-old blood, shooing away the baby that had wanted to emerge from my legs and crunch my breast in her tiny mouth. My stomach had been a baby. And all along my mother had encouraged this baby to persist. She whispered things in the hall or late at night in her own bed. She held seances in her own mind. She spoke to herself as a child on Foster Road, a child, who, many ages ago, had witnessed babies sprouting from the insides of fraught, unwilling women, and who, along with her mother, had mopped up bowls of blood, snot, tears and joy as the grown people looked on in sympathy.

Four weeks ago, a doctor and nurse had reassured me in lackluster tones while I cried, watching the hospital walls shake and the windows crack like ice. All there would be, they told me, was a brief moment of suction, then a lifetime of relief, fulfillment, less foolhardiness. I wept like crazy at the mention of that word: fulfillment. My mother, who stood at the nurse's side, eventually came round to saying that everything would work out for the best.

A lie.

Now I wanted to flop into Mae's arms. I wanted to feel her hand brush up against my face in love. She'd once been my best cousin-friend in the world.

All of it was lies.

Because the doctor had tapped me on the shoulder and smiled down as if he were floating on a cloud and said, —You made the right decision, Cookie. Now take care of yourself. One day you *will* have a normal baby just like any other normal woman.

—*Cookie, there you gone daydreaming again! Folks'll be here any moment! You best go get the girls and dress them in their clothes.*

I went back to my white Corelle plates. The sausage sizzled greedily in the pan.

—*Gone now*, Mae said, grabbing me by the shoulders and pushing me out the door into the yard. —*Forget the cherries. Go find the girls. Go get you and them ready.*

—Sure thing, I said, turning to face her, wanting to reach up and touch her somewhere, an arm, a cheek; but then strangely, Mae slammed the screen door on me, sending a swirl of red dust and pebble into my face.

She used to be my best cousin-friend. That was in the early Seventies, when I would come down here to spend the summer helping with tobacco. Twenty-seven years had gone by; and then it was yesterday evening, as I stepped into the small house and filled her arms with white roses from the train station. —*Sorry about your loss. Miss Amy was one hell of a mother*, I said.

In life, Miss Amy had liked to call herself a daughter of Linda Devine. In the old tobacco days, she felt it was her duty to remind Mae and me of our debt to Linda Devine. We needed to be mindful of those who'd come before, who'd lived life in more desperate ways—Linda Devine had been such a person. Did we realize that she once walked forty miles and back each day to see some of her eight spread-out girls at neighboring farms? That Linda Devine was born knowing how to read and write, and helped the abolition when she could? That Linda Devine once saved a town from burning to the ground? It sure would be good if some black folks these days had one ounce of Linda Devine's sense, Miss Amy liked to say. All this talk about Liberation. If you didn't know Linda Devine, you had no idea what Liberation meant.

(And so on, and so forth. The problem being that eighth grade girls in 1971 often don't truly appreciate certain parts of the past.)

After a day of tobacco, Mae and I squeezed into the old wrought-iron bed in the parlor and discussed our pubic hair (smelly) and our breasts (microscopic) and the sway of our upper arms (enough to drive a man crazy). We talked about getting jobs at the sewing factory one day, and about the smelly egg farm across the forest, and about the way boys could never really be trusted with your recklessness. We talked about the children we would have one day. We never mentioned heartache. We never mentioned husbands. We imagined sex flowing in and out of our lives like a birthright.

Linda Devine, our grandmother's grandmother's grandmother, was a woman that went back far into time; her face was captured in one of the oval insect-ridden, water-stained portraits that hung along the back hall of Miss Amy's one storey house, alongside sepia portraits of other high-necked, busty women whose dreamless faces stared straight into the camera. Mae and I did not care about these women. We did not care about escapes from slavery or secret abortions or forbidden marriages or abolitionists with hearts of gold or roads traveled by glint of moon. Those things were old-time things, to be laughed at underneath the stale, yesteryear quilts of the old iron bed. Linda Devine was a woman to be laughed at. She could never have known happiness, not like me and Mae imagined it.

When I arrived last night, my cousin was not at all sullen. She told me she was glad to see me. I had missed the births of her children, as well as the tears she'd cried over Hattie Mabel's Mark, but she said that was water under the bridge.

Instead, she laughed and took me in her arms, kissing me on the cheeks and forehead. She sat me in the parlor, where she poured burdock tea spiked with whiskey and served up Vienna Fingers on a platter. We sat again on the old wrought-iron bed, only now Mae complained about her hips, and wondered how I'd stayed so skinny, and then asked me if I thought her face was her age. I looked. Her face was smooth as a rock in the Cow River, no lines whatsoever, but in truth it was old. Everything about Mae was old. Her hair was piled into an old-fashioned braid on the top of her head. The faded running suit she wore had to have belonged to her mother, so flaccid was the seat of the pants. When she embraced me, I could have sworn her scent was Old Spice and mothflakes. So there was, under layers, the traces of unforgiving.

She wanted to know what all I had heard of her daughters, but then quickly ran to fetch them, the two girls who were named Essie and Winsome after some old can-and-preserve ladies who'd lived in the neighboring county. She screamed through the house for them to come out, to stop hiding if they didn't want their backsides tanned. My mother had warned me about these girls, especially the older one, the Downs girl; she'd said I should do my best not to be mean by accident. Not to stare. Not to say anything stupid. That I should remember that it took more to being a mother than an interest in good looks.

But last evening it was Rufus I spied first, standing in the corner of the room, still as a statue.—How you been, Rufus? I asked. He emerged slowly toward me, saying, —Hey, Cookie.

His old voice. His mouth was his old mouth. It looked like he was going to hug me, but what Rufus really did was slide his arms around me and slip them down my back. Perhaps he dipped around my behind.

—It's been too long, Cookie. But you come back.

—I'm here for your mother's funeral, I said, pulling away.

—I know why you're really here, Rufus whispered in my ear, running his palm along my spine; he kissed me with a tongue long and summer-hardened. Mae bounded back through the hall.

—*Don't worry*, he whispered, pulling back and smiling. —*Your secret's safe with me.*

—Look at my girls! Mae exclaimed, beaming. She held each girl by the hand and whipped them forth to give me a kiss on the cheek. The girls draped their arms around my waist, like loose chains. Mae could not stop beaming.

—Look at Essie! My beauty queen! Look at Winsome! See how far she's come!

—*Auntie Cookie*, the girls said in bloodless unison. One was tall, the other short. They did not look up into my face. I handed each a miniature Whitman's Sampler from my large duffel and turned away, hoping they had not noticed how fast and ugly my heart was beating.

—You're so lucky to have girls, I blurted at the wall. I didn't look up at Mae because I could feel her face well with tears. One of the girls had big hands, the other had hands the size of a fairy. Faintly I added, —I hear boys are the hardest to raise.

—I would've taken boys just fine, Mae answered softly. I looked up to see her close her eyes. She had the expression of a statue poised in the rain. The girls floated away from me and back into her arms. Then there was a long silence.

A trance.

II

Her amber face in the oval picture frame was unwavering: lips that swooned from one side to the other, a nose surprisingly dainty, a neck long as a table leg. It was said that her eyes were an amethyst blue straight out of heaven, but in the portrait you couldn't tell that. They sat half-closed on her face. Her dress was lace frill, the little we could make out at the shoulders. Her hair was a fat snake braid wound on top of her head. She was looking off to the side, and there was a softness to that look, a yearning. Otherwise there was nothing else of interest to note, other than the lack of love that seemed to outline her being like a halo.

One story went that she'd had eight children, an unlucky number for her, all girls; most had been sold away to other farms. The only one that managed to come back to her mother was not right in the head. So the story had been handed down to us.

That was Linda Devine's luck.

III

My mother had taken to warning me on the phone in the days before I left for Auntsville. Over and over she told me to be *humanly kind* when it came to Mae's girls.

—Why wouldn't I be? I'd asked.

—I heard that someone tried to talk her into an abortion with the second baby. I heard that Mae positively flipped.

I told my mother that I was just going down for Miss Amy's funeral. Nothing more.

—She's not like you, my mother continued. —Mae's a believer.

—I did my best, I said weakly, out of context. My mother did not reply, but over the phone I could hear the tapping of her newly done nails on her night stand table; there would be a vodka tonic on that table, next to a glass of water and a bottle of aspirin.

—Too many times you say what's on your mind, my mother sighed over the phone. —It'll cost you, Cookie.

When I'd had the final sonogram done, the doctor studied the neck of the baby and pronounced it too thick; soon afterward he spotted a cyst hovering over the baby's brain like a lily in a pond. *Stigmata*, he called them: signs for Down Syndrome. I'd have to rethink my plans. Handicapped babies were no picnic, and the cost to everyone involved—parents, schools, the state—was out of this world. The doctor's eyes were that glorious shade of blue that no real person ever seems to have. Only people in a dream. He told me to rethink my plan over a good night's sleep. Maybe have a fancy dinner at a restaurant. Put myself in better spirits. I left the clinic and did not stop walking, not when I got to the subway or to my front door or then to the bridge to the next borough, where the people on the streets all reminded me of worker bees in a hive. The necks, the heads, the faulty hearts, the eyes like flying saucers. I wasn't too old to get pregnant again. Babies were always a possibility. I turned the corner and headed back to my mother's home, despite the skeletal outlines of faces and flowers which I saw clearly in the grain of the pavement.

When I first told my mother I wanted to have the procedure, she begged me to think things through clearly. It was already a life, she maintained. Even if the test said Down Syndrome, it was already a life.

—I can't handle what this kind of life will require, I feebly countered back then. Because I knew what she would say. She was my mother.

—I bet you weren't thinking that when you lay down to get this baby. I bet it was only fun and games. Fun and games.

—Mama, I'm not sure.

—*Fun and games.*

And afterwards: when they'd suctioned the baby out and I awakened, it was my mother, cradling my face in her hands. She wasn't angry, nor was she regretful. She was simply white-haired. Perhaps silver, in the right light; tameable. She was looking at her own daughter. —They say you can't have anything to drink, she whispered, her hand on my forehead. —Not for a few hours, nothing to drink or eat.

IV

The sky opened up just as I put my foot in the yard. The rain roared treacherously, as if it were showing off. I'd only gone a short distance into Mae's seventeen acres, with its fruit trees and vegetable patches and poisonous snakes and firs so tall they stubbed the clouds; in spite of the downpour, however, I saw two heads in the distance, near the road. When I reached the girls, they lay flat against the reddish-gray earth in a flimsy patch of grass, with their eyes opened toward the sky, and their hands locked over their chests.

—*Girls!* I called. —*Girls! You don't want to get wet!*

But they were already soaked to the skin. And they did not move, not until I shook them out of their trances with my bare hands. Their dresses were torn, their faces muddy. Quickly the rain ceased—this was no more than a two minute shower. Both sets of eyes rolled open as I stood there, towering over them like a mountain. They were waiting to be punished.

Winsome sat up stiffly; she was the older one, the tall one. The Downs. Her skin was a tempered brown, like a European loaf, and she was already armed with a woman's hips and utilitarian feet. In every corner of her face, you could see her father, Hattie Mabel's Mark: the deep sideburns running alongside her cheeks, the smile sewn so un-evenly. I remembered him from earlier tobacco days. Back then I'd despised his poverty of imagination, the way he glared at me and Mae when we purposely tracked him down in the tobacco shed to blow him kisses. His daughter seemed different, at first glance: Winsome had eyes that moved like two sparkling suns over the plains of her face.

She jumped to her feet and then made a giant fist by locking her delicate hands together. It was an odd gesture. Winsome pressed this soft giant combined fist sharply into my chest, but it didn't hurt me at all. It didn't leave any mark or impression. She pressed forward, then let go, time after time, each with more force. And I just stood there, a blank instead of a person.

—What you up to, gal? This was Essie asking, winking an eye at me as if I understood the joke.

Winsome opened her arms wide, as if to embrace me. Instead, she scrambled her fingers around my chest in a spidery motion, like a boy's first overtures of love.

—That's her favorite thing to do, Essie said. Her dark brown face was pocked with the residue of ringworm. —She my baby. She like titties. I know everything she do.

I felt like crying.

—My mama said you might was gone call us retards or some-thing, Essie said.

—I would never do such a thing, I said, snapping my head back at her. —Why would your mother even think such a thing?

Essie shrugged.

I said, —Do you know that there was a time before you were born, before Winsome here was on the earth, when your mother and I had other lives?

The girl narrowed her eyes at a piece of bark on the ground.

—We were happy together, I said, then bit my tongue. I didn't know how I'd meant this, or how the girls would take it. But it was a fact: together we had known happiness, twenty-seven years ago.

Essie bowed her head, as if to consider this carefully, but then Winsome let out a roar as fierce as an elephant. I started, and Essie did too, though she took pains to cover her fear, quickly laughing at her sister and rolling her eyes. Winsome pulled her hands away from my chest, where a burning sensation had worked its way from my spine to my sternum, a crackling of electricity, a dash of used lightning. In my mind I wondered why I had really come back.

—You weren't always Mae's daughters, I continued. —You used to be a part of your mother's mind.

—We was just about to find out what the clouds wanted, Essie said, ignoring me, scouting heavenward with a hand shielding her eyes. —Then you interrupted us. So please say you're sorry.

—I'm sorry, I said. There was a stillness then, in which you could hear the insects underfoot in the red mud laughing at us. Essie reached out and took my hand. —We gone to take you someplace, she said. —You ready?

Winsome smiled sweetly and clapped her fairy hands.

When the wake breakfast was over, all the relatives headed down Foster Road for the church. Mae and I were left behind, clearing the last of the Corelle dishes into the sink.

—You see something, Cookie? How those folks barely looked at

Winsome in my mother's kitchen and God knows they each one of them have their own little version stashed away in their own house!

—The world's not fair, Mae. Just ask me.

—They look over her like she a crumb. Fucking fuckers! My own mother loved her to the bottom of her very soul may she rest in peace even if it took her years and years and years. God save her soul.

—Your mother was a fountain of love, Mae.

—It's a scientific fact that a Downs kid can go to college these days, Cookie. Not like in the old days. My Winsome can even be on a tv show, she put her little mind to it.

—The world is her oyster, Mae. I know she will go far.

—Essie is normal as the day is long but folks like to think of her as slow, too. Makes it easier for them.

—*Don't you sometimes hate the world?*

—No one is born a mother, Mae continued. —Don't you forget that. You have to be made into a mother, nail by nail, plank by plank.

Then she was quiet. The whole house was quiet. The daisy clock quit its ticking. Foster Road had emptied itself of people. I sat on a chair and chewed my nails until there was nothing but skin, thinking how lucky it was that I'd gotten the girls back in the house on time, and wondering why I had listened to the doctor, to his statistics. Why I'd thought happiness would ever be possible as long as I walked the earth. Numbers were as faulty as feelings, ideas.

—It's hard, specially the diapers on a grown girl, Mae continued somberly, —But I am a mother. I do what a mother needs to do. I feel what a real mother needs to feel.

—The world's not fair. Just ask me.

—*Just ask you what?*

She adjusted the daisy clock on the wall, making the time one o'clock in the afternoon. —I *made* Miss Amy love her granddaughters, she said. —Because how could you not love your own flesh and blood?

I sighed, thinking about how, as girls, we'd laughed at Linda Devine. Though she surely didn't count as flesh and blood.

Mae poured out the last of the soda cans down the sink drain, and my thoughts switched to my mother, and I remembered how she looked as she sat next to the hospital bed on a metal folding chair, squeezing my hand. Her gray hair seemed to have whitened in the night; in the past, she'd always remarked how much better black people looked with a natural silver on their head instead of a pressed brown. And so here she was, not beautiful but resilient, mournful.

During the procedure I'd had a dream of a plantation, the kind I used to see back when I was in the eighth grade and had ridden in the tobacco truck across the land. The mansion—in my dream no more than a hollowed out husk—contained beams from which hung azure ears of corn. From those cobs rained a torrent of kernels smack onto a bed of rotting leaves—large, ugly leaves that I couldn't quite recognize. Stalks of something brown and yellow sprung up in the leafy mulch. You could die if you touched those stalks—I knew that that was law in my dream.

I stood at the door of the mansion, marveling at a swirl of bats I saw flying near its ceiling. I wondered if I should go in, but then in my dream, there was no time for a decision; the beams shook wildly, the floor rose and fell, as if an earthquake had hit, and the air became thick with fire and hail stones. A voice, loud as a clear Sunday, began to cry,—*Is it snowing? Has the snow already begun?*

It was a woman's voice, and the sound of her supplication broke my heart. An ordinary woman asking about plain snow. A day like every other in creation.

—*It's probably all for the best, as you say*. In the real world, my mother was repeating this, wiping her eyes with a piece of hospital paper towel. The doctor had told her to try and wake me up because it was time to move out of the recovery room.

V

After I'd found them, the girls would not be deterred. Though it was time to get dressed for the wake breakfast, they insisted on leading me by the hand to the back of the old barn, which was no longer used for tobacco but for storage: in it, there were old-fashioned wire hoops, a bundle of yellow-brown letters, some rusted harnesses, inner tubes, a set of barbells, glass panes, a wringer, a broken telescope, empty cans and Mason jars. Among these ruins I found a few pictures of me riding on the back of a tractor, and a few of Mae as a cheerleader, and inexplicably, a copy of my high school yearbook. *The Amity Warriors, 1976.* In it, I had been dubbed the Girl Most Likely To Be Likely—something I'd at the time taken for a pretentious joke. The girls pointed to a huge stack of magazines. These magazines belonged to Rufus, and Essie was only too happy to show them to me, one by one: torn pages in which grown women with breasts large as cow udders straddled one another, and men with dicks like flagpoles cavorted happily with one another. In one magazine, both men and women posed together like creatures on an obscene carousel. The sex was old, dusty, uninspired. But the girls laughed hysterically. They'd been through them all. I grabbed the bundle of yellow-brown letters as the girls pulled me back into the daylight.

———

Dear   , You will do me an eternal favor to attend to this matter for me As soon as possible, if God bee willing. I am weak of body and spirit and have no money for clothing & misc. Food being my daily concern. Pleas keep my girl until she is 21 years of age. I have herd of your kindness and would be entirely indebt. Your servant.

They dragged me to the other side of the house, to one of Miss Amy's older gardens, untended now for some years, a grove of fruit trees and vines and junked metal—we stood at its edge, but nevertheless got a bird's-eye-view of the devastation of growth within. The girls pointed out the prehistoric skeletons of tractors and other machinery that had long been consumed by vine and ruinate; some clothes lay in buried heaps. There was the heat-strangled cries of birds traveling the periphery. Then there were other sounds, other haunted intimations. The girls laughed at my face and the shock they seemed to think was there. It was then that they came up with the plan.

It was all so simple you could've called it *child's play*: one of them would go and get fruit from the grove to offer up to the ghost of Miss Amy. If the girl was swift, she could run in and grab some cherries from the tree and not feel a thing. Yes, it could be done. It had been done plenty of times before. Fruit from the branch was nary a problem. Fruit from the vine could be tricky. Swooping a handful of wild blueberries from the ground was a big risk, thanks to those devilish water moccasins (one bite and your leg could go in a cast, Essie pointed out). But mostly everything else—including sitting in one of those junk heaps and pretending you were a boy—was easy enough, you put your mind to it.

—What if a snake came and bit you, I asked. —What if you died?

—I would take it in my bare hands and strangle that mother till he don't know night from day, Essie answered coldly. —And if I needed help, I always got my sister.

Winsome nodded glumly, stepping back from the grove into a patch of drying mud. Essie shrugged, deciding that she would try and make it to the sweetest cherry trees, maybe fifty yards deep into the grove. There were vines and snarls and garbled shadows every inch of the way, but she claimed to have feet like lightning. Winsome would stay behind with me.

—You really shouldn't, I began, as Essie disappeared in the flash of an eye.

Winsome gripped my hand—it felt as if a door had slammed shut on my fingers. I pulled away. The girl was nowhere to be seen. It was as if the darkness and vine had swallowed her completely. —*Hey Essie! I cried. You really shouldn't! You have to come back!* I felt my lungs go up and down. I didn't want to feel that fairy hand again. My mouth was dry for a vodka tonic.

—*ESSIE!* I screamed.

—*Hush Auntie Cookie, do you'll wake them snakes!* Essie's voice hissed back.

—*Essie come here this minute and don't you give me any lip! I cried. —Essie! There's the wake breakfast waiting on you! You and your sister have to get dressed!*

Winsome regained my hand, and I could tell, in my mind's eye, that there was a smile on her face. I didn't want to care about either of these girls. I wanted to close my eyes. There was a faint memory of Mabel Hattie's Mark stealing an egg truck that somehow landed Mae and me in trouble from Miss Amy. We'd both been whipped with peachtree limbs. Mabel Hattie's Mark later reprimanded us for getting into everyone else's business—his voice was just as nasal and unforgiving as any adult's. He accused us of trying to be "cute."

—*Essie! Essie! Think of the funeral!*

Winsome pressed a fingernail into my skin. She whispered, in a voice no bigger than a thimble, —*We pray. We pray.*

The skin had broken, and my hand was now bearing a tiny river of blood across the back of the palm.

—*We pray.*

—*Essie, get your stupid ass out here right now! You want to be late to your own grandmother's funeral?*

Before I could do anything else, Winsome rubbed her fingers against the blood, gently, as if she were polishing her fingertips. I looked on in hopelessness.

Once Miss Amy had regaled Mae and me with a story about Linda Devine in order to show how devout she was, how authentic—we of course couldn't have cared less. The time of Miss Amy's story was right after the War, and the entire village—including the whites—had come to Cow River to hear her famous prayer of peace. Linda Devine stood knee deep in the white water and shouted her words across the heads, the trees, the clouds, even the stars in the universe; she was talking directly to God. —*It's all in Your hand!* She shouted. —*It's all in Your hand!*

Of course, Mae and I insisted that no such thing had ever happened—whites coming to a nigger gathering!—and for saying our thoughts aloud, we were made to kneel in pebbles.

Now there was no sound in that darkness. It was truly as if Essie had been swallowed whole. I stepped backward and looked at Winsome, wondering if I could see a trace of my mother in the girl's sudden and brilliant smile. It would be a long shot. The girl looked as if she were about to erupt.

—Stay calm, I whispered to her, taking her other hand in mine.

—Emergency, she whispered back.

VI

The funeral was short and sweet. Folks spoke of Miss Amy in remembrance and misremembrance—Hattie Mabel's Mark broke down in tears on more than one occasion. Mae stiffened when she saw him like that.

Later he acknowledged her by tipping his hat in her direction—no embrace—and some time after that, when the real singing began, Hattie Mabel's Mark fell into Miss Amy's coffin, crying his eyes out like a woman. Mae stormed out of the church, and did not say another word to me until dark, when she was turning down the old iron bed.

The stars were out in small number against a black brocaded sky. She asked,—You never found a man in these years? Cookie, you sure do look good enough.

—I'm too demanding, I lied, picking up a pillow.

Mae pressed the sheets deep into the mattress with her hand. —Hattie Mabel's Mark comes by now and then, looking to see how Winsome and Essie's doing, but he's not no real father. He just looks, is all.

—You can do better than him, I said.

—It's nobody down here better than him, Mae laughed, daintily placing a lavender satchel in the center of the bed. —Mostly he's not all bad.

—Love always seems to pass me by, I then said, thinking of the few men I'd had affairs with. They were all bad. The last one, Jacob Martin, had said to me, —*Cookie, why don't you just forget it? You're just not mother material.*

—When Hattie Mabel's Mark and me used to get together, I used to could see the whole entire universe in my little pinky, Mae said thoughtfully.

—Your girls are wonderful, I cried suddenly. —They are your entire universe! Those awesome girls!

Then I said softly, —If I was smart, I could have had one of my own.

Mae sighed. A frittered cousin's love blew out of her mouth in that sigh. She got up to close the light.

—Don't talk about things you don't understand, she said. —The world's one fucking unfair place.

The next letter flew out of my hand as if a wind had blown it away. It landed on the floor near the bed, and I swooped like a bird to pick it up out of the dust balls.

Dear____: It is ben a wile and tho I am far away in body I am near in spirit. Would you pleas be so kind as to give my girl pen and pa-per and avail upon her a letter for me? I am alone now accept for her.

She with you five year today. Being my last hope and yet I have not receiv'd word and feel lonely like the hills. Pleas be so kind. A mother love is like God's Own. Your servant.

I wept tears of a baby.

And later that night, both Essie and Winsome lay in bed, smiling under their covers. Old wounds had been forgiven. They were recalling the look on my face when Essie first went in the woods. All along it had been their plan to fool me, to make me think that Essie had got bit by a snake and was lying somewhere in the grove, bleeding to death. As good as she could, Winsome had been able to keep the joke.

The first scream that morning was real enough. Perhaps I might've mistaken it for a wild bird, or a lost mountain lion, and been scared out of my mind. The girls were keen on my reaction. Essie would scream again, and Winsome would say, —EMERGENCY.

They would make me jump to the right conclusions. They would make me think Essie had been wounded or bit or crushed and they would make me cry my eyes out. Those girls were some wild practical jokers.

The second and third screams were real, too. A girl's screams— Essie's. Once I heard them, though, I did not move to save her. I did not lift my foot into those vines and branches and snakes and go after her, the way I should've done, according to the plan.

Instead, I stood there at the brink of that ancient darkness and held tightly to Winsome's hand. There was a river of blood on the back of my palm, and I was feeling the slow tense of Winsome's body just by her breaths, which grew shorter and shorter. —Emergency, she finally said, in a quick whisper to me.

I began to cry, and likely she was wondering why I acted this way: a grown woman looking the fool, with nail-bitten hands and mouth foaming over like a rabid dog. Likely Essie wondered why my eyes had shut themselves and why I kept repeating someone's name (my mother's name: *Linda! Linda!*); or why my nose ran with streams of ugly, orphaned snot; or why, as Essie screamed those last few times, I jumped to cover Winsome's ears with my hands.

—Don't, Winsome said to me, pulling my hands off of her. —Don't. It ain't nobody's fault.

Essie eventually came running from out the trees with real tears on her face; she thought we'd left her behind. At the sight of her sister, Winsome fell to the ground in a trance. Perhaps the clouds had told her to do that. Perhaps it had been my hands. I couldn't look to find out, because just then, Essie was upon me, slapping me in the stomach and shouting garbled words in my face—I was sure I'd made out the words *granny* and *blast*. Down on the red earth, on my knees, I covered my face and let her rain her blows. The girl slapped and hollered. (Later she would tell me that I had spoiled what should have been the best damn joke in Auntsville in years!)

After a few moments Essie grabbed hold of Winsome and began to shake her arms, as if Winsome were nothing but rags. —*Wake up, wake up,* she cried. —*You don't want for us to get in trouble, do you, fool? Wake the hell up.*

VII

And deep into that night, when the first birds began their singing, I sat at the edge of the old iron bed in my nightgown and packed my things. There was nothing left for me to do now that the funeral was over. In a few hours I would find my way back to the station. I would leave Mae and her girls and pretend we never met. I would take the letters from the barn with me. I would find my mother and run my hands through her hair. I would cry. Babies were eternally impossible. I'd return to the nothing I'd left behind.

But would there be something? I thought of what Mabel Hattie's Mark had said at the funeral, the Scripture he had chosen to recite: they are blind and yet can see.

—I've dreamt of you, Cookie. And here you come back, trying make my life whole again.

It was Rufus suddenly, hovering above me at the old iron bed, his knees touching my knees.

—We were children, I said, turning my head toward the window as the sound of feathers flapped off into the night sky. Rufus did not move. He smelled of baked food and sun and the wood of the barn— a lasting, lonely smell, one I would later remember when I found myself back in Brooklyn, disappointed over new men. Rufus put his hand on the pulse of my neck, which beat with the same need as years before. The sun would be up soon.

—Children grow up and remember, Cookie. And I've kept your secret.

—*What secret of mine do you know?* I rose to my feet so fast, he nearly toppled to the floor.

—I know you come back for me at last, he said, pulling me into his arms. —I know you loved me all these years. Ain't nobody's secret no more.

—Rufus, I began. —You aren't a child. That time is past.

—Come here. I want to kiss you. He was looking at my belly.

—There's something I have to tell you. Something you should know. Everything.

—*Everything*, he repeated, circling my breast with his hand. —*I already know what I need to know.*

Lonelier than ever, our hips pumped into each other like there was no tomorrow. We kissed our way from the bedroom into the back hall, where the old sepia portraits hung, where the oval picture frame containing sad Linda Devine brushed silently against the wall. Miss Amy had often told us that the only child out of her unlucky eight who'd returned to Linda Devine—the youngest—had been retarded in the head. Otherwise, why would she have returned? These were slavery days we were talking about, remember.

Miss Amy said that this last girl had eventually gone missing, never to show her face again, as if the world had eaten her like a big old snake. That was the blow Linda Devine could never recover from. Love was a child's face, and it didn't matter who that child was. Miss Amy warned us to remember that always.

We hugged, we kissed. In a matter of minutes Rufus and I fell full on the floor, not wet with passion, but dry instead, like two pieces of friable wood rubbing together for warmth.

He assured me that Mae was a hard sleeper. Never in a million years would she hear us, or abandon her nighttime dreams: her girls as nurses, or movie stars, or managers in the sewing factory. On the floor, he spread my legs apart with his knee, like in the old days.

—I'm ready for you, Cookie. You ready for me?

His dick was large, too cumbersome to find its way into me without my hand, but when I touched him down there, he pulled away. My nightgown was up to my hips, and I struggled to get it up further. I moved his hand with the tips of my fingers, but suddenly he stiffened, refusing to travel his hand anywhere along my body, even though there was so much on my body I could point out to him: *right there*: lovely, lush, viable. *And over there*: the place I'd had the baby borrowed right out of me. *There, there, and there*: I can begin again, if you tell me I can.

(Yes, oh yes, oh yes. It is not necessary to be a mother all the time. But some of the time, yes, that would be perfect.)

Rufus leaned his face into my neck the way some men do to women when they are overcome by memory. Hickeys, earlobes, knees, belly buttons, butterbeans, tongues, stolen eggs and cigarettes. Because that was all I was: memory. His graying breath, the grip of his fingers: that was pure, petulant memory, too.

—It's no laws against finally doing what is right, he whispered.

—We can do it right this time. We grown, Cookie. We made our mistakes in life, but we grown now.

—Yes, I answered, because he was the only lover left in the world.

—We grown, Cookie. Love is all it's left.

He fumbled with my underwear, pulling at the waist elastic, but not taking it off.

—We grown, Cookie, he said softly. Hesitantly.

Yes. Yes. Love *is* all it's left.

One moment, then two moments, then three: I looked into his sun-dappled gray—he did not move. My back was aching against the hard wooden floor, and all I wanted was for Rufus to make up his mind, and make me do what was right.

VIII

Some of the truths spoken about Miss Amy at her funeral included the following:

A) She'd loved those girls, the Downs one and the regular slow one, with all her heart. Miss Amy begged Life to have mercy on her.

B) She let Mae forget the past and concentrate on the future.

C) Miss Amy hated those girls. She would not wear a locket with a likeness in it to save her life. She begged Life to have mercy on her.

D) Miss Amy never let the past be forgotten. She was a good mother in that way.

E) In her heart of hearts Miss Amy wished she hadn't been so hard. She wished that words, once spoken, could simply vanish into the sky, beyond the clouds, to the inky corners of the universe, where the heart of our maidenly world is often said to beat.

The last one of the yellow-brown letters in the bundle was creased a number of times, as if the writer had meant to destroy it. The ink was splotched, the penmanship creaky; and if you touched any part of the paper in the wrong way, the letter crumbled in your hand like mist. I tucked it carefully into the pages of my yearbook, but then ripped it out again.

> *Dear____:*
> *You say you have not seen her in days that turn to weekes. If you see her you will pass on that I never give up hope. It is my last girl week of body but rich of mind. She travel to me in dreams & I misses her mor then a Husband. Do tel her. I am here & repeat: Pray without ceasing in everyThing give thanks.*
> *One Thessalonians 5.*
> *Your servant.*

Life didn't deserve to be a mystery. How to live should be a lesson engraved in tombstones. All of us had been born blind as girls, and without these lessons in granite, all of us would remain blind as grown women.

The Round:
Rowing Gently Down the Stream

This section explores the symbiotic relationship between mother and child, how each, as in round form, sings the song of the other, deepening with each turn, the melody and meaning of their duet. A daughter's near-death illness forces a mother to coddle and protect, then rise to the challenge of freeing her to face her destiny; single motherhood requires a mother and son to open up to one another emotionally and grow in understanding of each other and themselves; a mature mother anticipates with grace and wisdom yielding to her adult child the right and the privilege of caring for her. Our children are always changing, but so are we mothers, and despite the occasional dissonances, our raised voices swell to their final choral blessing echoing sweet harmonies for generations.

From "The Children of the Poor"

BY GWENDOLYN BROOKS

VERSE 6

Life for my child is simple, and is good.
He knows his wish. Yes, but that is not all.
Because I know mine too.
And we both want joy of undeep and unabiding things,
Like kicking over a chair or throwing blocks out of a window
Or tipping over an icebox pan
Or snatching down curtains or fingering an electric outlet
Or a journey or a friend or an illegal kiss.
No. There is more to it than that.
It is that he has never been afraid.
Rather, he reaches out and to the chair falls with a beautiful crash,
And the blocks fall, down on the people's heads,
And the water comes slooshing sloppily out across the floor.
And so forth.
Not that success, for him, is sure, infallible.
But never has he been afraid to reach.
His lesions are legion.
But reaching is his rule.

1949

Dancer of the World

BY PATRICIA SMITH

It is time for the performance. Mikaila whizzes around the house, dramatically lowering the lights and triple-checking to make sure that the CD is cued to the right track. The one and only audience member, I have been placed in the very center of the couch and warned to sit perfectly still and to refrain from commenting. After punching a button on the boom box with one stubby finger, she retreats to her room in a flash of grin and bumble, slamming the door and allowing herself a moment to deal with last-minute jitters and costume adjustments. After a dramatic pause, she announces herself in a grandiose scream that is barely muted by the thick door:

"NOW PRESENTING MIKAILA SMITH,

DANCER OF THE WORLD!!!"

The knob twists, twists again. There's another twist, followed by an anxious pull. A huff. Twist, twist, twist. A twist that rattles the knob. A kick. I calmly relay directions from my seat in the small audience. "Twist and pull at the same time, honey." There are uneasy seconds of nothing but the sugary strains of the Love Unlimited Orchestra's "Love Theme." I fear I have broken some cardinal rule by speaking directly to the star.

"You're not supposed to talk to me."

I apologize with a single word. There is more silence as the diva decides on a course of action. Finally, she takes the advice I wasn't supposed to offer. Twist and pull. The door flies open, so forcefully she almost falls back into the room. After a bit of flustered stumbling, she closes it again without pulling it shut. I hold my breath.

"NOW PRESENTING MIKAILA SMITH,

DANCER OF THE WORLD!!!"

And the dancer of the world skitters out, fingers laced gracefully above her head. In her five years, she has seen ballet dancers, and this is sort of what they do. But this is not how they look.

Mikaila has wiggled into a pair of dingy white tights with an ever-widening hole at the left ankle, cranberry patent leather stompers with huge bows and 2-inch heels, and a pair of lime-green capris winking wildly beneath a lavender tulle tutu. A favorite midriff top from two summers ago, which mysteriously keeps finding its way back from the Salvation Army donation pile, strains against her belly. Three head-bands barely contain an explosion of raven curls. Her lipstick is twenty sizes too pink. She's slathered blush on her cheeks and chin, and the rest of her exposed skin is adorned with some manner of Barbie-endorsed ain't-it-great-to-be-a-girl glop. Her forearms sparkle furiously.

She pirouettes slowly, giving me time to be stunned by the sight of her.

Then the dancing begins.

It's a dazzling blend of modern interpretive dance, disco, ballet, Tae-Bo and the hokey pokey. She remains serious throughout, her eyes glazed in concentration as if each dip, swirl and spin were memorized. Every spill is finished with a flowery flourish, as in "I meant to do that." Her gyrations leave the music behind. She whirls, pivots and leaps, and I want to comment on how amazing this all is, but she eyes the audience carefully, watchful for any sign of disobedience. I sit straight up. I smile a lot, a full-fledged belly laugh rumbling behind gritted teeth.

Too soon, it is time for her final bow. She curtsies with clumsy grace, letting applause wash over her. I'm known to be stingy with my standing ovations, but I am prepared to cheer her forever. The curtsies continue. Elastic pops, tights run faster, glop glitters. "OK, you can stop clapping," she says abruptly, and suddenly we're back to just-before-bedtime and she's her and I'm me again. She runs to the couch, arms spread wide, grin at full voltage.

"Was I good, mommy?" she says. The she stops, blinks her eyes. "I mean, *grandma*, was I good?"

I feel my heart bending. It stops just short of breaking, and somehow that hurts more. I hoped that this one time she would call me mommy and know in her heart that it's true, that I have given birth to every moment of her with every moment of me.

I *am* someone's mother. I remember the Chicago summer day it happened, a day that was all steam and chaos, warm water rushing down my legs, etching rivers in the rust. My unflinching Baptist mother, exhilarated and accusing, rode silently with me in the back of a meandering city police van. We could have gotten there faster on foot. On both sides of me in Cook County's maternity ward, other unwed mothers, their undone hair writhing and their eyes shiny with pain, screeched expletives as their sons and daughters battled to the surface. I breathed in numbered beats, haughty with natural childbirth. No numbing shots. No help. I had vowed to sweetly suffer.

Once you have given birth, once your body has expanded, found flame, bellowed and slammed shut, you earn the right to be a mother to anyone. You carry the card. I remember waiting for my son to be brought to me to nurse; another child cried out, and my breasts flooded with milk, became rock, strained against my skin. That child, too, was mine.

When I left the hospital for home, my son Damon was mummified in powdery blankets. None of him showed. This was per terse instruction from one Miss Annie Pearl Smith of Aliceville, Alabama, who has spent most of her life as my mother. In Aliceville, it's common knowledge that no sun or wind should touch the skin of a newborn. "Can't let the world in too fast," was my mother's rationale for just about everything.

Only 20, I signed on to her loving down-south insanities. I spat on the broom whenever someone accidentally swept my foot. I never walked to the right of a pole. When I had a cold, I ate the Vicks VaporRub that my mother served up on a forefinger. I was certainly in no position to question her about this mysterious, spitting squiggle that now belonged to me.

Numb with not knowing, I walked behind her as Damon fretted in his cocoon, his tiny fists punching for air. It was summer in Chicago. His little life was already crazy. He was only days old, and we were already loving him to death.

It's also an Aliceville tenet that the hollowed and feverish new mother stay in bed for at least a week after coming home, sipping peppery potlikker, chewing Bayers and listening to the elders. The elders, not exactly the wizened matriarchs the name implies, were mostly prying church hens assigned the tasks of molding the baby's head with their withered hands, pinching its nose to get rid of that dreaded flat spread, and reporting back to the congregation about the texture of the child's hair. It was either nap or silk, and that information was critical when it came to predicting its future.

The hens didn't much care for my one sassy rebellion, the decision to breastfeed. The very thought was an affront to their Delta sensibilities. Visiting one Sunday after church, my mother's best friend, Miss Alberteen, stared incredulously as Damon found my nipple and began to feed. She moved in so close I felt her breath on the skin of my breast.

"Don't look like nuthins comin' outta that thang," she insisted. My smug mother clucked, nodded knowingly. Faced with this disapproval, which at the time felt very much like the disapproval of all women everywhere, I began to doubt my own abilities. My body balked at the betrayal, and the flow of milk stopped like someone had twisted the knob of a faucet. My son widened his eyes, scrunched his face, bawled.

I want to tell you how he grew, but I can find no language large enough to encompass both the pain and pride. Damon read his first book at three; the slim volume was called "City Fun," a phonetically-slick tale of pink-cheeked children who frolicked on concrete walks, gazed in awe at skyscrapers, whirled in the chilling spray from open fire hydrants. He devoured new words, found poetry on his own, filled notebook pages with worlds he had never seen. And he wept when his goldfish, the inimitable SweetCheeks, was found floating upside down in his bowl.

I had inherited my mother's belief that placing my child among white folks would somehow anoint him, and, at my insistence, he slipped on the blue blazer of prep. I was a fascinated witness as he flailed somewhere between the world of ski vacations and Boy Scouts and the lure of drooping denim and 40-oz. Screw-top bottles.

If I squeeze my eyes shut right now, I can almost see the moment when the city swallowed him. It opened its maw and he walked in, practicing his pimp, wondering who he was.

I have seen him shuffling toward me in shackles. I have seen gang love burned into his bicep with a wire hanger first twisted into symbol and dipped into fire. I have heard the barely bridled panic in his voice after a cellmate threatened to bash his skull with a tube sock crammed with dead D batteries. I am mother to the ghost of someone. Know that I have played Peter to his Jesus, I have denied him, quickly changing the subject when friends regale me with stories of their sons, finishing those PhDs, skipping up the corporate ladder, on European tour with their jazz bands. During visits, in rooms that are always too hot, I look down the row of mothers who all look like me, and behind the mesh, at men who all look like him. They are swagger, freshy muscled, in jumpsuits the color of storm. They are discarded children; I am mother to them all.

Mikaila Smith, dancer of the world, is my son's daughter. She was conceived in a blur of street swagger, the product of one over-anxious cock whose owner found redemption in the folds of plump, sluggish, emotionally scarred white women, women who would ask absolutely nothing of him beyond that one sweaty moment of pre-tend. In this instance, the woman was built thick and flat, like a wall. She spews expletives through holes that have rotted in her mouth, lumbering on shoplifted Adidas, Nikes, Timberlands, K-Swiss, run-ning from her own fisted history. Even after it, she was mother to no one. She did not birth Mikaila as much as expel her.

The two of them, my son and this woman. *Making something means you exist.* Imagine their limbs tangled, all the lies in their throats. And out of this madness dances one perfect child, pinchable cheeks and songs gleefully off-key, an angel with their sin in her every cell.

The last time I saw true joy in my son was on the day Mikaila was born. It was he who graced her with the middle name Chalice. "That's a king's cup," he told me proudly, as if that fact scripted the child's fate.

"I saw her coming out," he said. His whole face was flustered from that glimpse of a woman's secret. "I held her, Ma. She was so little and sticky. And she knew me. She knew who I was." For that white-light second, his world was wide open, his eyes sweet and star-tled.

The next day, he was still crazed with the knowledge of his daughter. But he avoided her gaze.

I too tried not to look at her. I never wanted to lock eyes with the mistake they'd made, never wanted to witness the sweet void of a toothless smile, never thought I'd press my whole face to her skin and just be still there. I wished my horny son and his clunky amour months of squalling and colic, diapers drooping with poisons, the dawning knowledge that their lives would never again be theirs.

I had raised one child. He was scarred and clueless, but he was in the world. With that glorious failure behind and before me, I day-dreamed another, blissfully detached, life. I could be an expatriate scribe, strolling stone paths in Paris. Perhaps I'd discover a penchant for gourmet cooking, spend languid afternoons chopping herbs and releasing their light. Or I could simply slouch and read the desperate writing of others, rest my colored gal hips on a perfumed pillow.

Whatever I became, I would do so gleefully unencumbered. Alone.

But even as I crafted this giddy distance, I felt the tiny thing aching toward me. My idle breasts remembered milk.

Snapshots: Mikaila at three weeks in a tiny apartment smelling of old inches left behind in liquor bottles. Mikaila buttressed by two pillows in a steamy closed bedroom, imprisoned there to avoid the resident Rottweiler, who licks her and growls at the smell of her skin. Restless mother and child move from place to place as if God's huge hand is lifting them up and plopping them down. They move. A dead mouse rots beneath the stove. They move. Mikaila's mother, depressed and death eyes, scuffs through the day in night clothes. They move. She shows up on my doorstep at least once a week after being tossed unceremoniously from her last hiding place: "I don't want to sleep on the street with her. Can she stay here tonight?" I give doses of my home to the child who is not yet called my granddaughter, watch as the woman who expelled her walks away.

By this time, she and my son are strangers again. They have packed up their history, moved to the opposite ends of their daughter.

During the spring just before Mikaila turned 2 years old, she and her mother disappeared. They simply slipped the bounds of the world and taught my heart to howl. On Mother's Day, the phone rang and there was one singing syllable from the child, unrecognizable as a word. Then the connection was broken. Something was teaching my heart to howl.

When they finally emerged from a homeless shelter weeks later, I wrapped my arms around Mikaila, curved my body over her, and would not move or let go. I carried the card. I could not walk away from how real my granddaughter was. She moved like heat in my arms. She wore a raucous crown, both nap and silk. There was a space in my soul—the size and shape of my mostly absent son— where she fit perfectly. I was like my mother during those long-ago church days, surrendering to the thick wall of organ wail, steeling her body for the Holy Ghost. I didn't ask *why me*, I didn't question where it came from, I just let my unbridled love for the child settle over me like a clinging quilt.

For the next three years, across a courtroom from her mother, I tried not to dwell on the hurt of it, on the image of two women fighting for a female child. I tried not to feel that I was shattering what had yet to build between them. At first, I believed that I was simply temporary, providing haven while the woman grew stronger, until she could look at her own child and see a pulsing heart, up- turned eyes and perpetually open arms. But then I sensed the dam- age, Mikaila's darkening corners. And I made up my mind to be what I had always been, to do something tall and wide for this child who is threaded through with my blood, the blood of my son.

And so I take her. I pull her into my chest and hold, bury my nose in her hair, swear to kill anyone who is not sugar in her world. I am prepared to fight. I am 3:15, denims rolled to my knees, a bottle cracked on the curb. I am all in the world's face. I am jumping to its chest. I'm hiding a straight pin in my hand. I am furious whirling, showering sparks, making everyone keep their distance. You will not touch her with your wrong hands.

Now the two of us are together on yellow paper with a fancy gold stamp. Occasionally, Mikaila's mother swells forth like static on the line. She moves in close with memorized motions, then disappears for weeks at a time. The child loves her, and the idea of her. In fact, she is so full of love for everyone she dances out loud simply to release it.

However, a recent addition to the diva's routine disturbs me. Mikaila has discovered her hips, obviously inherited from the colored side of the family, and their plump fluidity fascinates her. She pouts, turns her back to the audience, rolls her butt experimentally. Then, tired of trying on the world, she sheds her stage persona and pulls me to my feet. We dance relentless disco. She won't let go of my hand. The music beats in both of us, rattles that one place we touch.

A Miracle Every Day

BY MARITA GOLDEN

I always wanted to be a mother. To one child. And I was not afraid to raise that child alone. I planned to be a mother one day, even at the age of twenty-two, while living in New York City and studying at the Graduate School of Journalism at Columbia University and daily discovering and reconfiguring my ambition. I would be a mother, even if I had to do it alone.

This yearning was intertwined, quite compatibly and quite logically it seemed to me, with the determination to write and to explore and claim as much of the world as I could. And through some act monumental or miniscule, I would, as well, contribute to the progress of my people, and maybe even of the world. Race-woman with a baby at her breast, the fingers of her free hand resting on the typewriter keys. The image filled me not with fear but with greedy anticipation. I secretly knew, even then, that to have a child was a profoundly important act of narration. Yet I never felt that the story I would write as "mother" would subvert the articles I was writing then and the books that would lay in wait.

A child is a chronicle. As in any saga, the one composed by mother and child revises assumptions and unsettles the too-neat line of demarcation we often draw between what is possible and what is real. Motherhood offered me another way into the world, even as it demanded and required everything and then forced me, like a weary scavenger, to search for still more. Honor thy mother, thy father, thy child.

My own mother was unprepared and, she once confessed to me, absolutely amazed when she became pregnant with me at forty-two. It was in the summer of my nineteenth year that my mother told me she had never thought of aborting me, although her relationship with my father was turbulent and I was an unplanned child. This secret history spilled forth in the aftermath of my revelation that I feared I was pregnant and was thinking of having an abortion. As a counter-narrative, my mother told me that I was a child who became, once my existence was confirmed, retroactively longed-for and totally desired. The year of my birth, my mother owned several boarding houses, played and often won at the numbers, drove her own Pontiac, and frequently hosted parties that featured marathon games of poker and bid whist on the first floor, and games of craps in the basements of the houses she owned.

As we sat on my mother's chenille-covered four-poster the day I spoke of a pregnancy I feared, and my mother of a pregnancy she embraced, she recalled, nonetheless, with chagrin and a pain she could not camouflage, how her friends teased her about her middle-aged pregnancy. Years later, after I had become a mother, I searched through all the black-and-white photos of my family in vain for a picture of my mother pregnant. There were cracked and aged pictures of my mother lying on a blanket on the sand of some segregated beach with friends, or standing before her mother's modest house on McConnell Road in Greensboro, North Carolina, in the summer when she came to take me home to Washington after I'd spent six weeks with Granny Reid. And there was the three-by-five black and white photo of her guiding my five-year-old hand in the cutting of a cake at my first big birthday party, a picture I always searched for first each time I opened the album. But there were no photos of my mother, a large woman, made larger still because her body was filled with me.

Those nine months were not (as far as I know) captured on film and, by the snapping of the lens, honored, legitimized, saved. The body of a pregnant woman is lauded as a temple in cultural mythology, yet evokes the oddest, most intense mixture of obsession and revulsion. The body supposedly held sacred is vulnerable to blatant assessment and even mockery. The body of a woman "with child" sometimes seems to belong to everyone in the world, really, but her. When I failed to find any photo of my mother pregnant, I searched through my own photo album and found none of me carrying my son. Is this erasure, or willful amnesia, or a conspiracy to somehow obliterate the act that perhaps more than any other defines the lives of so many women, women like my mother, women like me? The stiff pages of the photo album I kept in honor of the family my husband and I had created held scores of christening pictures, dozens of photos that captured every moment of my son's growth; but the bulky, weighty, "foreign" body that had been the site of the most astonishing incubation was nowhere framed or frozen in time by either me or my mother.

I did not want the child I feared I carried at nineteen. I was still in college and had cast myself, and been cast by the cultural eruptions of that time, as an unalterably modern woman. Controlling my fate was everything to me. I was young, filled with the hubris and vanity of the young, and thought controlling my destiny was purely a matter of determination. I wanted a child when I could make promises to that child, and to myself, that I was sure I could keep.

If I had had an abortion, it would not have been an illegal, possibly lethal operation, the kind my mother had described to me as common for many of the women of her generation. I could walk openly into a legal clinic. I could safely and freely make an appointment for a qualified doctor to abort my child. My mother argued against the abortion I was considering, if I was indeed pregnant. In fact, my period was horribly, uncharacteristically late, but I was not pregnant. My mother's relationship with my father often sapped much of what was strong and pure and beautiful in her. Still, as she later recalled, when she knew that she was pregnant, "It never occurred to me to have an abortion because I thought if I did, I'd be denying the world someone who might do great things. What if I killed a scientist, a doctor, someone who could make the world a better place?" My mother asked this question rhetorically, but with an arc of emotion that in its strength echoed the feelings of nearly twenty years earlier. "I would never forgive myself," she concluded.

Some may hear in those words an elitist valuation of human life. What if my mother had aborted a being who grew into a man or woman known only for the unremarkable nature of their life, someone who steadfastly shunned the extraordinary? Wasn't that a life worth saving too? But what I hear in my mother's plea are the awesome expectations she possessed. She was a black woman in 1950, carrying a child for whom she could predict and assert only the ability to amaze, to act upon and in the world in powerful, positive ways.

I can imagine how awkward my mother must have felt wearing maternity clothes, how morning sickness must have struck her as a cruel, twisted joke at forty-two, when, as she told me, "I thought I had gone through the change of life. I didn't even know I could still get pregnant." Even her language is revealing, the way she spoke of "the change of life" rather than menopause, moving from fertility to infertility, growing out of youth and into age. Even as chagrin and embarrassment competed with wonder, my mother imposed upon me—foetal, existent though only partially formed—the grandest of expectations. Maybe I wasn't a full person yet, but she must've felt the presence of my soul as well as my heartbeat.

In her decision to give me life, my mother christened and launched herself. I assume she felt that I would be some kind of miracle poised against the heartache of her tumultuous and sometimes violent relationship with my father. The odds might have been stacked against my birth as the inspiration for the kind of love she hoped for, but never knew, with my father; but my mother said yes to me to see what would happen. A talented, skilled gambler, she convinced herself that those nine months were a bet she could win. My mother was brave enough to have left the South; thousands of dollars had been placed in her large eager palms by numbers backers; she regularly came to the rescue of friends and family with succor and financial assistance; she was a mini-legend among her friends; and she loved and had married my father, a man who considered himself the eighth wonder of the world. My mother must've felt that I was a sign, a portent, a charm. Clearly her luck hadn't run out yet.

It ran out when she left my father and became a single mother at fifty-five. But I saw my father every week. My mother had walked out of his life. He refused to leave ours.

When I vowed to become a mother and to parent a child "by any means necessary," as it were, the ease with which I imagined myself with child and without a husband was rooted, I am sure, in the lives of the many women surrounding me as I grew up.

My two most cherished childhood and adolescent friends were raised by single mothers, as was the cousin to whom I am closest. In the boarding house in which we lived before my parents separated, my best friend among the roomers was a young nurse raising her two-year-old son, Tommy, in a single room on the second floor, a room furnished with a bed, a crib, a chest of drawers, and a record player.

I grew up surrounded, it seemed, by female invincibility, by women who were workers and mothers and sisters and friends and the children of their own mothers. These were women who belonged, I always felt, to the children they raised, the supervisors who paid them, the pastors they praised on Sunday morning. Somehow I could not imagine them belonging entirely to themselves. Courage was the password in countless small dramas staged impromptu in the grocery store, negotiations with the landlord, the phone company, conferences with teachers, expeditions to buy school clothes, wiping up a fevered child's sickness from the bathroom floor. I never thought these women ached with weariness in the darkness at night; or mastered the art of weeping completely yet silently, so no one could hear; or chiseled deserved anger into a stark object of beauty so perfect they were afraid to even touch it.

The battlefields were domestic. The rate of attrition high. Few medals were given. After all, they were merely mothers. Valor was assumed. Every family has some ancestral loss woven into its bloodstream that would tell, if anyone asked, of some female cousin or aunt or sister who couldn't or wouldn't give in to motherhood, who lit out for the city, the North, or some territory inside herself, and left the children behind. Then there were the few "chosen" women, beautiful or smart or both, who had had "accidental" children gently pulled from their breast so as not to encumber their march toward a place in some Negro college or a job with "the government" or the yearning to make it as a singer, a dancer, anything that would save them from a colored woman's fate, or a single mother's destiny.

But those women are spoken of in whispers, if at all. There are sporadic, partial requiems for the children left behind. It is the mothers—single, singular, solitary—who formed, as it were, an army we never had to acknowledge because everyone knew they would always be there. I felt no fear at the prospect of raising a child alone, for I was once a little black girl imbibing the dogma of independence and forewarned of the world's dangers, embedded in my mother's teachings and in her touch. She would have been derelict to have transmitted any other lesson to me.

Many of my childhood friends were raised by single mothers, who appeared to me as tight-lipped stoics, graceful and long-suffering. Only when those friends and I grew into young women did the secrets tumble forth, in tales of mothers who raged openly and often about what motherhood had denied them, who chose never to look back, held their progeny too close, protected too much, never spoke of or forgave absent fathers, took too many lovers or none at all.

With no children of their own to fail, these mothers' daughters sometimes concluded that a terrible wrong had been done. Their childhoods had been warped, corrupted—unintentionally perhaps, but the damage had been done. Still, the mothers had remained, steadfast, flawed and human.

These women, the mothers of my friends, were neither Sapphire nor Sojourner. In the end maybe they were both, hands on hips, berating the forces that would deny them, righteous warriors capable of all and anything for their children. Like me, they were spiritual daughters, too, of slave mothers, America's original "single mother," and of every mammy bound by the love of her own child, burdened by the affection and power of another's. I saw all that, and wanted to be a mother still.

Did I long for motherhood because of genes programmed to save the species, the undeniable call of the womb, a conspiracy of culture and conditioning and every doll my mother ever bought me?

Yet many of my girlfriends spoke openly of not wanting children. They did not shun the heresy, were not afraid of blasphemy. I admired those girls for their renegade spunk and daring. They knew who they longed to be instead of Mother, had chosen already their own name. But for me a child would complete my name, not censor or inhibit it.

Motherhood cleansed and baptized me like some necessary massive tidal wave I hungered to meet and to know; it sharpened my sense of myself, and of all the women residing within me. None of the men I've loved, the countries I've lived in or journeyed to, the books I've written, transformed me as did loving and raising my child for a decade as a single parent. The years that I was mother/father/sister/brother/everybody/everything to my son were a crucible and a gift. I raised my child and parented myself as well. We grew up together in startling, never-to-be-forgotten ways. Each attempt to shape a healthy childhood for my son altered who I was and would be as mother, as woman, as person. Learning to love my son unconditionally, I embraced myself wholeheartedly. The ongoing process of teaching my son, Michael, to love himself, and others, with respect and charity, opened my own bruised heart to the love of men.

I divorced my son's father a year after my son was born. I remarried when my son was twelve. The years between that divorce and remarriage bound us and shaped us into an entity that sociologists and bureaucrats and cultural critics thought they knew. But we resisted those definitions and became something singular yet collective, whole, and linked to others in ways that allowed us to make a miracle every day. As an African American single mother, my poster girl was not Murphy Brown, educated, affluent, in control, challenges and obstacles overcome in thirty minutes. My symbol was a second-generation teenaged mother portrayed as single-handedly draining the National Treasury because she was on welfare. Of course, Murphy Brown was a fantasy even for most *white* single mothers; and the young sister was a corruption and a lie.

I mothered and fathered my son during our sojourn together, and in amazing synergistic ways, my son made me. He made me brave, and smart and wise, and creative and cunning. Being a single parent is a job, a calling, an avocation. It is impossible, yet millions of women master its intricacies, and turn it into an expression of genius. It is rewarding, and it is at its essence as much about your soul and your spirit as it is about your child.

Several years ago, I was invited to lecture at a large Midwestern university by a female professor of African American literature. During the long drive from the airport, and in subsequent conversations as the professor, Andrea, shuttled me around the sprawling university during my two-day visit, we talked about our lives. She was an articulate, attractive young woman, made more endearing by her passion and enthusiasm for teaching and literature.

The evening of my departure, as we drove to the airport through several inches of snow, Andrea announced, "By next week, I'll be a mother." She was awaiting finalization of her recent adoption of a three-month-old baby girl. "I thought I'd be married by now," she explained. "But I've been looking. I've been waiting. I've been praying. I don't know when or if it'll happen." With a sweep of her hand toward the wide expanse of now-dormant corn and wheat fields for which the state was famed, she said, "There aren't any black men out here. I got tired of waiting. I wanted someone to love."

Then Andrea giddily told me about the girlfriends who had volunteered to be godmothers and aunts, the baby shower her friends had thrown for her, and the African-inspired christening she planned. When we arrived at the airport, we took leave like old friends, hugging one another and wishing each other well.

As I sat on the plane, returning to Washington and my own son— the someone I loved as much as Andrea already loved the daughter she was adopting—I thought of how incredible and transformative was the journey that Andrea had embarked upon. Even armed with her intelligence, her confidence and her courage, Andrea could not have suspected how shattering and how redemptive raising her child as a single parent would ultimately be. She would be remade every day, and she would be shaken to the nub and the heart and soul of herself as a woman.

Absolutely everything in her life would change. The single-parent experience is a life, not a lifestyle, one that possesses more gifts than burdens, more opportunities than sacrifices. For the woman with the capacity to live in permanent evolution, who approaches motherhood and parenthood with imagination and bravery and compassion, single parenthood can save and expand her life. Nobody will tell you that, unless they have been there—where yes, the nights are long and the days are too, and success is measured in the incremental, nonstop development of two human beings, both mother and child. Family therapist Audrey Chapman calls single mothers "people makers," referring to the ways in which they create and shape their children's lives. But single mothers are also creating and making themselves. The shaping of a whole, powerful, mother/woman self—that is the real challenge of single motherhood, and the implicit reward. Paying the bills, finding day care, a good school, clothing, feeding a child; these tasks are peripheral to the real challenge for single mothers—creating a healthy whole self out of which you can love and "grow" your child.

The challenges are real, inescapable, hard to deny. Male children raised in single-parent homes are statistically shown to perform less well in school and have more trouble with the law; girls raised in single-parent homes more frequently get pregnant in their teens and often have problems bonding emotionally with men. These statistics are race-neutral and are advanced as a defining commentary on the lives of all female-headed families. But where are the studies that analyze single-parent families for the strengths of the mothers, the positive coping and adaptive skills learned by the children, the support systems that help make these families "work"? Until complementary data exists that attempts to scientifically find and explain single-parent success—with the same diligence applied to stereotyping through analysis of "failure"—any conversation about the effect of single-parent families on children or mothers is incomplete and suspect.

No one can deny that poverty is greater among single-parent families, that the material, physical, sociological, and psychological stresses on single-parent families are significant. But for all the women I know who have been remade and transformed by their lives as female heads of families, these statistics simply did not matter; for they were too busy loving themselves and their children, and thereby making themselves the exception to what is supposed to be the rule. When I was a single mother, I decided that the conventional wisdom was irrelevant to my life and son. We were not a statistic. We were a family.

During my son's teenaged years, I experienced the kind of moment that is impossible to plan or predict, and which informed me that I had accomplished much of what I had hoped to while raising my son as a single parent.

One January weekend, six months before Michael's graduation from his Pennsylvania boarding school, Westtown, I traveled to New York to publicize the paperback edition of one of my books. My husband, Joe, had planned to take the train up from D.C. on Friday, and Michael would also join us, as he had a long weekend break from Westtown. Joe came down with the flu and stayed home. The Friday morning that Michael arrived, after he got settled in the hotel, we walked around Broadway and had lunch at the Motown Café, where, while singers impersonated the Temptations and the Supremes, Michael shared his exploits on the basketball team and spoke of already missing Westtown and the friends he had made and would soon leave behind when he graduated in June. After lunch, we went to see *Waiting to Exhale* and, walking back to the hotel, talked about men and women and love and choices.

That night the first game between the Chicago Bulls and the Los Angeles Lakers, retooled with a returned Magic Johnson, was scheduled to air at 10 P.M. While waiting for the game to start, we watched the movie *To Wong Foo, Thanks for Everything, Julie Newmar*. The tame, lifeless comedy starred Wesley Snipes and Patrick Swayze as two of three transvestites on an elaborate road trip through the South.

At one point, I sighed in frustration at the predictability of the plot. Michael, his six feet two inches sprawled across the other bed in the room, agreed and then said, "But look at them, Mom, they're dressed up like women, so they can show their emotions. They're walking around in high heels and they can cry."

I instinctively lowered the volume and turned to look at my son. At seventeen, he was lanky, baby-faced, yet trying hard to grow a mustache. I looked at his face and saw gazing back at me his father and myself. I had bought him dolls along with trucks and video games, all to try to foster his feminine side. As Michael moved into adolescence, I had initiated and maintained a consistent dialogue with him, sometimes a monologue, about the sexism in rap music, the objectification of women in MTV and BET videos, the need to respect women and to embrace his own feelings of vulnerability, fragility, and fear. While I was a single parent we had been through counseling together, and whenever a crisis loomed on the horizon of his life, I urged Michael to open up, not to shut down; to cry or talk through his anger rather than to ram his fist through a wall.

My son's totally unexpected yet passionately felt observation informed me that he had been listening. Now it was my turn to hear him. Michael confided how, as he watched the film, he felt a perverse envy for the freedom of the three men. "On the basketball court, if I get injured I can't cry if I'm in pain. The other guys would razz me about it. But if a girl trips up the stairs she can bawl like a baby," he declared with a vehemence that startled me. "If a girl breaks off with me and I'm hurt, I can't admit that to my buddies. I have to lie. And you know, Mom, sometimes when I'm with them I lie so much that I begin to believe I am not hurt too."

The outrage and visceral sense of inequity Michael obviously felt at the socialization he had to endure, despite my best efforts, heartened me. For it revealed that, while perhaps at that moment in his life he was not able to permit himself to weep in the presence of his friends, or to honestly reveal his feelings to his buddies, he could at least critique the false, dangerous values of masculinity that trapped him and so many other males. He had at least formulated a language to name the problem, even though he could not yet solve it. That moment was an instant of epiphany for me. For it confirmed that the struggle I had waged to influence a portion of my son's soul had not been in vain.

I shared my own anxieties around gender issues, told Michael that women paid a high price for being female, and that it cost men even more to be male. But I also told him how a few weeks earlier, Joe had come home from the high school where he teaches and informed me that one of his former students had been shot and killed. Joe wept freely and at length as he remembered the young man. I told Michael of Joe's male friends and how they all shared moments of crisis and defeat with one another, and were as honest and intimate and lovingly supportive as any women could be.

We watched the Bulls-Lakers game when it came on. But to me it hardly mattered. I had scored the points I needed. During the years when I was raising Michael alone, talking to him endlessly about women, about men, even as I struggled to sort out the meaning of love and life for myself, my son was listening. With no husband beside me, with fingers crossed, propelled mostly by faith, I believed that I could raise a son who would want to honor what was feminine in him as well as that which was masculine, and who would someday learn that all of it belonged to him. I laid the foundation for who I wanted my son to become—a sensitive, thoughtful, perceptive young man who would not take the world at face value. This is what he became.

For all the warnings that the odds are against you, the most critical enemy faced by a woman who is a female head of family (the term I prefer) is doubt. The doubt is in many ways justified when the immensity of the task is considered, but it need not be paralyzing or persistent. We shepherd our children through their lives with the aid and the love of family; of friends and neighbors; and of institutions ranging from school to church. Are you truly a single mother, or are you a woman working in tandem with a community and a world full of personal and material and institutional resources to help you "grow" a healthy child?

The inner journey, however, which so powerfully defines the meaning of single motherhood, is the adventure that we feel least equipped to initiate. Many single mothers who work energetically and quite successfully to provide materially for their children, neglect their own emotional wounds, inflicting them on their children like a dreaded inheritance. Above all, a single-parent home requires a mother/parent intent on opening herself and her child to the qualities of compassion, love and respect for themselves individually and as a family unit. The single mother must develop the ability in herself and in her child to extend those qualities to others. These are the tools both mother and child require, like psychological oxygen, in order to avoid the traps of self-pity, anger, bitterness, or a sense of betrayal—emotions that fester beneath the calm exterior that many single mothers and their children present to the world.

Every child wants a father they can know, can bond with, and who is always near. Many women feel that a happy marriage is their due. Navigating the treacherous path through the lives we have received, as opposed to the ones we planned, is the test for everyone. It is a challenge especially difficult for single mothers, because so often they feel that they must do it alone.

But developing an inner emotional life as a single parent is the first step in helping your child to do the same. Learning to be reflective and self-critical, to assess one's own choices and actions as objectively as we would judge a stranger's, and in the process to extend charity and understanding to oneself and others, is an evolution that is lifelong. It is a way of living one's life, and it is the most important thing our children can see us do. It is a skill that single mothers need in abundance in order to avoid making martyrs of themselves and demons of absent fathers. We need to chisel a safe space in the hearts of our children where they can feel and explore and shape the myriad complex and contradictory emotions they feel about themselves and their lives in single-parent homes. Help them realize that they carry a safe place within them, in their own hearts and minds.

The greatest strength of single mothers, is in their ability to allow their children to re-create them; their genius lies in their willingness to recognize the interdependence of self-love and maternal love; their wisdom is in the recognition that mother is one of the most awesome and generous and life-giving designations they could ever have.

Elementary Lessons

BY RITA COBURN WHACK

In the mid-Eighties, you could fly from Pittsburgh to New York on the weekend for nineteen dollars one way. I was living with the man who would become my husband at the time and we had just relocated to slower, more provincial Pittsburgh. Having no children to consider, we would hop a plane whenever we felt Manhattan call. We would spend Friday night in Harlem, make our way to Greenwich Village for an afternoon of jazz at Sweet Basil's on Saturday, then, after shopping for groceries at Jefferson Market and Balducci's, we'd visit our former neighborhood before departing to return home.

One Monday morning after such a weekend, I became concerned about my fiance's desire to start a family immediately after we were married. I was producing a television series on women climbing the corporate ladder. Standing on the emerald lawns of the University of Pittsburgh as fall teased summer's last days, I interviewed three students on the impact of career women in business and the resulting effect on family life. The young white male student was even-tempered, sure of his future, which included an Ivy League university for graduate studies. Although I can't recall his words, I remember his posture: solid, unfettered. Nor do I recall the comments of his white female counterpart, but I'll never forget the young black woman. Her words pierced the afternoon's complacency.

"Until my niece and nephews have the same opportunities as their children," she pointed to the young man, who continued to lounge comfortably with no change of expression, and to the young woman, who reddened, "the corporate ladder and networking will leave my children out. And I will fight this racism so that they won't have to. And I will raise them with everything I have."

This young black woman's anger disturbed me. I had borne no children to teach me about life's dreams, fulfilled or thwarted. Yet I recognized that her sensibilities spoke to our reality as African Americans. Pittsburgh was then behind the times, but in Chicago, where I was born, and in New York, things were the same for blacks: A few of us were unfolding linen napkins to feast at the table, but far too many were waiting for crumbs. Her words also evoked the community where I grew up. We were poor, hardworking, blue-collar people, descendants of field Negroes, decent and proud. Children were the well from which our water came. But was I obligated to fight for children that were not mine? I was more tired from climbing than thirsty from want; some discretionary income had provided a reprieve from memories of struggle and fight. Surely, a few years as a petty bourgeois Negro couldn't hurt? Or could it?

Children.

I filed the tenor of the conversation along with her words.

Three years later, I watched my son and daughter, seventeen months apart, sleep sweetly in cribs on either side of their butter yellow and light oak nursery. I understood then that those emerald green lawns were of a pasture where my children might never linger. I too vowed to fight. I had no idea then that every time I fought for my children, I fought for all children and, most surprisingly, I fought for me.

I found a part-time opportunity working with teen mothers and their children, along with the too-young grandmothers, often single as well. The community center where I worked was nestled in Pittsburgh's Hill district, where poverty was a given and the way to improve the lives of children had to be paved through generations. As we talked, laughed, wrote and learned together, my sisters held up a mirror. Though I had not coped with the pain of being unloved by having babies prematurely, I found I was not different from these women. Indeed, we had much in common.

Shhh! Shhhh! You have to be quiet to hear this secret, as it is quietly kept. Ensconced in our own nurseries, many women slumber. In the face of our lives, we mothers sleep, cradled in the arms of fear, or lulled by the intimidation that gently rocks us into a dark submission so that we can never quite become who we are meant to be. We rest. Some of us reveal the wear and tear of our tattered dreams on our faces. Some of us manage to look the part we play, clean up nicely, although there are days when we can barely make the effort to look at ourselves honestly and embrace the person we see. We choose to be somnolent rather than alert so that we might consciously resist and defy the tidal pull of our oppression. In society, mothers are still too often invisible and ignored because we underestimate our power and dismiss our worth.

To sleepwalk life, we consume denial and believe we are not hurting anyone. We are not loud and foolish, simply languishing. The words seem harmless "to sleepwalk life." In reality, they are demons that belie a great truth: we yearn for awakening. Now, while my antidote—motherhood—is not for all my sisters, it worked for me, and I send a shout out to the sisters who fought hard as mothers and became women in the process. For many of us, our renewed, enlightened consciousness was born in the love of our children.

When our son, Lee, was almost 2 years old and our daughter, Christine, was a baby, we enrolled Lee in an ethnically diverse daycare program two days a week. We wanted to help him adjust to being around other children. One late afternoon, I picked Lee up from daycare, strapped him in his car seat next to his sister and drove home. I noticed the area around his mouth was red. I asked him what had happened but his words were limited. He tried to show me and started to cry. I drove back to the daycare center with Christine on one hip, Lee clutching my hand. As I took him around the center, a cook finally confided the truth. One of the workers had grabbed him by the face in anger. A few more questions and I discovered that the woman who grabbed him was going through a divorce and angry.

Why my child? I screamed inwardly, but I knew the answer. I confronted the racism of a white woman who could not respect my son in a room of children where only one other looked like him. I took my son out of the school only to experience a similar incident a few years later. Was there a war on young black boys? Through letters and meetings, with a shrill, relentless and quietly insistent voice, I faced adversity and won. As I completed this lesson, I gave voice to my sisters and served folks notice that our sons and daughters must be treated fairly.

For some mothers, a child becomes a guide from the sleepy place. We discover that when we put children to the breast, out true selves are nurtured. We find our own feet with a baby, eventually taking grown-up steps. We awaken, and become confident in order to teach confidence.

I marvel at God's grace and hope that there are fewer and fewer souls who, seeing our color, lose sight of what it is to give another human being respect, but I find it a joy to give us voice. Those of us who found our strength in our children will not be judged by anyone. What we could not do for ourselves, we learned to do because there was another life that depended on it. With motherhood, we find we can speak, softly or loudly, whether poor and affluent, with and without rage. We are no longer afraid, and the children in our care are well protected.

Ahhhh! This is the way my daughter would sigh as she awakened, finished playing with a toy or hearing a story. It was a sensuous sigh and I noticed it when she was not quite a year old. At one, she took to trailing her hand gracefully through the air to accompany the melodious sound of her voice. As years passed, I realized she was a girlie girl, loving her brand of femininity. No soccer or basketball teams for her; she took to dresses rather well. In later years she developed a lean tomboyish-ness, and with her ladylike disposition, meshed the two into a style of her own.

My daughter reminded me that if Esther bathed six months in

milk baths before she could even see the King, then I, too, deserved to be pampered inside and out.

I have several friends that seem never to have enough time to keep their hair in place and fingernails manicured. For them, matching underwear every day of the week would be a monumental achievement. For some who want this type of femininity, a few have been blessed with daughters who lead the way. A daughter's ability to define the beautiful they choose to be helps teach us that time for self is attainable, profitable and, if we don't take it, we can't effectively support them in doing so. If we run ourselves ragged taking care of everyone else's needs, leaving no time for ourselves, we teach daughters that other people are worth more than they. And sons learn that women are only for the beck and call of men.

My son taught me that you could march and sing and knock down walls with faith that the Kingdom belongs to you. When a brain X-ray revealed scar tissue and he received an early diagnosis of multiple sclerosis, I learned how to pray. I called on the saints of my church and joined a minister and my husband in anointing our son with oil. Reared in a teaching church, our ten-year-old son was asked and gave his permission for the anointing. I was nervous, how much did I really believe in my faith? Was James 5:16, *the fervent effectual prayers of a righteous man avail much*, really true? Was the Bible to be believed? I prayed and trembled until I had no choice but to believe. Hours later, a spinal tap showed clear liquid and later tests left no traces of scar tissue. Then I realized that church meant having people I trusted to call upon, that fellowship was real and faith was something you did not just claim, but practiced.

This year, as my son prepared to leave for Morehouse College in Atlanta, he met with several pastors and the prayer partners who were to be his college roommates. Under the guidance of their elders, these young men vowed to practice their faith and to share it with those inclined to listen. After watching them work as JAM (Jesus And Me) leaders for four years, mentoring, entertaining and guiding more than one hundred youth on Monday nights, and spending Fridays 'chillin' in our basement with fifteen to twenty kids, I knew they would do well on their own. They gave me hope in a world that shows distorted images of young black men, visions that often skew toward violence, drugs, and sex. These young men have a truth, and they also have a possibility. When I watch my son toss his shoulder-length dreads back and laugh, it strengthens my voice for all my brothers.

As my daughter completes her senior year in high school, I see her compassion. Her love of young children and of her peers commits her to service. After she discovered that an acquaintance had begun to cut herself, a form of self-mutilation, she called me and explained the problem. We encouraged the young lady to seek counseling that in time unraveled years of abuse. We learned that there are no "bad" children. If a child is acting out, find out what causes them to do so. Then fight with everything you have. Awaken to the need for change and trust in your intelligence, perseverance, and courage.

As I watch Christine embrace her peers and young children with hope, I am both sad and joyful. I will soon miss interacting with this young woman, my daughter, who has more patience that I ever had and who believes, above all things, that to be great is to be a servant. /

Now, I'll tell you what I think of me.

There are many lessons I have taught my children, but there are many more that they have taught me. The day-to-day care of children is a phase of my life that is ending; I can not say I am without regrets. If given the chance, I would have loved them harder, discerned more and fussed less. But I have fought well. My son is not a predator and my daughter is not a young woman to be used. I am strong enough to fight for others because I remember when I was too weak to fight for myself.

I am learning yet another lesson. Time to let the teachers go. They are stronger than I was when I was their age. They are not fearful, and thanks to them, neither am I. I get up each day knowing that there is a God. I raise my hands and pray for enough children each day that I can lower my hands, wrap them around my shoulders and love myself a while. I know the difference between having discretionary income and true prosperity rests in having relationships of love. I know that better than finding the best material things for children is finding the places and people who nurture and guide them. I know what it is to love being black.

My husband has come to know a new woman and we like her. My children believe that all the hard lessons they had to learn were worth the challenges, and that those lessons prepared them for a victorious future. Now, as I watch them leaving my arms to embrace life's classroom, I know that their journey will always be a part of my own. I wonder if they know that they are not only students, but the best of teachers.

My Girl

BY BETHANY M. ALLEN

*R*achael is my *girl*. She's one of my best friends—she's funny, talented, smart and kind. Beautiful inside and out, she's a generous, supportive and sweet person. Her smile and personality can light up a room. We tell each other our secrets, make each other laugh, and have our share of fights. We grew up together. And she's my daughter.

I know all too well that there are times when a kid needs a parent, not a friend, but I also know that that fine line that can be drawn even finer by single parenthood. When raising a child alone, there is no partner to share in the "good cop/bad cop" dynamic, in which one parent plays the heavy and the other has the soft touch. As a single parent, I'm it. I have to dole out reprimands and punishment right along with kisses, lunch money and birthday presents. And believe me, with three kids, I give out a lot of all of those things.

In true maternal fashion I profess to love all of my kids equally, and I do, but I have a special relationship with Rachael, my oldest. I had her when I was 18, and motherhood forced me, reluctantly, to grow up. Despite the fact that I sometimes resented my overnight maturity and longed for the carefree lives my peers took for granted, I am grateful now for what she gave me during those early years. More than anyone else, she taught me how to be a mother. Now that she's a teenager, I am hoping to teach her what it means to be a young black *woman* in this society—and, perhaps most importantly, how to avoid making the same mistakes I did.

It is a bit tricky to explain to a child, who ultimately exists due to one of said "mistakes," that she is not a mistake herself. In fact, in hindsight, it is hard to believe that the circumstances that led me to be an unwed teenage mom were not in some way divinely orchestrated. Even though it is a path I wouldn't recommend to anyone, and would be devastated if any one of my children were to follow, Rachael and I have an amazing relationship that was borne out of our reliance on each other back in the days. However, it is important for her, and for other children from families of single mothers, to understand the implications that come along with having and raising a child alone: the quite likely financial, emotional, and social isolation, confusion and fear. Those implications are intensified when the birth is unplanned and the mother is extremely young.

When it happened to me, I went into denial. I couldn't believe that I was about to become a statistic—a young, unwed black woman with a baby. To make matters worse, I lived in a small rural New England town where I was not only the sole black kid, I was the only person of color period. In my mind, and perhaps in reality, I represented my race to all the inhabitants of that small town, and unfortunately I was exemplifying a stereotype I just knew they were so ready to believe. Even if the entire town *didn't* look down on me for having a child out of wedlock, I felt as though I had let the larger black collective down.

I was smart even, Ivy League college–bound, and yet I still managed to mess up in this typical, expected way. Maybe it was feeling like such a huge disappointment that led me to believe I would be able to give up my child after she was born. Throughout my pregnancy, I convinced myself that there was no way I was ready or fit to be responsible for this new life. My plan was to give custody of the baby to a relative who was unable to have children and get my life back on track like nothing had ever happened. I might have been able to go through with it, too, if I hadn't laid eyes on her. The change of heart was instantaneous; after months of telling myself I could never live with a child all it took was a moment to concede that I could never live without her.

Since I hadn't planned on actually keeping her, two weeks after she was born I was expected to show up at Harvard College. A reflection of my immaturity, I had my mom call to find out what my options were, and because it was so late in the game deferring entrance wasn't among them. So off I went, halfhearted, regretful yet somewhat relieved. I was able to resume my life as a "normal" teenager temporarily. My mom, who had only supported my decision to give up my child out of respect for my wishes, enthusiastically accepted the role of primary caregiver for my daughter. Going to college seemed the right thing to do. I didn't want to waste the opportunity to get a degree from Harvard because I had gotten pregnant, and I believed that ultimately my daughter and I would be better off once I graduated.

My freshman year was a disaster. Not only was I dealing with the usual pressures of learning to adapt to collegiate life, I was missing my girl. In the short time I had with her before I left for school, I rarely put her down, rarely broke the gaze that was fixed to that tiny face that looked so much like mine. I went for weekend visits every chance that I got, even missing a mid-term once because it was given on the only day that I could catch a ride home from the bus station. I paid for that and other academic discretions by being asked by the University to take the following year off. Being at home full time for a year gave me my first real taste of motherhood.

I had always been of the mind that I didn't want to have kids "when I grew up" because it seemed like a thankless task. My daughter was indeed a handful, yet I inexplicably loved every minute—once I got used to it. She surprised me with her quick wit and easy disposition. She was an angelic child. So charming was she that I considered not returning to school the following year when it was time to go back. My father convinced me; I think the line went something like, "If you don't, we'll both need to go to the hospital. Why? Because it will take a surgeon to get my foot out of your ass." So, I went. But this time I wasn't alone—I had my girl in tow.

That's when things got rough, and "angelic" became a word less frequently associated with Rachael. Running her back and forth to day care around attending classes and studying was more challenging than I had expected. She had a hard time adjusting to being separated from my mom and other relatives whom she had grown close to at home, and my inability to devote my full attention to her caused her to start acting out. She shred my papers, pulled all the tape out of my roommate's answering machine, and wet the bed. A lot.

I decided that I wasn't ready to be both a student and a mom, and a few years went by before I felt up to the task. By that time, a failed long-term relationship had grown my family—I was now the mother of three—and we were living in off-campus housing, so there was a more pressing need for steady income. I wish that I had a formula that I could have shared in response to the recurring "How do you do it?" query, but I never quite figured it out myself. While I may not have always done it well, I called upon the age-old tradition of the black everywoman, doing everything simply because *I had to*. Things were tough: We stayed broke, ate cereal for dinner, and I struggled to stay on top of homework (mine and Rachael's, since she had started school by then). My other two children were in day care, and my attention was spread so thin that the staff at the center knew my youngest was potty trained before I did.

Being a single, working, matriculating mom wasn't all trials and tribulations, though. There are plenty of good memories, anecdotal moments that we all recall in stories that bind us as a family. One time I was studying for an exam when my daughter went on a sugar-induced high after clandestinely drinking half a bottle of chocolate syrup. Tearing around our microcosmic apartment, she paused briefly to ask, "Mommy, I been drinkin' syrup, is that okay?" Another time I was relaxing in my room, eating the aforementioned ever-popular bowl of cereal, when my son came flying into the room and turned a miraculous flip onto the bed. I was momentarily impressed, until his foot came down and caught my bowl, sending Cheerios spewing to the far recesses of the room. I would have snapped if not for years of performing the juggling act that is single motherhood, which has taught me, if nothing else, not to cry over spilled milk. Or cereal.

While I would be heartbroken if any of my children were to break the dreadful news to me that I spilled to my mom fourteen years ago, I want them to know that I did more than live with my choices; I learned to treasure my role as a mother. Pride in my children and my will to defy the bleak prophecy of single motherhood made me work hard to overcome the humiliation of my condition. I had to learn that being a single mom doesn't mean that I am ethically void, and it doesn't mean that I can't have great kids with deep commitments to traditional family values. Most importantly, I discovered that being a single mom doesn't necessarily limit the possibilities for me or for my children.

To some extent, my two youngest children's father has assumed the father-figure role in Rachael's life, but she knows the deal. She resents her "real" father for skipping out, and has yet to realize that *he* is the one that is missing the most by his absence. He has no idea that he parented this wonder-child, this beautiful, spirited young girl with ebony eyes and his cleft in her chin. He may never know how athletic she is, or how articulate and compassionate she is, how brave she is or that she always finishes her vegetables and her favorite television show is *I Love Lucy*. He will never know how special she is or that she is the way she is today in part because of the way she came up, the way we came up together: without him.

Even though we've done all right so far, I want more for my kids. I want them to be able to enjoy their young adulthood unfettered from the dense responsibilities of parenthood, and to take advantage of that time in their lives in ways that I couldn't. I especially worry about Rachael. I know that young women who grow up without fathers can suffer from abandonment issues, and often fall prey to a vicious cycle that leaves them young, poor single mothers as well. She knows that it's been a strain for me to raise a family alone, so I try to impress upon her that I wouldn't want her to struggle the way that I have and sometimes still do.

While I worry about her modeling negative behavior, I also know she is proud of my perseverance and the strength of our family. It boggles my mind whenever I realize that she feels this way, and not just because most of the time she acts as though it's my goal in life to embarrass her. Even though all those years ago I felt like such a complete disappointment for having her, now I couldn't be more proud to be her mom. I have somehow managed to make her proud of me, too, and that may end up being my greatest accomplishment. She's my daughter. And she's my girl. There's no mistake about that.

Welcome to the World

BY DAWN TURNER TRICE

*I*t is a hot July afternoon. My daughter Hannah and my mother are seated at the kitchen table. I am in my home office. I can't see them but I can hear them chatting about Hannah's day at summer camp. Their voices ride the warm breeze and they sound like girl-friends relaxing under a beach umbrella. My mother, a 60-something who's cute and quite busty, sips iced tea. My seven-year-old slurps milk in between run-on sentences.

"Grandma Barbara, Joseph says he's older than me, but he's much shorter, so I know he isn't older, so I asked him his birthday and he wouldn't tell me, so I asked his brother and he's younger and he said he didn't know, so . . ."

"Take a breath, Hannah," I yell to my only child. Hannah is lanky and tall for her age. Her hair is parted down the middle and her two ropey braids jiggle when she talks.

"That was good thinking," my mother says to Hannah.

At this moment, I sense that my mother's entire being is in tune with my child. She smells Hannah's chocolate chip cookie–laden breath. She watches her little girl gestures—arms flailing the same way in resignation or triumph. And when Hannah's cascade of words slows, my mother waits for her to continue wide-eyed, like she's watching floats in a parade.

Since my mother began coming out to our house to lend a hand during the week, Grandma Barbara and Hannah have become girl-friends of a sort. At some point during the afternoon, Hanna will say: "Grandma tell me a story." Grandma will talk about wanting to be an actress or ballerina when she was a child, then settling for singing in the church choir and rearing two daughters on Chicago's South Side.

One story she doesn't tell is how she saved Hannah's life. Hannah isn't quite ready for that yet. It's a gift that will be unwrapped when she's older. For now, I will share it with you:

It is late February 1996. Hannah is a healthy 14-month-old until the day she gets an ear infection and then a fever. Even after a day's course of antibiotics, her little body is a flame that resists extinguishing.

On the first sleepless night of her illness, my husband and I alternate giving her fever reducing medicines and bathing her in cooling towels, according to her pediatrician's instructions.

On the second sleepless night, my husband has been up and down the stairs to the kitchen for water and juice so many times that around dawn, he misses a step and slices open his foot on some loose wood moulding at the bottom of the staircase. He leaves me with our sick child and drives himself to the emergency room.

At about eight o'clock that morning, my mother calls. An hour later, she's on our doorstep. The weight of the past few hours—Hannah's fever unrelenting; David in the emergency room getting thirty stitches in his foot—makes me collapse, sobbing into her arms.

That afternoon my mother and I take Hannah back to the doctor's office. By now, she is lethargic. Her appetite is waning. The antibiotics still have not taken hold.

The waiting room in the doctor's office is filled with children who appear sicker than Hannah. One child has green mucous oozing from his eyes. Several others hack and wheeze uncontrollably. My mother and I attempt to shelter Hannah, who's uncommonly quiet and still, from the fog of germs.

I have no idea my child is by far the sickest.

So after a while, I whisper to my mother; "Maybe we should go and come back tomorrow. I don't want her to catch what they have."

My mother looks down at Hannah then back at me. She recognizes that I am both sleep-deprived and drunk with denial.

"We're going to wait," she swaddles Hannah in her blanket.

"But . . ." I say.

"No 'Buts'. We should wait."

When we see the doctor, Hannah's pupils are nearly fixed. He tells us to get her over to the emergency room of a nearby hospital, one of the best in the Chicago area.

My husband meets us there. He's on crutches and potent painkillers.

After a couple of hours, a pediatric neurosurgeon tells us that Hannah's ear infection has spread, like a wayward spark, to her brain. Her brain has begun to swell and they are trying to stop the swelling with powerful antibiotics. If that fails, the brain will begin to press against her skull. The skull is hard and resistant, he says. The brain will have no place to expand into, so she will die.

While the doctors talk to us, nurses wheel Hannah into the intensive care unit where she lay in isolation. Arms and legs splayed, she wears only a diaper. A complex web of wires and tubes extends from her little body to nearly ten machines. She is in an induced coma and breathes via a respirator.

Helpless, we pray. In the lounge area, there's a bank of telephones and we call all of our relatives and friends and ask them to pray, too.

Throughout the first two days, doctors tell us that although Hannah might not survive, at least we got her to the hospital in time to give her a fighting chance. She would have died had we waited until morning.

Hanna spends ten days in intensive care. As the infection responds to the antibiotics, doctors slowly wake her up. We won't know what damage, if any, the infection has wrought until later. But what's immediately noticeable is that the right side of her body is much weaker than the left, and her left eye is no longer mid-line.

I can't help but think about how when Hannah was born, her eyes were the starkest thing about her. She was very fair with humongous dark, dark eyes that seemed ill-fitting in their size and hue.

Now, as she awakens, we joke that her left eye is a great big brown marble that wanders, crouching from time to time in the left corner. It seems to have a mind of its own.

A couple of weeks pass. She begins to move about and her movements resemble those of a stroke victim. Her right arm is limp like a rag doll's. Although, at 14 months old, she had mastered walking, she has to re-learn how to take a first step. And when she does, her right leg drags slightly.

To top it off, she has this huge cowlick. An arc of hair is missing from where a device, called an intra-cranial pressure monitor, had been inserted into her brain to detect swelling.

All in all, she looks like the walking wounded and we don't care. We couldn't be happier. She is alive.

We learn later that the few children who do survive brain infections rarely do so intact. Some lose limbs; others, their hearing or sight.

It is Easter Sunday when we leave the hospital. More than a month has passed since we arrived. A big white rabbit stops by the room and hands Hannah an Easter Basket. Her smile is slightly crooked as she rummages through the fake grass for chocolates.

Before we leave, her pediatrician reminds us that we are very lucky to have gotten her there in time. I do feel lucky, blessed even, but I can't help thinking about how I wanted to leave and come back the next day. The thought chills me and nearly breaks my heart.

On the way out of the hospital, I promise Hannah that when she's well enough, we will have a garden this spring. We will plant lots of flowers.

It is September, a couple of years later—the beginning of preschool. Red and yellow leaves rain down on the schoolyard. Children run through a sandbox and swing from monkey bars.

Hannah and I are standing on the edge of a playground. I'm

holding her hand, feeling her gently pull away. As she pulls, my grip tightens.

She knows that I normally hesitate before I let her go. Today is no different, so she looks up at me curtly, impatient that I am the one who stands between her and fun.

Truthfully, I'm afraid she'll fall and hurt herself, or get some germ. We've skirted death before. She has emerged so far with what amounts to little more than minor scratches. Her right leg is still weaker than the left, but her walking, for the most part, is fine. She's left-handed, and we attribute this to her weaker right hand, which has less dexterity, but works well enough. Two surgeries and eyeglasses have erased nearly all of the deviation in her eyes, and her cognitive skills are humming right along.

One evening, days before, my mother plants a seed: "I know you don't want to hear this, but Hannah's going to have to scrape her knees and fall down and get colds. You've got to let her be a child. You can't protect her from life. She'll be all right. She's proven, she tough." My mother pauses. "It wasn't your fault that she got sick. But it will be your fault if she fails to thrive."

Now, when I let Hannah's hand go, she runs over to the kids on the playground. She has sprouted wings. My stomach has butterflies.

I watch her play on a jungle gym. She travels with ease from one bar to the next. The wind kisses her cheeks until they are rosy. When she swings, she pumps her legs and she begins to create new heights for herself and a new playing field.

If you don't know her story, you can't imagine what she's been through. She looks as "normal" as any other child. She negotiates an obstacle course. She trips and falls and gets back up laughing, chasing her shadow.

I hear my mother say again: "Hannah will be just fine."

I repeat those words to myself over and over. My ability to trust that she won't get sick again has been wounded. Hannah is well on her way to recovery. Now it's time for me to heal.

It is Christmas Day, Hannah's seventh birthday. Our family converges on our house for Christmas dinner. As relatives arrive, they bring desserts that are piling up on the kitchen counter. Sweet potato pies, apple cobblers, and homemade spice cookies ring the centerpiece cake, decorated with the words, Happy Birthday, Hannah—Merry Christmas to All.

Each birthday, my husband and I are reminded of how she was born on Christmas day and reborn on Easter Sunday.

We are reminded that when you've come close to losing a child, you never fully recover. Even if that child, like ours, is healthy and the effects of her illness are few.

We view the world through the prism of that near-disaster. And when illness comes, even common colds, light splinters into fine pieces and once again we're blinded by what we now know are the possibilities: that a fever isn't just a fever; a cough isn't simply a cough.

My challenge is to remember the entire story—not just the brink, all those days in the hospital uncertain of her future—but also the happy ending.

When it's time, we sing "Happy Birthday" to Hannah and she basks in the glow of the moment. Later, I watch Hannah and my mother munch cake together. Hannah says, as if she hasn't been told this story a thousand times, "Grandma Barbara, you were in the hospital when I was born, right?"

"I was there," Grandma Barbara says. "I was standing right behind your daddy and I watched you shoot out with your one arm stretched way up in the air. Like you were waving to your public."

Hannah smiles at this and finishes on cue: "And the doctor said, 'It's a girl and she's got big feet and hands.' And then I started screaming, right? And Mama was tired and kind of out of it, but she said, 'Oh, Hannie. Welcome to the world.'"

Too Blessed to Be Stressed

BY REVEREND DR. SUZAN D. JOHNSON COOK

I had always wanted a family and my husband Ron and I prayed about children from the beginning. God answered those prayers even sooner than we expected. He also answered our prayers for a safe delivery and a healthy baby. On October 4, 1992, little Samuel, whose name means "gift of God," came kicking and crying into this world.

This new gift brought much joy, but it also changed my life—dramatically. I was so excited about giving birth, but somehow my brain had not grasped the fact that after the delivery there would be a lifelong process of raising a child. I thought having a baby was kind of like playing basketball: You toss it through the hoops, somebody gets the rebound, everybody cheers, and the game goes on.

I was used to getting on and off airplanes at least twice a week, with no responsibility for anyone but myself. As a single woman, I had covered almost everything I wanted to do: I traveled abroad, worked as a television producer, obtained my doctorate of ministry from Union Theological Seminary, and entered the full-time ministry. As a pastor, I had resuscitated a dying black church in Chinatown, Mariners' Temple, the oldest Baptist church in Manhattan. Suddenly, another human being was completely dependent on me, and I couldn't even leave the apartment and take the elevator down to the mailbox without making arrangements for someone to watch him. And this tiny little creature could not tell me what he needed or wanted. He just cried, and I had to learn how to figure out what was wrong; More than that, I had to figure out what to do about it.

Perhaps the most startling revelation for this unprepared new mother was this: poop happens. And it happened with such frequency that I was appalled. Now, my husband is a gem. He has always shared responsibility for household duties, and he was wonderful with the baby. But in those first few weeks I pawned off so many dirty-diaper changes on Ron that he finally said, "Suzan, get over it. You are this baby's mother. You've got to learn to deal with poop!"

Another thing nobody told me was that you need to have Plan B ready for your Sunday wardrobe. Because as soon as you put your church clothes on and start out the door, the baby will throw up all over you. When you happen to be the pastor, having a backup outfit is not just a nice idea, it's critical. You don't want to stand in the pulpit with baby puke adorning your best silk blouse. And you can't make excuses to the congregation for being late because you had to go back and change clothes. I learned about Plan B the hard way, and I want to tell you: It was stressful.

The stresses of combining marriage, motherhood, and ministry drove me deeper into God's Word. As I spent time allowing Scripture to confront my innermost feelings, I came to understand that it is important not to become distracted from my true mission. Stress is a distraction that keeps me from fulfilling God's call on my life. I can't be all things to all people; I have to focus on being who God wants me to be and doing what he wants me to do.

We can demonstrably reduce our stress levels when we learn to understand the seasons of our lives. To do that, we must know ourselves. We must listen to our bodies not only intellectually but also emotionally and spiritually.

It is most important to know God. Each day God is trying to tell us something. Each day we must listen. Often I have asked God to help me identify and understand the seasons of my life. Is this a time to move, or a time to stay put? Is this a time to work hard, or a time to rest and relax? "To everything there is a season."

It was after the birth of Samuel, that I began thinking about my dream of a White House fellowship again. When I had applied for the fellowship during the George H. W. Bush Administration, I was interviewed in Boston. Wearing a stylish purple suit, I walked confidently into a room full of interviewers dressed in cookie-cutter black business suits and a few navy blue blazers, which seemed almost daring by comparison. Although my interviews went well, it was obvious that I was a little too liberal and had a little too much pizzazz for that conservative crowd. It was not my season to be in the White House then. Instead, it was my season to fall in love, get married and start a family.

But after the presidential election in the fall of 1992, the incoming Clinton administration promised to be much more diverse—my purple suit might even seem too stuffy for the young Clinton crowd—and interested in the issues that really motivated me.

That was the season for fulfilling my dream. My first interview was in the White House with Carol Rasko, a domestic policy advisor to President Clinton. As we were talking, her eyes caught the lapel pin I was wearing. It held a tiny picture of Samuel, who was then nine months old. "Who is that?" she asked, pointing to the pin.

When I told her it was my son, she said, "You know, out of everything you do here in Washington, the most important thing is that you go home at five o'clock and pick that baby up and connect with him. Even if you have to come back to the office late at night or take extra work home, make sure your child sees you every day."

I never forgot her words; they kept me on track. The glamour of being a Fellow would fade, but motherhood would always be there. God began to confirm in my spirit that if she were that caring and sensitive about my child, then that was the place for me. I had prayed earnestly about this year in Washington because I knew it had to work for Samuel and Ron in order for it to be right for me. Ron and I were married in 1991, so ours was still a young marriage. We would commute on weekends, and I would be a single mother during the week. I knew that it would be stressful. I asked God to give me favor and put me with the right people and places, and he had. The right apartment, the right child care—everything had fallen into place. I suddenly knew it would be the same with landing the right position.

Some of the most vital lessons I've learned have been about understanding, and following, God's direction. While God's general instruction may be to go forward, he sometimes signals us to slow down, to yield, or to stop completely for a period. And when we learn to go with God's traffic flow, we get rid of a lot of the stress in our lives.

In addition to the White House interview, six more interviews in the new administration had been lined up for me, including one with the late Ron Brown, who was the Secretary of Commerce. Every interview went well, and when I returned to the White House Fellows office, the placement counselor said, "What did you do? How did you pull it off? All seven places offered you jobs."

"I didn't do anything special," I said. "I was just myself."

They thought I must have done something very unusual. But the Holy Spirit had prepared the way for me, and I just went with the flow.

I was very tempted by the offer from Secretary Brown at Commerce and the one from the director of AmeriCorps, the new national volunteer program. But my preference was the job at the White House, working with the domestic policy council. It had not even occurred to me that every single fellow wanted to be in the White House, and that the competition for that job would be the most fierce. But the Baptist preacher from the Bronx landed the top position.

In September 1993, I began working as a domestic policy advisor to President William J. Clinton. It was an outstanding year and provided everything I was looking for. I needed to be stretched, and it stretched me. But I always let everyone know that at 5:00 or 6:00 P.M. I was going home to Samuel. On weekends, I let everyone know I wasn't available because Ron was flying in and that was family time. And, as I had hoped, once I made the extent of my availability known, everyone respected and supported my priorities.

One weekend I was invited to the Kennedy Compound along

with the other White House Fellows. I really wanted to go, but I had no babysitter. I was not going to forsake my child by leaving him with someone I didn't really know. I was a White House Fellow, but I was a mother first.

Ironically, it was during my White House fellowship that I learned to place the boundaries that would allow me to nurture my family life in years to come. My current ministry at Bronx Christian Fellowship is built around my family needs and my congregation has respected those needs. Still, it is amazing how people pressure you to make appearances at the expense of your private life. I've really worked through the guilt. Public figures often lose their families in the process of helping everybody else, and our leaders really need to look at that. When you don't place boundaries you become worn down and fatigued. God never intended anyone to be on call twenty-four hours a day, draining herself to the point that she was resentful or sick.

Family time is a part of who you are, as is time for relaxation, dreaming and prayer. I make sure that we have time for one another: I may work on Sundays, but nobody touches my Saturdays or evenings. And we take wonderful family vacations. I want my children to have the freedom to talk to me and to know that I will listen.

When I became a mother, I changed biologically and spiritually, I came to understand stewardship; I was the steward of this family and together we must walk in a balance of mind, body and spirit.

Toward the end of my fellowship year, I stood at the living room window one Sunday night with Samuel in my arms. Ron had just returned to New York for the week. The trees in the park were beginning to change color; autumn was arriving. Sam squirmed and cried out, reaching toward the window. I thought he was curious about something in the park and stepped closer to the window. Then I realized that what he was reaching for was the photo of his father on the windowsill.

I thought: "We need to be together again, united, as a family." My dream had come true and my year in the White House helped me to answer some tough personal and theological questions. But my season was changing: God called me back to the pulpit, for now the political arena was not where He wanted me to be. And He called me home, where Ron, Samuel and I could grow together.

Even when we have a clear direction, even when we reach our target destination, we sometimes find that God keeps us there only for a season. So we have to know where we're going in life, and we have to know when it's time to leave.

When I returned to Mariners, I was pregnant with my second child and I began to pray about how I could restructure my ministry to make more time for my family. I was determined that I would not miss out on seeing my children grow up. I did not want the babysitter to be the mother figure. I did not want them to say someday, "I didn't know my mom. She was always out there helping other people, but she didn't have time to help me."

While I was in labor with my second son, Christopher, in May 1995, the Lord revealed to me that I was going to give spiritual birth to a new ministry. I was so preoccupied with giving physical birth that I could not clearly determine God's direction at first.

But every time I looked at my newborn son, I heard God's voice whisper, "New Birth." At the time, Mariners was helping an associate launch a new church. "Lord, does 'new birth' mean helping her?" I asked.

"No, you are going to build a new church," He said.

In June I traveled to Virginia for the Hampton Ministers' Conference. It was always the highlight of my year, and I didn't want to miss it, even though it was so soon after Christopher's birth. And having a few hours alone on an airplane allowed me to have some quiet time with God. During the flight, the Lord began to give me a vivid picture of the new birth he had in store for me. He gave me the name of the new church, the neighborhood, even the bylaws. I saw the people who would be coming. I saw the kind of ministry I would be building. I wrote down everything I was seeing and hearing in the Spirit. None of it resembled, even slightly, where I had been. God was definitely doing a new thing in me and through me.

When I made the decision to venture into new waters with God, he led me step by step and confirmed every single decision. He brought the right people and situations into my life to let me know without any doubt that I was doing the right thing. God even gave me the benefit of time, allowing me to begin to build the new ministry while I was still pastoring at Mariners.

I went to our denominational leaders and presented my plan to start a new ministry, Bronx Christian Fellowship, in the community that nurtured me as I was growing up. I shared with them the need for new birth in my old neighborhood, the Yankee Stadium area. They gave their blessing—reluctantly at first, but I got the green light to proceed.

Even though I was serving two congregations—both Mariners' and Bronx Christian Fellowship—preaching five times weekly, and trying to hold it all together, I wasn't stressed out. I wasn't burning out. My inner peace and joy increased.

By June 1996, I had resigned my position as pastor of Mariners' and became full-time pastor of Bronx Christian Fellowship. We had established a solid base for the new ministry with about 150 members. In the first year we saw more than 200 people give their lives to Christ.

Most of our members are previously unchurched African-American and Latino professionals. The church is in an established working-class neighborhood with many intact families. Our congregation has two themes: One is "Bringing the Best to the Bronx," and we bring speakers and performers from all over to expose our membership to the best the world has to offer. Our second theme is "Celebrating the Family." And with this theme we acknowledge that, regardless of our family structure, we are all part of the family of God.

Members look out for one another. We provide playdates at the church, single men have to help the single mothers. We run the church in the Black tradition, celebrating our African heritage and providing a positive affirmation of our culture and history.

I am certainly celebrating my family. What I have asked God for—more time with my family—I now have. The first location of the Bronx church was just four blocks from my home. I could take Samuel to school in the morning and pick him up on my way home. The babysitter could bring Chris by the office any time. My husband's office was ten minutes away—just a short cab ride, one subway stop, or a brisk walk.

More than two hours' daily commuting time vanished. I did not realize just how stressful that trip down FDR Drive to Mariners' was until I didn't have to make it anymore. Most evenings I am home by six o'clock. I am a "new and improved" pastor with much more energy to tackle problems and find solutions.

As my boys grow, one of the biggest adjustments I've had to make is learning how to write sermons with cartoons blaring in the background. Sam and Chris know that Mommy is a preacher and that I go to church all the time. But that's the extent of their concept of my role as a pastor. It doesn't matter if I'm in a very high spiritual moment with God, when that purple dinosaur comes on TV, they want Mommy to watch Barney with them. So I do because I understand that I won't ever have a second chance to go back and relive lost moments with two precious little boys.

God still gets some good sermons out of me, but I occasionally lose my peace of mind in the process. Then I have to allow His grace to give me the serenity to accept that my boys' need for my attention is something I can't change right now. All too soon they'll be grown up and won't need their mommy. Then I'll have to make another adjustment and learn how to write sermons without the jarring background noise, without sticky little hands pulling on my skirt and without sweet little voices yelling, "Mom, Barney's on!"

Maybe that lesson won't be as hard to learn. Or maybe it will be even harder. But God's grace will help me accept it with serenity.

Whatever you are called to do in life, you must learn how to keep stress from distracting you or destroying your peace of mind. You can learn to live with what Scripture describes as the peace that "surpasses all understanding" (Phil. 4:7). I'm not an expert. Not a doctor. Not a psychologist. Not a supersaint. I am a woman who has rediscovered some spiritual principles that helped me adjust my priorities and change my thinking. In the process, I discovered I was too blessed to be stressed.

A New Balance

BY FLORENCE LADD

It seems like yesterday, as they say, when I went shopping for a bicycle with my son, Michael. Actually, it was ten years ago. He was then a student at Hampshire College in Amherst, Massachusetts, and he needed a new bike to speed him to and from Northampton and South Hadley.

Last week Michael and I went shopping for a bike again. This time he was buying a bike for me. Our excursion to Wheelworks, a Boston-area supermarket of cycling, involves a back-story: In years past, Michael was responsible for the loss of two bicycles that were mine. My beloved Sprite, a brown bike with perhaps more than three speeds (I only use three, no matter the number available), had been stolen from a construction site where Michael had a summer job when he was in high school. He had left the Sprite unlocked, inclined as he was to trust in the goodwill of others. I had encouraged his sense of trust; but after the theft, I realized it was time to teach him the importance of being cautious, indeed, vigilant, especially when my property was at risk.

Recently, I was unnerved by the "disappearance" of my second-hand red Univega, which Michael had left in the apartment of an acquaintance who suddenly moved (or was evicted). Both bikes were lost in Cambridge, Massachusetts, arguably the bike-robbing capital of the world. Again in mourning for a beloved bicycle, I reviewed my lectures to Michael on vigilance and accountability. Inwardly, I worried. Did Michael have a willful disregard for property, his as well as mine, (for two or more of his bikes had also been stolen)? Or was he becoming one of those creative types for whom the practicalities of life prove elusive? I realized that this time my lectures would be neither effective nor, from my perspective, satisfying. I insisted that he buy a bike for me.

When Michael was in high school, I hadn't expected him to replace the Sprite. At that stage, I would have had to give him the money and that wouldn't make sense. Now an adult, Michael had money in the bank, income earned as a poet and performance artist. Not a lot of money, but enough to purchase a bicycle.

At Wheelworks, a muscular young salesman greeted us brightly. Michael said, "We're looking for a bike for my Mom. A lady's bike." With a skeptical glance, the salesman took in my mature proportions, not sufficiently concealed under my long, black linen dress.

While I browsed among the low-end bikes, conservative in appearance and modestly priced, Michael cruised up and down rows of high-tech, expensive models.

"Come over here," Michael summoned. "Better bikes are over here." He selected two from the rack, compared their handlebars and gears, told me about the advantages and disadvantages of tires with different treads and widths. "You won't be doing any off-road riding, will you?" he asked. Hearing more of a command than a question in his tone, I took notice of who was advising whom, and stiffened.

After comparing features, Michael decided that the more expensive model would be better for me. "You'll be safer on it," he said. Under the fluorescent lights, the platinum-finish Specialized Roadrunner had a glamorous sheen. It looked capable of speeds unsafe for a woman of a certain age.

"Take it for a spin around the block," the salesman suggested as he turned to another customer.

"That's okay," I murmured. I glanced at the trucks and busses zipping along the avenue, then down at my long dress. "I'll try it at home."

"You've got a helmet. You'll need a mirror and a bell, but you won't need lights. You won't be riding at night," Michael concluded.

It was a seismic moment. Something inside me shifted. Layers of conversations and conventions that had shaped our thirty-year relationship were repositioned. A revolution in the scale of things. My authority and responsibility seemed diminished: Michael's magnified.

An experienced biker and woman of the world, I felt indignant about this unceremonious transfer of power. But I realized that it was not spontaneous and should not have been unexpected. In a flash, I recalled that Michael had gradually gained more authority in our exchanges over the years. And gradually, I had yielded.

"I definitely want a basket," I asserted belatedly, to exercise an option among the few choices remaining.

From the array of baskets, mirrors and bells, I selected those I liked, with Michael telling me not to get anything "cheesy."

"Do you need biking shorts?" he asked with a giggle.

"No, but what about this?" I said, reaching for a yellow cloth cap with a red and blue logo, the type the Tour de France riders used to wear.

He said: "Put that cap down." It was a perfect imitation of that stern voice I used when I needed to curb Michael's inappropriate behavior two decades ago. We both burst out laughing at the role reversal. But again, the insight into our changing relationship stifled my laughter. The prospect of being the more dependent one sobered me.

The salesman reappeared and announced the sum of our purchases, looking to me. "I'm paying," said Michael, pulling out his checkbook.

Michael wheeled my new bike to the car, secured it on the bike rack and drove us home.

There is very little traffic on our street, a safe place to try out a new bike. Michael adjusted the seat. I got on and cautiously pedaled a few hundred feet, the front wheel wobbling wildly. Gradually, with more force and confidence, I was cruising steadily before turning around to pedal toward home. Toward Michael. Standing at attention, he was ready to leap to my rescue should I tip or tumble, watching with the same heart-felt encouragement I expressed the day we took the training wheels off of his bike and he pedaled uncertainly toward me on the same street. His proud smile showed that he was pleased; I appeared steady and sure of myself.

With an affectionate pat on my shoulder, he said, "I hope you'll ride a lot Mom. Try to ride every day."

I wheeled the bike into the garage where I lingered to admire it, as well as to come to terms with the new balance in our relationship. Each time I ride, I am reminded that the bicycle symbolizes a turning point for us. I anticipate future shifts in our relationship, as Michael grows more wise and worldly, and we grow older. There may come a day when he will tell me to stop driving my car, when he will advise me to reduce my domestic responsibilities and move from our house to an apartment; when he may tactfully suggest a transfer to a nursing home. I hope I will have the grace and good sense to accept those transitions with a measure of the insight I gained the day Michael bought my new bike. I trust I will continue to feel as I did then: Protected, secure and reciprocally loved.

Journeys

BY MAXINE CLAIR

here are few things as personally rewarding as journeys, yet they seem to fall so flat when we try to describe what happened to us along the way. It's sort of like an ad for a feature presentation that turns out to be slides of somebody's trip to the Everglades. Well, I'm telling you right up front that I've got slides. I've filed each set according to the degrees of gratification from most to least. I'll flip fast and show only one, my number-one-set:

The first one is of me. I'm on my way. I'm wearing one of those green, backless numbers. That's my mother. She's plying me with crushed ice. My husband was out of town and so he isn't in the picture. That sign—can you make it out?—it says "Delivery Room" but it's really the universal sign for "One-Way Street." What I don't know here is that I will do this three more times. Each soul that finds its way through this body will be like a separate country that I must find my way across. Each will have its own language, its own spectacular mountains, active volcanoes, and vernal places. Each will have swamps and seas as calm as oil.

This one is of son number one, pedaling his very first tricycle. When he grows into a flower he'll be a bird of paradise.

I'm downright fat in this one, walking through the same door in a different city, and my mother isn't there. It's another son, this one more like a bouquet of baby roses, all bud and thorns, but give him time.

And here, a few years later, still another son—the sunflower— wild and radiant, hard to miss.

You've seen one like this before, but this time it's a girl, and her trip has been taxing. If she were a flower she'd be African violet— stunning fragile—quietly insinuating herself into the land.

Here's me sitting on our kitchen counter reading *The Yellow Wallpaper* on a sunny afternoon. The four of them are making their own peanut-butter-and-jelly sandwiches at the table and making their own towers and tunnels with the jars.

This one seems out of place. It's the five of us at the dinner table. That's son number one. If this were a video you would catch the attitude in his voice. He's saying how nobody else's mother goes out on dates, and when his brother—the one with the fork in his hand—points out that Mrs. So-and-So down the street has a "friend," number one says that's because Mr. So-and-So is dead, and "Dad's not dead," he says. "He's just divorced from us and living somewhere else."

This one is of me with Webster's Collegiate in my lap. I'm looking up the word "heartfelt," or was it "patience"?

At first glance at this one you think "adorable, so handsome, so intense." Look closer. He's swallowing a worm and he's grinning.

This one is of us ready for church. I have just buttoned my daughter into her cute pale blue outfit. That's not blood down her front. It's red shoe polish. She wanted her Stride-Rites to shine.

There she is in her plaid jumper, her hair in braids with a riot of barrettes, her first book bag slung over her pink Huffy bike.

Here it's autumn and we're out back. I'm supposed to be teaching them touch football, but tackle is all the boys know. See how the oak tree blazes? I never fell. I've got the ball. They're hanging on, and their weight holds my feet on the ground. I've thrown my reading aside on the stoop: *Wouldn't Take Nothin' for My Journey Now.*

This is me on the phone disowning number two the time he locked the principal out of her office.

This is me on the phone to the poison control center with my finger down number three's throat.

This is me calling 911. The skewed angular thing attached to my daughter is her arm.

This is me holding the phone that cannot ring again until the bill is paid.

This is us on leftovers night—lasagna and mashed potatoes.

This is me with *American Heritage* this time. I'm looking up the word "endure."

Now here's my son number two, the thorny one who locked out the teacher. We're at his baccalaureate. He has earned that piece of paper he's got rolled up in his hand. He's asking me why I cried the whole time.

Here's my son number three, seeking his fortune, painting sunflowers on blue jeans for a fee.

This is Miss African Violet, skipping school to be with her friends.

Here's son number one, away at school. Far away.

Here's the girl who wanted to marry him.

Here's the guy he ended up with.

Here I am, practicing my smile in the mirror.

Here are the five of us that winter in the backyard. I'm trying to get them to stomp the word "Joy" into the snow. They're trying to get me to make a snowball.

This is the Cross pen set they chipped in for when I got my MFA. An investment, they said. Make us rich.

That's my first-born son, my six-foot bird of paradise and me—two faces on a park bench in April. I'm holding on to him, he's crying. The test has come back positive. Let me flip back to the slide of him on his first tricycle where he's pedaling fast.

There's number two! That's New York, in front of Spike Lee's place. He's the young businessman come full bloom.

There's number three on MTV, my son—would you believe—doing a commercial in his sunflower jeans.

And that's my baby girl with her book bag, heavy with Torts and Civil Procedure.

Finally, here are the five of us playing touch on Christmas Day. I asked for an *Unabridged*. They've given me a Coach bag instead, and a walk-around telephone. But, thanks to them, I know the definitions by heart.

That's the end of the set. Don't worry if you fell asleep. They say it's the way of journeys. You'd have to have been there.

Permissions

"Our Grandmothers," copyright © 1990 by Maya Angelou from *I Shall Not Be Moved* by Maya Angelou. Used by permission of Random House, Inc.

"My Daughters and Me," by Faith Ringgold, copyright © Faith Ringgold. The material herein was adapted with permission of the author and was previously published in *We Flew Over the Bridge: The Memoirs of Faith Ringgold*, copyright © 1995, Little Brown & Company.

Margaret: A Mother for All Seasons copyright © 2004 by Jewelle Taylor Gibbs.

"Ernestine: A Granddaughter's Memories," copyright © 2000 by Jewell Parker Rhodes, appears by permission of the author. The story was previously published under the title "Georgia on Her Mind" in *The Oxford American,* vol. 36, Nov/Dec. 2000.

"Everyday Use," from *In Love & Trouble: Stories of Black Women*, copyright © 1973 and renewed 2001 by Alice Walker, reprinted by permission of Harcourt Inc.

"Nineteen Thirty-Seven" by Edwidge Danticat Reprinted by permission of Soho Press from *KRIK? KRAK!* by Edwidge Danticat © 1995. All right reserved.

"Daystar," from *Selected Poems*, Pantheon © 1993 by Rita Dove. Reprinted by permission of the author.

"Mother" from *Sarah Phillips* by Andrea Lee, copyright © 1984 by Andrea Lee. Used by permission of Random House Inc.

"Slip and Fall," copyright © 2004 by Cecelie S. Berry.

"An Unnatural Woman," Copyright © 2002 by Martha Southgate.

"When Wild Southern Women Raise Daughters," Copyright © 2002 by Evelyn Coleman.

"Unmasking Step-Motherhood," copyright © 2003 by Deborah Roberts.

"The Complex Mathematics of Mothering," copyright © 2003 by AJ Verdelle.

"Goin' Round the Bend," copyright © 2003 by Melba Newsome.

"the lost baby poem," from *good woman: poems and a memoir*, 1969–1980, copyright © 1987 by Lucille Clifton. Reprinted with the permission of BOA Editions, Ltd.

"Many Rivers to Cross" from *On Call: Political Essays*, copyright June M. Jordan; Reprinted by permission of the June M. Jordan Literary Estate.

"Mother, Unconceived," copyright © 2001 by Erin Aubry Kaplan.

"Good Night Moon," copyright © 2000 by Felicia Ward appears by permission of the author. It was previously published in *Nimrod International Journal* and *The Beacon Best of 2001*: *Great writing by Women and Men of all Colors and Cultures*.

"Mother's House," copyright © 2003 by Tananarive Due.

"Linda Devine's Daughters," copyright © 2003 by Carolyn Ferrell.

"*The Children of the Poor*," *Verse 6*, from *Blacks*, copyright © 1991 by Gwendolyn Brooks. Reprinted by consent of Brooks Permissions.

"Dancer of the World," copyright © 2001 by Patricia Smith.

"A Miracle Every Day" from *A Miracle Every Day* by Marita Golden, copyright © 1999 by Marita Golden. Used by permission of Doubleday, a division of Random House, Inc.

"Elementary Lessons," copyright ©2003 by Rita Coburn Whack.

"My Girl," copyright © 2003 by Bethany M. Allen.

"Welcome to the World," copyright ©2002 by Dawn Turner Trice.

"Too Blessed to Be Stressed," reprinted by permission of Thomas Nelson Inc., Nashville, TN, from the book entitled *Too Blessed to Be Stressed*, copyright © 1998 by Reverend Suzan D. Johnson Cook. All rights reserved.

"A New Balance," copyright ©2002 by Florence Ladd appears by permission of the author. A version of the essay was previously published in the *Boston Globe*.

"Journeys," by Maxine Clair, copyright © Maxine Clair, appears by permission of the author. *Journeys* was also published in a limited, signed edition of *Quill and Brush*, a publication of the Pen/Faulkner Foundation.

Contributors

BETHANY M. ALLEN is a working mother of three who hopes to graduate from college before her daughter does. Her biweekly column, "Brown-Eyed Girl," appears on Africana.com, an online magazine. She is currently working on her first novel.

MAYA ANGELOU is hailed as one of the great voices of contemporary literature and as a remarkable Renaissance woman. She is the author of twelve best-selling books, including the memoir, *I Know Why the Caged Bird Sings*, and the sixth installment of her autobiography, the current best seller, *A Song Flung Up to Heaven*. In 1981, Dr. Angelou was appointed to a lifetime position as the first Reynolds Professor of American Studies at Wake Forest University. She became, in 1993, only the second poet in U.S. history to have the honor of writing and reciting original work at the presidential inauguration. In 2000, she was awarded the National Endowment for the Arts Medal of Arts. In addition to her many successes as an author and poet, Dr. Angelou is an educator, historian, actress, playwright, civil-rights activist, producer, and director.

CECELIE S. BERRY is a graduate of Harvard College and Harvard Law School. Her personal essays have appeared in the *New York Times*, the *Washington Post, Newsweek, Newsday, New Jersey Monthly*, and on Salon.com. Her commentary has been broadcast on National Public Radio's "Morning Edition." She lives in New Jersey with her husband and two sons.

GWENDOLYN BROOKS was born in Topeka, Kansas, on June 7, 1917. She was the author of more than twenty books of poetry, including

Children Coming Home (1991), *Blacks* (1987), and *The Bean Eaters* (1960). In 1945 her first book of poetry, *A Street in Bronzeville*, was a critical success. She won her first Guggenheim Fellowship and became a fellow of the American Academy of Arts and Letters. With her second book of poems, *Annie Allen* (1949), Brooks became the first African American to win a Pulitzer Prize. In 1962 President John Kennedy invited her to read at a Library of Congress poetry festival and in 1968 she was named the Poet Laureate for the state of Illinois. She also wrote numerous books including a novel, *Maud Martha* (1953), and *Report from Part One: An Autobiography*. She edited *Jump Bad: A New Chicago Anthology* in 1971. During the sixties, she became a leading articulator of the Black Arts movement. Her poetry is protest poetry, and her terrain is, most frequently, the unforgettable characters who populate the underclass of the nation's black neighborhoods. Gwendolyn Brooks died on December 3, 2000.

MAXINE CLAIR grew up in Kansas City, Kansas, one of nine children. She attended the University of Kansas as a medical technology major and later attained the position of chief technologist at Children's Hospital National Medical Center in Washington, D.C. After attending a writing workshop at George Washington University, she decided to pursue a Masters of Fine Arts degree in creative writing. This she did, while working as a medical technician to support her four children. Clair's first novel, *Rattlebone*, won the Friends of American Literature Fiction Award, the American Library Association's Black Caucus Award for Fiction, and the *Chicago Tribune*'s Heartland Prize for Fiction. She is currently a Professor of English at the George Washington University in Washington, D.C., and the recipient of a Guggenheim Fellowship for work on her second novel.

LUCILLE CLIFTON was born and raised in Depew, New York. In 1969 her first book of poetry, entitled *Good Times*, was hailed by the *New*

York Times as one of the year's 10 best books. Clifton worked in state and government positions until 1971, when she became a writer-in-residence at the historically Black Coppin State College in Baltimore. She produced numerous award-winning books of poetry, including *Blessing the Boats: New and Selected Poems, 1988–2000*, which won the National Book Award; *The Terrible Stories* (1995), which was nominated for the National Book Award; *Good Woman: Poems and a Memoir, 1969–1980*; and *Two-Headed Woman* (1980), both of which were nominated for the Pulitzer Prize. She has written more than sixteen books for children, including a series of books featuring the life of Everett Anderson, a young black boy. Clifton has served as Poet Laureate for the state of Maryland and in 1999 was elected a Chancellor of The Academy of American Poets. She has raised six children.

EVELYN COLEMAN, a former psychotherapist, has written nine children's books. Her most recent works for young adults include *Born in Sin, Mystery of the Dark Tower*, and *Circle of Fire*. Her adult fiction and nonfiction have appeared in *Essence, Black Enterprise, Southern Exposure, The Utne Reader*, and the *Atlanta Journal and Constitution*. In 1989, she was the first African American to receive a fiction fellowship from the North Carolina Arts Council. Her first novel in the mystery genre for adult readers is *What a Woman's Gotta Do*.

SUZAN D. JOHNSON COOK served on President Bill Clinton's Initiative on Race and Reconciliation and has been named by *Ebony* as one of the top 15 women in ministry in the nation. She was the first African American woman elected senior pastor for the American Baptists, the first woman chaplin for the New York City Police Department, and the first woman officer of the historic Hampton University Ministers' Conference, the largest gathering of African American clergy in the world. She is the author of *Too Blessed to Be Stressed*, editor of *Sister to Sister: Devotions for and from African-American Women*, and co-author of *Preaching in Two Voices*. She lives in the Bronx, New York, with her husband and two sons.

EDWIDGE DANTICAT was born in 1969 and came to the United States from Haiti at the age of twelve. She received a BA from Barnard College and an MFA from Brown University, where she wrote her first novel, *Breath, Eyes, Memory*. Her short stories have appeared in 25 periodicals. She has won a 1995 Pushcart Short Story Prize as well as fiction awards from *The Caribbean Writer, Seventeen*, and *Essence* magazines. At twenty-six years old, in 1995, her short story collection, *Krik? Krak!*, was a National Book Award Finalist. Recent works include *The Farming of Bones*, about the massacre of Haitians at the Dominican Republic border in 1937; *After the Dance: A Walk through Carnival in Jacmel; Behind the Mountains: The Diary of Celiane Esperance*; and in the spring of 2004, *The Dew Breaker*.

RITA DOVE, Poet Laureate of the United States from 1993 to 1995, was born and raised in Akron, Ohio. She has published a novel, *Through the Ivory Gate* (1992), a collection of stories, a verse drama, a book of essays, and five books of poetry, among them *Thomas and Beulah*, which was awarded the Pulitzer Prize in 1987. The recipient of numerous literary fellowships and awards, she is Commonwealth Professor of English at the University of Virginia and lives near Charlottesville with her husband and daughter.

TANANARIVE DUE is, most recently, the author of the haunted house novel *The Good House* and co-author of *Freedom in the Family*, a mother-daughter memoir of her family's contribution to the civil rights movement. She is the author of the novels *The Black Rose, My Soul to Keep, The Between*, and *The Living Blood*, which won a 2002 American Book Award. A two-time finalist for the Bram Stoker

Award, the former *Miami Herald* columnist now lives in Washington state with her husband, novelist Steven Barnes.

MARIAN WRIGHT EDELMAN, Founder and President of the Children's Defense Fund (CDF), has been an advocate for disadvantaged Americans her entire professional life. Under her leadership, CDF has become the nation's strongest voice for children and families. The mission of CDF is to leave No Child Behind and to ensure every child a healthy start, a head start, a fair start, a safe start, and a moral start in life, and a successful passage to adulthood with the help of caring families and communities.

A graduate of Spelman College and Yale Law School, Ms. Edelman began her career in the mid-60s when, as the first black woman admitted to the Mississippi Bar, she directed the NAACP Legal Defense and Educational Fund office in Jackson, Mississippi. In 1968, she moved to Washington, D.C., as counsel for the Poor People's Campaign that Dr. Martin Luther King, Jr, began organizing before his death. She also founded the Washington Research Project, a public-interest law firm. For two years she served as the director of the Center for Law and Education at Harvard University, and in 1973 she began CDF.

Ms. Edelman has received many honorary degrees and awards, including the Albert Schweitzer Humanitarian Prize, the Heinz Award, and a MacArthur Foundation Prize Fellowship. In 2000, she received the Presidential Medal of Freedom, the nation's highest civilian award, and the Robert F. Kennedy Lifetime Achievement Award for her writings, which include seven books: *Families in Peril: An Agenda for Social Change; The Measure of Our Success: A Letter to My Children and Yours; Guide My Feet: Meditations and Prayers on Loving and Working for Children; Stand for Children; Lanterns: A Memoir of Mentors; Hold My Hand: Prayers for Building a Movement to Leave No Child Behind;* and *I'm Your Child, God: Prayers for Our Children.*

CAROLYN FERRELL teaches creative writing at Sarah Lawrence College. Her short story collection *Don't Erase Me* won the 1997 *Los Angeles Times'* Art Seidenbaum Award for first fiction. Her stories have been anthologized in *The Best American Short Stories of the Century*, edited by John Updike, *Children of the Night: The Best Stories by Black Writers, 1967–present*, edited by Gloria Naylor, and *Streetlights: Illuminating Tales of the Urban Black Experience*, edited by Doris Jean Austin. She lives in New York with her husband and children and is at work on a novel.

JEWELLE TAYLOR GIBBS is a clinical psychologist and sociologist. She began her teaching career in 1979 as a professor at the University of California Berkeley School of Social Welfare. She became the first African American professor to be appointed to an endowed chair in the University of California system as the Zellerbach Family Fund Professor of Social Policy, Community Change and Practice. She is a regular commentator on issues relating to youth violence, adolescence, urban education, affirmative action, police misconduct, and racial profiling. She is the author of numerous academic and popular texts, including, *Preserving Privilege: California Politics, Propositions and People of Color; Children of Color: Psychological Interventions with Culturally Diverse Youth;* and *Race and Justice: Rodney King and O. J. Simpson in a House Divided*. She also served as editor of *Young, Black and Male in America: An Endangered Species*. She is the mother of two sons.

MARITA GOLDEN is the author of four novels, most recently, *The Edge of Heaven*. Her autobiography, *Migrations of the Heart*, explores the contradictions and rewards of returning to Africa from the perspective of an African American woman marrying into an African family. She has also written, *Saving Our Sons: Raising Black Children in a Turbulent World;* edited *Wild Women Don't Wear No Blues: Black Women Writers on Men, Love and Sex;* and co-edited, *Gumbo: An Anthology of Black Writing*. She is Executive Director of the Zora Neale Hurston/Richard Wright Foundation.

JUNE JORDAN was born in New York City in 1936. Her memoir, *Soldier: A Poet's Childhood*, was published by Basic Books in 2000. Her books of poetry include *Kissing God Goodbye: Poems* (1991–1997); *Naming Our Destiny: New and Selected Poems* (1989); *Living Room* (1985); *Passion* (1980); and *Things That I Do in the Dark* (1977). She is the author of children's books, plays, a novel and *Poetry for the People: A Blueprint for the Revolution* (1995), a guide to writing, teaching, and publishing poetry. Her collections of political essays include *Affirmative Acts: Political Essays* (1998); *On Call* (1985); and *Technical Difficulties* (1984). The recipient of numerous grants, awards, and fellowships, Ms. Jordan taught at the University of California, Berkeley, where she founded Poetry for the People. She died of breast cancer on June 14, 2002.

ERIN AUBRY KAPLAN is a reporter and columnist for *LA Weekly*. Her writing has appeared in *Salon, The London Independent, Black Enterprise*, and *Contemporary Art Magazine*. She is the recipient of the 2001 Pen West Literary Award in the journalism category for her work, "Blue Like Me," a personal essay exploring the roots and modern consequences of depression among African Americans. Also a creative writer, she is, most recently, a fellow in creative nonfiction at the Sundance Institute.

FLORENCE LADD is an author, social critic, and psychologist. Her novel, *Sarah's Psalm*, received the 1997 Best Fiction award from the American Library Association's Black Caucus. From 1989–1997 she was Director of the Bunting Institute at Harvard University, a multidisciplinary center for women in higher education. She lives in Cambridge, Massachusetts, and Flavigny-sur-Ozerain, France.

ANDREA LEE'S most recent collection of short stories is *Interesting Women*. She received the Jean Stein Award from the American Institute of Arts and Letters for her first book, *Russian Journal*, and is the author of a novel, *Sarah Phillips*. She lives with her family in Europe.

MELBA NEWSOME is a freelance writer whose work has been published in *O, The Oprah Magazine; Ladies' Home Journal; Essence; Vibe; Family Circle;* and the *Los Angeles Times Magazine*. She received the 2002 Outstanding Article Award from the American Society of Journalists and Authors. She lives in North Carolina.

JEWELL PARKER RHODES is a professor of Creative Writing and American Literature at Arizona State University, where she has served as Director of the Master of Fine Arts in the Creative Writing program. Her latest novel, *Douglass's Women*, was published by Pocket Books in 2002. Her short fiction has been anthologized in *Children of the Night: Best Short Stories by Black Writers*, edited by Gloria Naylor, and *Ancestral House: The Black Short Story in the Americas and Europe*, edited by Charles Rowell. Her work has been nominated twice for the Pushcart Prize. She is also the recipient of the Yaddo Creative Writing Fellowship, the National Endowment of the Arts Award in Fiction, and two Distinguished Teaching Awards.

FAITH RINGGOLD began her career more than thirty-five years ago as a painter. She is best known for her painted story quilts—art that combines painting, quilted fabric, and storytelling. She has exhibited in major museums in the United States, Europe, South America, Asia, Africa, and the Middle East. Also an acclaimed writer and illustrator, her first book, *Tar Beach*, was a Caldecott Honor Book and winner of the Coretta Scott King Award for Illustration. She has written and illustrated eleven children's books. She has received more than seventy-five awards, fellowships, citations, and honors, including the Solomon R. Guggenheim Fellowship for painting, two National Endowment for the Arts Awards, and seventeen honorary doctorates. She is a professor of art at the University of California in San Diego, California.

PATRICIA SMITH is one of the nation's foremost slam poets. She is a five-time champion of the Uptown Poetry Slam in Chicago; four-time champion of the National Grand Slam and a co-founder with her husband, poet Michael Brown, of the Boston Slam. Her poems have been anthologized in numerous collections. She began her career as a journalist at the *Chicago Sun-Times* and became a columnist for the *Boston Globe,* where she earned a Pulitzer Prize nomination in 1998. She has published three books of poetry: *Big Towns, Big Talk* (1992); *Life According to Motown (1991)*; and *Close to Death.* Her writing has also appeared in *The Nation, The Paris Review, Agni,* and *Tri-Quarterly.*

DEBORAH ROBERTS, an ABC news correspondent, joined the ABC newsmagazine *20/20* in June, 1995. Since then, she has served as a substitute anchor on *World News Weekend* and *Good Morning America.* She won an Emmy in 2002 for "Her Lost World," a report for *20/20* in which she accompanied an Ethiopian-American woman on her return to her war-torn country in search of her mother. Ms. Roberts has also contributed to *Self.*

MARTHA SOUTHGATE, a former editor of *Essence,* is the author of two novels, *The Fall of Rome* and *Another Way to Dance,* which was awarded the Coretta Scott King Genesis Award for Best First Novel. She received a 2002 New York Foundation for the Arts grant and has won fellowships from the MacDowell Colony and the Virginia Center for the Creative Arts. Her nonfiction articles have appeared in the *New York Times Magazine; O, The Oprah Magazine; Premiere*; and *Essence.*

DAWN TURNER TRICE is a columnist for the *Chicago Tribune*. She has published two novels, *Only Twice I've Wished for Heaven* and *An Eighth of August*. She also contributes commentary to National Public Radio's "Morning Edition."

AJ VERDELLE began her career in statistics and data analysis. She is the author of the novel *The Good Negress*, a finalist for the *Los Angeles Times* Book Award for First Fiction, and the Pen/Faulkner Award. She is the recipient of a Whiting Writer's Award and a Bunting Fellowship from Radcliffe College at Harvard University. She teaches creative writing at Princeton University.

ALICE WALKER has, most recently, authored a collection of stories, *The Way Forward Is with a Broken Heart*. She has published numerous works of fiction, essays, and poetry, including *In Love and Trouble: Stories of Black Women* (1973); *Meridian* (1976); a novel, and the essay collection, *In Search of Our Mother's Gardens* (1983). She is perhaps best known for her Pulitzer Prize–winning novel, *The Color Purple*.

FELICIA WARD lives in Oakland, California. She has served as an associate editor of *Equal Means*, a grassroots journal for women, and for many years was director of the Bay Area Black Women's Health Project. In 2000, she was awarded the Katherine Anne Porter Prize for Fiction and, in 2001, she received a Stegner Fellowship in Creative Writing from Stanford University.

RITA COBURN WHACK is a series producer and writer for CCC City Edition, a program of Chicago Public Radio's WYCC. She is a two-time Emmy award–winner for her documentaries *Remembering 47th Street, Chicago's answer to the Harlem Renaissance during the 1920–1950s*, and *African Roots, American Soil: African Americans in Agriculture*. She is the author of the novel *Meant to Be*.